Legislative Research on the People's Supervisor System

Qin Qianhong

Legislative Research on the People's Supervisor System

WUHAN UNIVERSITY PRESS
武汉大学出版社

Springer

Qin Qianhong
School of Law
Wuhan University
Wuhan, Hubei, China

Translated by
Da Lu
Human Rights Institute
Southwest University of Political Science
and Law
Chongqing, China

ISBN 978-981-95-7971-6 ISBN 978-981-95-7972-3 (eBook)
https://doi.org/10.1007/978-981-95-7972-3

Jointly published with Wuhan University Press
The print edition is not for sale in China (Mainland). Customers from China (Mainland) please order the print book from: Wuhan University Press.

This Springer imprint is published by the registered company Springer Nature Singapore Pte Ltd.
The registered company address is: 152 Beach Road, #21-01/04 Gateway East, Singapore 189721, Singapore

To my wife Liu Xinying and my daughter Qin Yihan

Preface

The judicial domain is often regarded as an area exclusively controlled by the legal elites. Many legal professionals may be familiar with the story from over 400 years ago when English Judge Coke defied the king: the king sought to participate in adjudicating a case but was refused by Chief Justice Coke. The king was furious and said, "As the sovereign of the nation, all the land and people belong to me—how could there be anything beyond my authority?" Coke replied, "It is not that Your Majesty lacks authority, nor that your intellect is insufficient, nor even that your knowledge is inadequate. It is simply because Your Majesty is not well-versed in the laws of the Kingdom of England. Judges handle cases that invariably involve the lives, property, and liberty of people—matters that cannot be properly resolved by natural reason alone but require artificial reason. The law is an art, demanding long study and practice before one can truly master it." While this story may be interpreted in different ways, one thing is certain: legal matters require expertise. Then why do common law systems like those in the UK and US have jury trials? And why has China also established systems of people's assessors and people's supervisors? Isn't this a case of letting amateurs decide cases or allowing ignorant judges to make arbitrary rulings? In fact, it is not. While these systems have their own historical origins—such as the *Magna Carta* (1215), which guaranteed the right to trial by one's peers (meaning a jury composed of neighbors), and *Interim Organic Regulations on the People's Courts of the People's Republic of China* (1951), which provides that "to facilitate public participation in trials, people's courts shall implement the people's assessor system according to the nature of cases; assessors have the right to assist in investigations, participate in trials, and offer opinions"—there is a shared underlying principle: allowing non-experts to participate in judicial proceedings is seen as a vital part of democratic governance. Indeed, modern states justify the legitimacy and proper exercise of state power through the principle of popular sovereignty. Judicial power, as an essential component of state power, is thus regarded as something that should be shared by the people as the sovereign. The legitimacy of these systems is further underpinned by the following considerations: in many challenging legal cases where evidence cannot fully reconstruct or conclusively establish the facts, judgment by individuals who share similar life experiences with the parties involved may yield outcomes more aligned with reasonableness and human sensibilities; through constant exposure to judicial proceedings, ordinary citizens will be influenced by the analytical frameworks, methodologies, and modes of expression employed by legal professionals, thereby facilitating the permeation of the spirit of rule of law throughout society; the selection of assessors and supervisors, to some extent, embodies the principle of party autonomy. As the Western legal adage goes, "Everyone must abide by the judgment rendered by a judge of their own choosing." Consequently, once a judicial process involving jurors or supervisors concludes with a decision, even if a party finds it deeply unsatisfactory, they must comply in good faith, provided the procedure is fair and proper. In contemporary China, the establishment of the systems of people's assessors and people's supervisors carries a more immediate impetus—addressing public discontent with judicial corruption. It must be said that China's current judicial system reform has fallen into a paradoxical predicament: one camp argues that the root cause of various judicial problems and dilemmas lies in the lack of judicial independence, with the judiciary facing too many internal and external constraints; another camp maintains that the fundamental issue stems from the relatively low professional quality and misconduct within the judicial ranks, so strict supervision is required, particularly through improving various supervisory mechanisms and measures. As to which constitutes the fundamental problem, opinions remain divided with no consensus reached. Currently, the mainstream view appears to favor the supervision advocates. However, this raises other questions: First, how can we afford the implementation costs of the systems of people's assessors and people's supervisors? For decades, people's assessors largely remained in name only, and since the mid-1980s, the system had become virtually defunct in some regions. To make people's assessors and people's supervisors truly play their role, we must establish feasible routine systems for selection and judicial participation, which requires substantial human and material resources. Can the already tight budgets of courts and procuratorates bear these financial burdens? Second, despite the fact that the *Decision of the Standing Committee of the National People's Congress Regarding Perfecting the System of People's Assessors* provides the procedures and criteria for selecting people's assessors, specifying that the basic people's courts shall recommend candidates to the standing committees of the people's congress at the same level for selection, several questions remain unanswered: How many people's assessors should each basic people's court maintain in its pool? How does the standing committee select them? Is it justifiable for the president of the people's court to conduct a self-review before submitting the list of candidates to the standing committee? These issues have not been adequately addressed in the Decision, so in practice, it is still possible to always see the same few "compliant familiar faces" in the courtrooms. The people's supervisor system faces greater challenges stemming from unclear positioning and a lack of consensus. As the originator and supervisee of the system, the People's Procuratorate initiates, guides, and facilitates the supervision process, ensures funding, and in certain regions, even selects the supervisors, which results in some degree of identity confusion and an awkward situation where they may not feel justified in their actions. Third, unlike the jury system in the UK and the US, which clearly delineates the functions of the jury, judges, and prosecutors, with the jury handling factual judgments and judges and prosecutors in charge of the application or enforcement of the law, the people's assessor system and people's supervisor system in China do not have such a distinct division of responsibilities. In China, people's assessors participate in the trial of cases as part of the collegiate panel, exercising their independent voting rights in determining facts and applying the law. Does the implementation of this system exceed the assessors' experience and cognitive capabilities, while also compromising the professionalism of legal judgments? Are people's supervisors merely exercising their democratic supervision rights, or are they substantially involved in the operation of procuratorial power, sharing a portion of it? When selecting people's supervisors, should the emphasis be on their democratic participation, or should greater weight be given to their professionalism, knowledge, and competence to ensure the accuracy of their supervision outcomes? Fourth, the involvement of assessors and supervisors in the judicial process necessitates a comprehensive set of supporting systems, such as the system of cross-examination and verdict announcement in court, as well as the system of supervision evaluation and voting. Without these, assessors and supervisors may continue to exist in name only, rendering judicial democracy and judicial civilization mere aspirations.

For an extended period in the past, constitutional scholars were absent from the discussion on the theoretical and practical aspects of people's supervisors and people's assessors. Nevertheless, based on the inherent nature and prevailing circumstances of these two systems, constitutional theory is badly needed to overcome theoretical and practical impediments, thus fostering continuous innovation in the relevant systems. The authors of this book, in their research on the legislative issues concerning people's supervisors, subjectively aim to embrace a fresh problem awareness and adopt novel research perspectives, so as to contribute their humble efforts to the attainment of the aforementioned goals. As for the objective impact of their work, the authors are open to fair comments of the vast readership.

Wuhan, China Qin Qianhong

Competing Interests The author has no competing interests to declare that are relevant to the content of this manuscript.

Contents

Chapter 1
Nature Positioning of the People's Supervisor System

1 Defining the People's Supervisor System

The people's supervisor system, as an institutional innovation introduced by the Supreme People's Procuratorate, does not form a universally agreed-upon definition in both practical applications and academic circles. We can gain insights into the operational status, normative establishment, and academic research of this system from the practical, normative, and theoretical perspectives. By rethinking on the viewpoints that define the system from these three perspectives, we can identify a method to delineate it, thereby clarifying the research focus of this book and laying a foundation for subsequent discussions.

From the practical perspective, the people's supervisor system, as a reform measure, is in a constant state of evolution and development, and only through a diachronic lens can the panorama of the system be appreciated. In accordance with the provisions of the Constitution and laws providing that all state organs must heed the opinions of the people and accept their supervision, the Supreme People's Procuratorate, after reporting to the Standing Committee of the National People's Congress and obtaining the approval of the Central Committee, decided to launch a pilot program for the people's supervisor system in October 2003. The original intention behind the design of this system was "to enhance external supervision and effectively prevent and rectify any unfair law enforcement issues arising from the procuratorial organs' handling of duty-related crimes."[1] Starting from the initial pilot implementation of the people's supervisor system in procuratorial organs across 10

Translator's note: As this book was published in 2010, the statutory provisions referenced therein have since been amended. To remain faithful to the original text, the English translation retains the wording as it appeared at the time of the book's publication.

[1] *Work Report of the Supreme People's Procuratorate on March 10, 2004 at the Second Session of the Tenth National People's Congress*, Gazette of the Standing Committee of the National People's Congress, 2004.

Q. Qin, *Legislative Research on the People's Supervisor System*,
https://doi.org/10.1007/978-981-95-7972-3_1

provinces, autonomous regions, and municipalities directly under the central government, including Tianjin, Hebei, and Inner Mongolia, by the end of 2007, 86% of procuratorial organs nationwide had embarked on this pilot. Both the macro-structure and micro-level institutional design of the system have undergone continuous refinement and evolution towards a relatively mature and comprehensive state through practical exploration. The changes in its macro-structure are primarily manifested in several aspects. Initially, the emphasis was on supervising "three types of cases," which has been expanded to encompass supervision of "five types of situations." Consequently, the involvement and engagement of people's supervisors in prosecutorial practices have extended beyond the stages of arrest approval and prosecutorial review of cases investigated directly by procuratorial organs to cover all stages related to the handling of duty-related crimes by these organs,[2] including the reception of complaints and visits related to procuratorial work,[3] investigative interrogations,[4] and even trials,[5] and appeals.[6] Additionally, there is exploration in practice regarding

[2] For example, The People's Procuratorate of Nantong Economic and Technological Development Zone, Jiangsu Province, adheres to the system of "no case without supervision". It invites people's supervisors to supervise activities such as the seizure of stolen funds and property, arrests, searches, follow-up visits to case parties, and the viewing of synchronized audio and video recordings of investigations, tailored to the specific characteristics of each case, so that people's supervisors participate in at least one activity of supervision for each duty-related crime case handled by the procuratorate, thereby placing the stages prone to illegalities under their supervision.

See Zhang Jie, *Nantong Development Zone: Comprehensive Safeguards for People's Supervisors to Fulfill Their Duties through "Two Systems"*, at http://www.js.jcy.gov.cn/read-news.asp?nid=10917, last visited on January 10, 2009.

[3] For example, the People's Procuratorate of Weiyang District, Yangzhou City, Jiangsu Province specifically invites people's supervisors to join in the reception of complaints and visits related to procuratorial work, so that they supervise this process.

See Tao Qin, Liu Wei & Dai Minghua, *Jiangsu Weiyang: Engaging People's Supervisors in Case-Related Complaints and Visits*, at http://news.jcrb.com/jiancha/jcdt/200810/t20081020_84274.html, last visited on October 20, 2008.

[4] For example, the People's Procuratorate of Hai'an County, Jiangsu Province invited people's supervisors to conduct supervision by viewing synchronized recordings and sign the audio and video work records.

See Yang Bosen & Liu Weiluan, *Jiangsu Hai'an: Inviting People's Supervisors to Supervise Investigative Interrogations*, at http://review.jcrb.com/200803/ca688002.htm, last visited on March 15, 2008.

[5] For example, the People's Procuratorate of Guangde County, Anhui Province, invited people's supervisors to observe a court trial. Following the conclusion of the trial, the supervisors assessed the prosecutor's performance in questioning, presenting evidence, cross-examination, debating, and their ability to adapt to changing situations throughout the trial.

See Zhou Lijun, *Anhui Guangde: Inviting People's Supervisors to Observe Court Trials*, at http://news.jcrb.com/jiancha/jcdt/200905/t20090527_225166.html, last visited on May 28, 2009.

[6] For example, the Weiyang District of Xi'an invited people's supervisors to supervise the review process of criminal appeals, marking a new initiative in implementing the *Provisions on the Procedures for the Public Examination of Criminal Appeal Cases by the People's Procuratorates (Trial)*.

See Mao Zhiwei & Zheng Ling, *Xi'an Weiyang: Inviting People's Supervisors to Supervise the Review Process of Criminal Appeals*, at http://www.spp.gov.cn/site2006/2008-03-16/0003817368.html, last visited on March 18, 2008.

the selection of supervision models,[7] such as the "same-level supervision model," "higher-level supervision model," and "centralized supervision model." Regarding its micro-level institutional design, the selection and appointment mechanism varies across regions in terms of candidate qualifications, methods for determining candidates, and the bodies responsible for selecting and appointing people's supervisors. Furthermore, means to guarantee the right of access to information for people's supervisors has emerged as a focal point of institutional innovation in various regions. From this perspective, some researchers define the people's supervisor system as "the process and system through which people's supervisors supervise the law enforcement of procuratorial organs in accordance with established procedures and rules."[8] They also highlight aspects of consensus about this system, believing that it conforms to constitutional provisions, meets the fundamental requirements of modern rule of law, follows the international trend of public participation in justice, and addresses the pivotal question of "who is to supervise the procuratorate." However, they also note that several issues remain to be explored, including the responsibilities and qualifications for people's supervisors, the objects of supervision (such as whether it's appropriate to supervise "three types of cases"), the scope of supervision (such as whether it extends to cases investigated by public security organs), and the efficacy of supervision.[9]

From the normative perspective, the current regulatory framework governing the operation of the people's supervisor system is primarily categorized into two tiers. The first tier comprises normative documents and decisions issued within the procuratorial system by the Supreme People's Procuratorate. These include the *Provisions of the Supreme People's Procuratorate on Implementing the People's Supervisor System (Trial)* (hereinafter referred to as the *Provisions*), approved at the 9th session of the 10th Procuratorial Committee of the Supreme People's Procuratorate on September 2, 2003, and revised at the 23rd session of the same committee on July 5, 2004, as well as the *Provisions of the Supreme People's Procuratorate on the Implementing the People's Supervisor's Supervision on the Five Types of Situations (Trial)*, approved at the 45th session of the 10th Procuratorial Committee of the Supreme People's Procuratorate on November 23, 2005. The second tier comprises normative documents issued by local authorities at all levels, encompassing normative documents issued by local people's congresses or their standing committees at all levels. These include local regulations, such as the *Resolution of the Standing Committee of the Sichuan Provincial People's Congress on Strengthening the Pilot Program for People's Supervisors in Provincial Procuratorial Organs*, approved

---

[7] In practice, the "cross-supervision model" is also adopted to address issues arising from the improving quality of case handling by procuratorial organs, including a decrease in the number of cases that require supervision, uneven distribution of such cases, and even absence of such cases in some regions, so that supervision resources can be effectively used.

See Xu Yingyan, Song Shijing & Jin Jian, *Cross-Supervision: An Innovative Model of People's Supervisors in Shanxi*, Southeast Academic Research, 2005.

[8] *Discussion on Several Issues Concerning the People's Supervisor System*, Fujian Law Science, 2005.

[9] *Ibid.*

by the Standing Committee of the Sichuan Provincial People's Congress, marking the first local regulation on the people's supervisor system in China, and relevant normative documents issued by local people's congresses or their standing committees without the authority to formulate local regulations, such as the *Implementation Measures for the Work of People's Supervisors in Hanyang District, Wuhan City (Trial)*, approved at the 5th session of the 13th Standing Committee of the Hanyang District People's Congress, Wuhan City, on June 22, 2007. This tier also encompasses normative documents issued by local people's procuratorates at all levels, like the *Implementation Opinions of the Shanghai Municipal People's Procuratorate on the People's Supervisor System (Trial)*, approved at the 6th session of the Procuratorial Committee of the Shanghai Municipal People's Procuratorate on September 16, 2004. It is these normative documents, which lack nationwide legal effect and vary in content, that govern the operation of the people's supervisor system. Based on existing relevant regulations, some researchers define the people's supervisor system as "a novel social supervision system that entrusts the supervision of 'three types of cases,' 'five types of situations,' and 'one specific situation' during the investigation of duty-related crimes by the People's Procuratorates to people's supervisors selected through democratic recommendation procedures, so as to enhance the supervision of the People's Procuratorates' investigation of duty-related crimes, elevate law enforcement standards and case handling quality, ensure the fair and lawful execution of procuratorial duties, and uphold social equity and justice."[10]

From the theoretical perspective, research on the people's supervisor system has evolved through several stages in tandem with the system's own development and improvement. Initially, it focused on justifying the system's legitimacy, celebrating its merits, and scrutinizing its shortcomings. This was followed by a stage of review and perfection of the system's details, then a stage of innovation and expansion. Ultimately, it culminated in the research on institutional legislation, which integrates insights from the above-mentioned three stages. Throughout this process, researchers derived different interpretations of the people's supervisor system from their distinct research perspectives. Some researchers categorize the viewpoints of academics and judicial practitioners into six types and, upon reconsidering on these viewpoints, define the people's supervisor system as "a novel social supervision arrangement established in accordance with the constitutional principles of democracy and the rule of law, which involves people's supervisors who are appointed by competent and organizational authorities pursuant to established rules and then, adhering to specific norms and procedures, conduct procedural supervision over the legal supervision organs' exercise of discretionary power in cases of duty-related crimes under their jurisdiction, with the aim to regulate the powers of investigation, investigation supervision, and prosecution in duty-related crimes, thus ensuring their orderly, fair, and honest operation and safeguarding equity and justice."[11]

---

[10] Zhou Yongnian ed., *Introduction to the People's Supervisor System*, China Procuratorial Press, 2008, p. 3.

[11] Xu Hanming, *An Economic Analysis of the Concept and Characteristics of the People's Supervisor System*, Fangyuan Rule of Law Special Issue on People's Supervisors, 2005.

The aforementioned viewpoints, which delineate the concept of the people's supervisor system from practical, normative, and theoretical dimensions, are highly enlightening. However, each of them still has room for further refinement. The first perspective on defining the people's supervisor system, grounded in its practical manifestations, exhibits inclusiveness yet is devoid of substance and overly broad. The second perspective, based on existing relevant norms, is precise and specific yet somewhat inflexible, failing to accommodate a wide range of vibrant and rational innovative practices. The third perspective at the theoretical level attempts to unveil the essential features, functions, and value propositions of the people's supervisor system, offering considerable insight. Nevertheless, the definition is overly abstract and somewhat detached from both the practical application and existing norms of the people's supervisor system, remaining to be improved in terms of accuracy. We believe that a more objective, scientific, and inclusive concept of the people's supervisor system can only be established by considering all three dimensions. Firstly, the people's supervisor system during the pilot phase should be viewed as a dynamically evolving system. We should embrace and observe all the institutional innovations and practical implementations across regions before a more specific screening and selection process, choosing the most appropriate institutional design from plenty of practical forms, rather than adopting a simplistic and rigid understanding of the model and content of the people's supervisor system. Secondly, by referring to the existing relevant normative documents, we can find that the people's supervisor system is a pivotal manifestation of judicial democracy, tailored specifically for the procuratorial organs' investigation of duty-related crimes. The evaluation conclusions, opinions, and suggestions offered by people's supervisors lack substantial and binding authority over procuratorial organs. The diverse normative frameworks of the people's supervisor system all revolve around this core, either aiming at its improvement in specific implementation and operation, or at its proactive expansion and cautious enhancement within a confined scope. Finally, the concept of the people's supervisor system must be established according to its nature positioning. Only on the premise of scientifically positioning the people's supervisor system and fully demonstrating its legitimacy can we comprehend its essential features and value propositions, so as to identify its niche and development direction. The nature positioning of the people's supervisor system is the very topic that this study will delve into next.

2 A Comparative Study of the People's Supervisor System and Comparable Foreign Systems

The institutional design involving ordinary people in procuratorial power is not exclusive to China, as similar systems exist abroad. As localized knowledge, these systems are closely tied to the national conditions, historical backgrounds, and cultural traditions of various countries, but a comparative study on their positioning is of great benefit to the nature positioning of China's people's supervisor system. Such a study offers indirect proof of our system's rationality and presents valuable resources for its enhancement, while also providing lessons on how to minimize the costs of trial and error in its implementation. To facilitate and deepen the research, this study only selects the Grand Jury system in the United States and the prosecutorial review commission system in Japan as two samples for comparison.

2.1 A Comparison of the Grand Jury System, the Prosecutorial Review Commission, and the People's Supervisor System

The Grand Jury system in the United States, which has its origins in the United Kingdom, is a system explicitly provided in the Constitution and constitutes a fundamental constitutional right enjoyed by the people. The *Fifth Amendment to the United States Constitution* provides: "No person shall be held to answer for a capital, or otherwise infamous crime, unless on a presentment or indictment of a Grand Jury, except in cases arising in the land or naval forces, or in the Militia, when in actual service in time of war or public danger." This provision has been interpreted by the Federal Supreme Court as solely applicable to federal cases, allowing state defendants charged with felonies to be prosecuted without undergoing a Grand Jury review.[12] Currently, the United States employs the Grand Jury system for felony trials at the federal level and in more than half of the states, with the number of jurors in those states allowed to be fewer than 23. The prosecutorial review commission system in Japan was established in accordance with the *Law on Prosecutorial Review Commission* enacted in 1948, and has been in use ever since, "offering an invaluable opportunity for citizens to engage in criminal justice."[13] While influenced by the Grand Jury system in the United States, Japan's prosecutorial review commission system is substantially different from it. The following table briefly compares the specific institutional designs of the Grand Jury system in the United States, the prosecutorial review commission system in Japan, and the people's supervisor system in China.

[12] Hurtado v. Cal, 110 U.S. 516 (1884).

[13] Matsuo Koya, *Criminal Procedure Law of Japan I*, China Renmin University Press, 2005, p. 153.

	Grand Jury System in the United States	Prosecutorial Review Commission System in Japan	People's Supervisor System in China[14]
Authority or Rights	1. File an indictment[15]; 2. Conduct independent investigations into criminal facts[16]	1. Review the appropriateness of the prosecutor's decision not to prosecute; 2. Make suggestions and recommendations on prosecutorial work	1. Supervise "three types of cases"; 2. Can offer opinions on the "five types of situations"; 3. Can give advice and opinions on "one specific situation"

(continued)

[14] The specific mechanism of the people's supervisor system here is based on the relevant normative documents of the Supreme People's Procuratorate.

[15] Since the mid-nineteenth century, the prosecutor's statement of public prosecution has progressively replaced the indictment filed by the Grand Jury, emerging as a significant and prevalent prosecution procedure, while the Grand Jury's prosecutorial function has gradually diminished.

[16] The Grand Jury possesses unique authorities, typically investigating intricate cases of organized crime, government corruption, and other offenses that are difficult to uncover through methods typically employed by the police.

Ellen Hochstedler Steury & Nancy Frank, *Criminal Court Process*, translated by Chen Weidong & Xu Meijun, China University of Political Science and Law Press, 2002, p. 392.

(continued)

		Grand Jury System in the United States	Prosecutorial Review Commission System in Japan	People's Supervisor System in China
Funding Source			As part of the court's budget, it is funded by the state	Expenditures are incurred from the operational funds of the People's Procuratorate and included in the financial budget at the same administrative level
Scope of Authority		Certain types of cases (major criminal cases)	All cases, excluding those related to civil strife or Antimonopoly Act	Cases investigated directly by procuratorial organs
Organization	Number of Members	A Grand Jury comprises 5 to 23 individuals	The Prosecutorial Review Commission is composed of 11 members	Three or more people's supervisors, with the total number being odd
	Member Selection Mechanism	Lot-drawing, merit-based selection, or both		Prioritization or random draw
Selection and Appointment Mechanism		Random draw	Lot-drawing	Democratic recommendation
Qualifications	Positive	Citizens who have the right to vote, meet certain age requirements, and are of sound mind	Citizens eligible to vote in elections for members of the House of Representatives	1. Uphold the Constitution of the People's Republic of China; 2. Possess the right to vote and stand for election; 3. Be aged 23 or above; 4. Be impartial and upright, with a reasonable level of education and knowledge of policies and laws; 5. Be in good physical condition

(continued)

(continued)

		Grand Jury System in the United States	Prosecutorial Review Commission System in Japan	People's Supervisor System in China
	Negative	No criminal record, etc	Individuals who have not completed primary school education, but those who possess primary school-equivalent or higher academic qualifications are exempt from this restriction; Individuals who have not had their rights restored following bankruptcy; individuals who have been convicted of a crime or sentenced to imprisonment for a term of over one year; 3. The Emperor, Empress, and their descendants, Ministers of State, judges, court personnel, public prosecutors, Public Prosecutors Office personnel, accounting inspectors, members of the Public Safety Commission, police officers, prefectural governors, heads of cities, towns, and villages, lawyers, as well as employees of postal, telecommunications, telephony, railway, and other relevant	1. Individuals who have undergone criminal punishment or are subject to criminal proceedings; 2. Individuals who have been dismissed from public office or dismissed with probationary retention
Term of Service		1 month, 3 months, 6 months, 1 year or 4 years	6 months	3 years (with a maximum of two consecutive terms)
Activation Mechanism		Convened in accordance with the judge's order (in some states, defendants have the right to waive the Grand Jury hearing)	On application (an application made by an accuser, a whistleblower, a petitioner or a victim of a crime to the prosecutorial review commission)	The supervision mechanism will be activated as provided when "three types of cases" arise
			Ex officio (based on news, whistleblowing, or other anonymous tip-off materials)	

(continued)

(continued)

		Grand Jury System in the United States	Prosecutorial Review Commission System in Japan	People's Supervisor System in China
Work Flow		Independent investigation, document review, deliberation and voting	Primarily listen to reports from case handlers, conduct a document review, deliberate and vote	Listen to the presentation and clarification from case handlers, pose questions to the handlers, observe or listen to statements and opinions from relevant personnel, deliberate and vote
Whether the resolution is enforceable or not	Procedural	Yes	Yes	Yes
	Substantive	Yes	Yes[17]	No

[17] The *Laws on Partial Revision of the Criminal Procedure Law* passed by the Japanese National Diet in 2004 and implemented in May 2009 explicitly provides: Following a resolution by the Prosecutorial Review Commission that "prosecution should be pursued" (requiring approval from at least 8 members), if the prosecutor fails to initiate prosecution, the Commission must conduct a review. Should the review again result in at least 8 members supporting a resolution that "prosecution should be pursued," the court receiving a copy of the Commission's resolution shall appoint a lawyer to serve as prosecutor and directly initiate public prosecution. Zhou Yongnian ed., *Introduction to the People's Supervisor System*, China Procuratorial Press, 2008, pp. 70–71.

Upon examining the table above, it becomes evident that while both the Grand Jury system in the United States and the prosecutorial review commission system in Japan are mechanisms designed to facilitate public involvement in the judicial process, they show numerous differences in their specific institutional frameworks and operating modes, each possessing its unique features. Their specific distinctions in institutional design and operating principle reveal their difference in nature positioning.

2.2 *A Comparison of the Nature Positioning of the Grand Jury System with that of the Prosecutorial Review Commission System*

2.2.1 Nature Positioning of the Grand Jury System and the Prosecutorial Review Commission System

The Grand Jury in the United States exercises a direct share of judicial power, possessing independent authority to investigate criminal facts and decide on prosecution, while also having the capacity to scrutinize and restrict procuratorial power. With the enhancement of procuratorial organs' prosecutorial power, the initial restraining function of this system to safeguard citizens against innocent prosecution has diminished. However, the restraining function aimed at preventing the procuratorial organs from declining to prosecute has been fortified, particularly in investigating crimes related to local government corruption and those difficult to detect through methods typically employed by the police. Regarding the Grand Jury system in the United States, as some scholars have noted, "the jury system serves as a mechanism for power restraint, reflecting the people's aversion to concentrating all power in the hands of a single individual."[18] In addition, to a certain extent, the Grand Jury system in the United States can be regarded as a judicial mechanism that embodies local autonomy.[19] The initial source of vitality for the Grand Jury system lies in the confidence that the people, guided by their conscience, can make impartial judgments. This trust is grounded in the common traditions, moral standards, beliefs, and values of the local community where the Grand Jury originates, and bolstered by the public's active participation with a sense of public moral sentiment and responsibility. Consequently, since its establishment, the Grand Jury has been endowed with a social character that stands independent of the state's public authority. It cannot be overlooked that just as society becomes increasingly diverse, so do traditional religious beliefs, values, morality, etc., leading to a gradual weakening of support from traditional and moral sentiments. In terms of power sharing, the Grand Jury

[18] Wang Pengxiang, *Criminal Procedure Law of the United States*, Peking University Press, 2005, p. 14.

[19] See Han Tie, *The Historical Evolution of Jury Nullification in the United States: The Conflict between Democracy and Modernization*, The Chinese Journal of American Studies, 2008.

readily comprehends the motives and actions of criminal suspects, and its conclusions are readily accepted by the public, which gives it democratic legitimacy. As for its restraint on procuratorial power, being distinct from it in nature, the Grand Jury is not susceptible to manipulation by procuratorial organs, rendering it a more potent external check.

The prosecutorial review commission system in Japan serves as an external supervision mechanism for the public to scrutinize the non-prosecutorial discretion within the procuratorial power, while also enabling the public to exercise their right to offer opinions and suggestions. Additionally, it shares the power to decide on public prosecution. In 2004, Law No. 62 made significant revisions to the *Law on Prosecutorial Review Commission*, adding provisions for lawyer assistance in reviews, that is to say, when the prosecutorial review commission deems it necessary to seek supplementary legal expertise during its review, it may appoint review assistants from among lawyers. During the second review, it is mandatory to appoint a lawyer as the one and only review assistant. The reason why the second review is added is that the prosecutorial review commission issues a resolution recommending prosecution and forwards a copy of this resolution to the chief procurator who is required to promptly consider the resolution and take appropriate action, but the procurator still decides against prosecution, or no notice regarding the procurator's decision is received within three months from the date of serving the copy of the resolution, which triggers the second phase of review. In cases where the prosecutorial review commission's resolution is issued in response to an application, and the applicant expresses no objection to the procurator's decision not to prosecute, the review may be terminated. After the second review, if the decision to prosecute remains unchanged, the prosecutorial review commission must draft a resolution detailing the recognized criminal facts and forward a copy of it to the local court. Then the court ought to appoint prosecutors and personnel responsible for sustaining the prosecution from among lawyers.[20] This significant revision has altered the previous effectiveness mechanism of the prosecutorial review commission, which was limited to offering opinions and suggestions without procedural or substantive decision-making authority. As a result, it now possesses the right to directly decide on prosecution on behalf of the public, thereby breaking the monopoly of the procuratorial organs over the right to initiate criminal proceedings and indirectly granting the public the right of criminal prosecution.

2.2.2 Insights Drawn from the Grand Jury System and the Prosecutorial Review Commission System for the People's Supervisor System

The Grand Jury system in the United States has restricted procuratorial power by means of public participation and direct exercise of rights from the beginning, while Japan's prosecutorial review commission system has only recently gained

[20] See Song Yinghui, *Analysis on the Latest Reform in Japan's Criminal Procedure System*, Hebei Law Science, 2007.

a share in procuratorial power. Despite ultimately serving the same purpose, the distinct development processes of these two systems are indeed thought-provoking, mainly attributed to their differences in institutional origin, litigation culture, and institutional conditions.

In terms of institutional origin, the Grand Jury system in the United States emerged as a result of the democratic efforts of the people of the British North American colonies to confront the common law tradition and royal authority of their suzerain. The Grand Jury, which represented the interests of colonial residents, gradually demonstrated its prowess amidst the conflicts between the colonial people and Britain,[21] earning a reputation for defending freedom. Therefore, this system won great popular support and was regarded as the most cherished right by the "British people" in the British North American colonies who would spontaneously and consciously adopt it to safeguard their own rights. In contrast, Japan's prosecutorial review commission system can be regarded as a specialized system that is designed predominantly by authority. Japan adopts the principle of prosecutorial discretion. Article 248 of Code of Criminal Procedure of Japan provides: "Where prosecution is deemed unnecessary owing to the character, age, and environment of the offender, the gravity of the offense, and the circumstances or situation after the offense, prosecution need not be instituted." Although the principle of prosecutorial discretion aligns with the concepts of litigation efficiency and modern "decriminalization policies" in criminal law, and helps to motivate prosecutors,[22] its improper application can lead to arbitrariness and recklessness among prosecutors, ultimately undermining the fundamental interests of the nation and society. Particularly in Japan, where the principle of state prosecution prevails, the exercise of prosecutors' discretion may leave victims and even the public interest of the country without adequate remedy mechanisms when harmed. Therefore, the principle of prosecutorial discretion has been the subject of controversy since its adoption. As a vital restraint on prosecutors' prosecutorial discretion, the prosecutorial review commission system has its own reason for being. It also serves to quell disputes and alleviate public concerns over prosecutors' potential for arbitrariness. The varying causes behind the emergence of the two systems significantly influence their positioning and operating modes. The Grand Jury system in the United States is designed to restrain power through

---

[21] In the eighteenth century, the conflicts of interest between the North American colonies and the British royalty intensified. As the representative of local residents, the Grand Jury struggled with the royal representatives in trials to safeguard the interests of the colonies. Especially before the American Revolution, the Grand Jury was often used by the colonial people as a tool to resist British rule. The Grand Jury's primary function lies in its exercise of jury nullification in practice, where it refused to bring a prosecution in accordance with British law against colonial residents who oppose British royal authority, thereby safeguarding the life, liberty, and property rights of colonial "British people." For instance, by incorporating Grand Jury trials in defamation cases to uphold press freedom, the British defamation law became nearly unenforceable in the British North American colonies.

See Han Tie, *The Historical Evolution of Jury Nullification in the United States: The Conflict between Democracy and Modernization*, The Chinese Journal of American Studies, 2008.

[22] See Chen Yuzhong, *On the Principle of Prosecutorial Discretion in Japanese Criminal Procedure*, Japan Research, 1997.

rights, so as to safeguard citizens' life, liberty, and property from arbitrary infringement by state power. In contrast, Japan's prosecutorial review commission system serves multiple purposes and maintains a closer relationship with state public power. While primarily established to uphold judicial impartiality and prevent the misuse of procuratorial power, it also aims to bolster the judicial system, at the cost of some independence.

In terms of litigation culture and institutional conditions, the Grand Jury system in the United States has evolved within a litigation culture that reveres due process of law, autonomy, and openness. Conversely, the prosecutorial review commission system has emerged and developed amidst a culture characterized by precision justice and bureaucratic monopolism, and operates under distinct institutional conditions. The distrust of power is ingrained in American constitutional culture. In addition to devising elaborate mechanisms to check and balance power, it is also important for people to participate in the judiciary and use their rights to restrict power, and the exercise of power must adhere to the principles of due process of law. Firstly, this contributes to the decentralization of the American judiciary, featuring numerous institutional designs that involve public participation, such as local autonomy in the operations of police and courts, the public election system of prosecutors, the jury system, etc., which embodies a fine tradition of openness to public participation, making it natural and easy for the public to accept institutional designs that share and restrict procuratorial power. Secondly, the exercise of procuratorial power is also restricted by the constitutional principle of due process of law. In many instances, this may lead to the sacrifice of the objective of punishing crimes. However, the Grand Jury, with its unique investigative means,[23] serves as a crucial complement to the power of procuratorial investigation. While the traditional role of the Grand Jury in guarding against prosecutors' abuse of their prosecutorial power to infringe upon the fundamental rights of citizens has gradually diminished, it remains an effective check on prosecutors' non-prosecutorial discretion and may even prove to be a beneficial tool for procuratorial organs in their pursuit of criminal justice. In contrast, since the Meiji period, Japan has essentially established a criminal procedure and judicial system that are uniformly administered solely by legal professionals, which has resulted in thorough investigations being conducted in Japan, with suspects in custody being subject to the utmost scrutiny within the confines of not directly conflicting with due process. Prosecutors generally only initiate proceedings when they are fully convinced of the sufficiency of the evidence. Court trials tend to rely heavily on documentary evidence, and with an annual conviction rate exceeding 99%, Japan's criminal procedure exhibits a distinctive characteristic of "precision justice."[24] The prosecution of criminal cases is deemed to serve the purpose of safeguarding the public interest, and vesting prosecutors with exclusive prosecutorial power ensures

---

[23] Several states in the United States have adopted some reform initiatives, a key aspect of which involves the integration of due process of law into the Grand Jury's inquiry procedure, such as allowing witnesses to have legal representation during such inquiry.

[24] See Matsuo Koya, *Japanese Criminal Procedure Law I*, China Renmin University Press, 2005, pp. 16–18.

maximum uniformity in the exercise of such power. To uncover the "truth of the matter" and impose punishment on criminals, a centralized and unified procedure is necessary, which imbues criminal justice with a pronounced bureaucratic flavor. Essentially, it operates within a relatively closed environment within the judicial system. Japan's philosophy of precision justice, coupled with its related institutional design and a relatively closed bureaucratic culture, contributes to the high quality of case handling by its procuratorial organs. The power restraint mechanisms for direct sharing or division of procuratorial power struggle to seamlessly integrate with existing systems, so the initial approach of adopting external supervision to offer opinions and suggestions is deemed more viable. The direct adoption of the American jury system met with strong opposition in Japan.[25] While the prosecutorial review commission system draws inspiration from American legal concepts, it possesses distinct Japanese characteristics in practice, enabling its continued existence and development.

The Grand Jury system in the United States and the prosecutorial review commission system in Japan share a common nature positioning: they are both judicial democratic mechanisms that empower citizens to participate in the judiciary and exercise their rights to supervise or restrict procuratorial power. And they serve not only as safeguards for citizens' rights but also as avenues through which citizens can exercise their rights. Their difference resides in the extent of public participation and the degree to which procuratorial power is shared, as well as their respective specific function positioning. Neither of them is targeted at all criminal cases. The original intention of the Grand Jury in the United States was to prevent the persecution of the public by the abuse of prosecutorial power. Later, it shifted its focus to actively investigating crimes, with "public interest" as its core concern. Japan's prosecutorial review commission mainly reviews non-prosecution decisions to prevent the abuse of non-prosecutorial discretion, aiming to provide civil remedies in the form of "switching from public prosecution to private prosecution" for victims and in the interest of social welfare.[26] The analysis of the distinct development processes of the two systems and the underlying reasons offers valuable insights into the nature positioning of China's people's supervisor system. Japan's experience is particularly instructive. For one thing, the origins of China's people's supervisor system bear similarities to those of Japan's prosecutorial review commission system. In addition to safeguarding judicial fairness, both are specialized systems predominantly designed by public authorities and serve to uphold the legitimacy of procuratorial organs' investigation power. "Behind this enthusiastic push for judicial reform may lay motives unrelated to the public interest, such as an attempt by the reformers to showcase their image as reformers and highlight their reform accomplishments."[27]

[25] For the reform of the Grand Jury system in the United States, see Zhou Yongnian ed., *Introduction to the People's Supervisor System*, China Procuratorial Press, 2008, p. 60.

[26] See Xin Peiyan, *Comparative Analysis and Practical Evaluation of the People's Supervisor System: With Reference to the General Characteristics of Extraterritorial Public Participation in Procuratorial Power*, Justice of China, 2008.

[27] Su Li, *Paths Lead to Cities: Rule of Law in Transitional China*, Law Press·China, 2004, p. 195.

For another thing, in the handling of cases directly investigated by procuratorial organs, their power is largely exercised in a closed manner, bearing strong elements of bureaucracy. Meanwhile, procuratorial reform has consistently sought to enhance case-handling quality and refine procedural precision. Japan's experience tells us that the nature positioning of the people's supervisor system should align with national conditions and meet the needs of judicial practice on the premise of respecting the constitutional principles of power restriction and rights protection and the democratic spirit of public participation in the judiciary, and the nature positioning of the system will become increasingly precise as it evolves progressively.

3 The Nature Positioning of the People's Supervisor System Within China's Constitutional Framework

3.1 Why Is Positioning Necessary?

The people's supervisor system is an institutional innovation independently devised by procuratorial organs and is constantly evolving and changing. The nature positioning of the people's supervisor system is of particular significance for its in-depth theoretical research, especially for its legitimacy argumentation, thereby promoting its practical progress. Generally speaking, positioning has two meanings, one is to measure the position of an object with an instrument, and the other refers to the position determined by such measurement.[28] We can see from its general meaning that positioning is used both as a verb, signifying the dynamic process, and as a noun, representing the outcome. And some methods and tools are needed to ensure the accuracy of the outcome. The positioning used in social sciences usually refers to the application of analytical tools and precise argumentation process in a defined field in order to place things in appropriate positions and make certain evaluations. The nature positioning is to find the immanent determinacy that reflects the essential attributes of things, so as to determine their appropriate position in a certain field. Therefore, positioning often serves as the logical starting point for discussion, and different positioning may yield entirely different outcomes.

3.1.1 Theoretical Level: The Underlying Need for Legitimacy Argumentation

Since September 2003, the practical implementation of the people's supervisor system has always been accompanied by doubts and endorsements. Various statistical data and individual cases can demonstrate the effectiveness and rationality of

[28] See Division of Dictionary Compilation, Institute of Linguistics, Chinese Academy of Social Sciences, *Contemporary Chinese Dictionary*, The Commercial Press, 1995, p. 255.

the system since its implementation, but its lifeblood consists in its acquisition and maintenance of legitimacy, and rationality can only serve as an auxiliary support for its legitimacy. Especially in a society ruled by law, the system cannot be implemented through state coercion, but needs to obtain legitimacy that practitioners, scholars and the public can agree on. The current legitimacy argumentation, which is not fully based on the nature positioning of the people's supervisor system, suffers from a scattered focus and a certain lack of persuasiveness. These arguments are either overly grand in their narrative or excessively confined to practical needs, particularly those related to the exercise of procuratorial power. Furthermore, the absence of a formal legal framework to provide substantiated backing adds to the inadequacy of the legitimacy argumentation for the people's supervisor system. As a result, in practice, there is a lack of confidence in the system's continued implementation, leading to a casual attitude or arbitrary modifications and adjustments in its implementation methods.

The nature positioning of the people's supervisor system is needed to establish a platform for communication and exchange during the process of legitimacy argumentation. In the absence of clear positioning, "debates among those holding different views resemble deaf people's dialogue, guiding the discussion towards a semblance of prosperity, lively but devoid of substantial content."[29] Habermas once provided a concise explanation of legitimacy in its narrow sense, asserting that legitimacy means the recognized value and de facto acknowledgment of some political order. To gain recognition and acknowledgement, there must be a platform for communication and exchange, and only through genuine communication and exchange can a true consensus be reached. The nature positioning of the people's supervisor system has laid a solid foundation for the construction of this discussion platform. Researchers can readily grasp the starting points of other researchers' argumentation concerning the legitimacy of the people's supervisor system, thus enabling mutual understanding and further discussion, and avoiding arbitrary criticism or repeated argumentation that is disguised as new argumentation by virtue of discourse transformation. At the same time, clear positioning facilitates the general public's acceptance and understanding, which in turn earns recognition for the people's supervisor system as it operates and develops healthily.

As an indispensable element and logical starting point for legitimacy argumentation, the nature positioning of the people's supervisor system embodies the value expectations embedded in the design of the system and shapes the system's development trajectory. Only by first grasping the immanent determinacy of the people's supervisor system can we proceed with its legitimacy argumentation. Its immanent determinacy is the primary aspect to be examined in the legitimacy argumentation. Only when its nature positioning meets the requirements of legitimacy will its specific institutional design have the potential to acquire and maintain legitimacy. Meanwhile, the nature positioning of the people's supervisor system is also a strategy to secure its legitimacy. Various nature positioning requires distinct proof paths. During the system's design phase, we can choose the nature positioning that can easily

[29] Charles Taylor, *Models of Civil Society*, Central Compilation & Translation Press, 2002, p. 3.

gain recognition and acceptance, so as to reduce the costs and obstacles associated with persuasion during system implementation. Therefore, the nature positioning of the people's supervisor system is also the logical starting point for its legitimacy argumentation.

3.1.2 Practical Level: The Inevitable Requirement for Overcoming Institutional Design Challenges

The people's supervisor system has undergone nearly five years of development since its pilot phase, during which it has achieved remarkable and widely recognized results, while also gradually maturing and progressing towards the establishment of a formal legal system. However, in practice, it still encounters many institutional design challenges. Firstly, the role of the people's procuratorate within the people's supervisor system. As the originator and supervisee of the system, the people's procuratorate initiates, guides, and facilitates the supervision process, ensures funding, and in certain regions, even selects the supervisors, which results in some degree of identity confusion and an awkward situation where they may not feel justified in their actions. Secondly, the selection and appointment mechanism of people's supervisors. Should we adopt the higher-level supervision model or the same-level supervision model for selection? Is it permissible for people's congresses at all levels to intervene in the selection of people's supervisors, and would such intervention exceed the authority granted by the Constitution and laws? Should we prioritize democracy, participation, and representativeness, or should we emphasize professionalism, knowledge, and competence to ensure the accuracy of their supervision results? Thirdly, to what extent can people's supervisors exercise their rights or authority during the supervision process. In order to guarantee that they can make informed supervision decisions, should people's supervisors be granted the exclusive investigation power of procuratorial organs to confront criminal suspects directly, and could this potentially lead to the emergence of non-professional "procurators"? To ensure the effectiveness of their supervision, should people's supervisors be endowed with the authority to make decisions on substantive matters? Fourthly, regarding the path selection for the institutionalization of the people's supervisor system, if legal form is not employed, would it constitute a violation of the principle of legal reservation? And so on.

These institutional design challenges arise from various subjective and objective factors, with one significant contributor being the lack of clear nature positioning of the people's supervisor system and the absence of a consensus. In fact, the solution to these difficulties relies on clear nature positioning of the people's supervisor system. The nature positioning of the people's supervisor system determines the value and functional expectation of its institutional design, while also addressing the issue of achieving balance in its institutional design and shaping its operational dynamics, as manifested in: the legal requirement of the system—whether explicit authorization by law is necessary or whether mere absence of legal prohibition suffices; the effectiveness support of the system—what degree of coercive force the state should provide to guarantee its effectiveness, or does it solely rely on the effectiveness given by its own legitimacy; the operating mode of the system—does it adopt a model of command and compliance, or one of communication, negotiation, and participation?

3.2 How Can the Positioning Be Done?

The nature positioning of the people's supervisor system is confined to China's constitutional framework, centered around civil rights and state power, and grounded in the structural and functional disparities between civil rights and state power.

3.2.1 The Core of Positioning—Based on the Evaluation of the Existing Positioning Theory

The nature positioning of the people's supervisor system has always been an issue that researchers continuously pay attention to and rethink on. At the beginning of the pilot program for the people's supervisor system, some researchers pointed out that the existing system is an internal supervision mechanism for procuratorial organs, but it also features a pronounced attribute of external supervision. The effectiveness of the people's supervisor system lies in its integration into the procuratorial organs' work procedure in the form of internal supervision. Instead of transforming the system into an external supervision mechanism for procuratorial organs, efforts should be directed towards refining relevant systems to uphold the external attribute of people's supervisors.[30] From the perspective of supervision classification, other researchers have positioned the people's supervisor system as supervision over the exercise of power, external supervision, and post-event supervision over cases directly investigated by the people's procuratorates.[31] After discussing the implementation foundation and characteristics of the people's supervisor system, and comparing it with the supervision by the National People's Congress, the people's assessor system, and the integrity supervisor system, some researchers have positioned the people's supervisor system as external supervision with independent legal status, which is social supervision of rights over power,[32] embodying the trinity of social supervision, democratic supervision, and external supervision.[33] This point of view is relatively

[30] See Zhou Hailin, *On the Nature and Improvement of the People's Supervisor System*, Journal of Fujian Police College, 2004.

[31] See Huang He, *Positioning of the People's Supervisor System—From the Perspective of Legal Supervision Classification*, Administration and Law, 2006.

[32] See Zhou Yongnian, *Reflections on the Legal Positioning of the People's Supervisor System*, Law Science, 2006.

[33] See Zhou Yongnian ed., *Introduction to the People's Supervisor System*, China Procuratorial Press, 2008, p. 41.

representative and comprehensive.[34] In addition, some researchers have attempted to mediate the conflict between the perspective of rights and that of authority, aiming to strike a balance between the democracy and effectiveness of the people's supervisor system. They position the system as quasi-authority supervision, "a right with elements of authority," as it's substantively rights-based and procedurally authority-based, and appeal for legislative action to facilitate the transition of the system from quasi-authority supervision to authority-based supervision.

Any attempt to position the people's supervisor system is valuable and highly enlightening, as we require a map to navigate our way through the territory of law. Even if a map is inaccurate overall, it can still offer some guidance, as without one, people would be unable to plan or organize their trips.[35] From the aforementioned views on the positioning of the people's supervisor system, we can see that these views emerge along with the practical implementation of the system and it's a time-phased process of constant thinking and rethinking. The views are put forward primarily from three perspectives: the authority-based one, the rights-based one, and the eclectic one. They also classify the system as external or internal supervision, social supervision, democratic supervision, rigid or flexible supervision, and pre-event or post-event supervision. These views often rely on comprehensive consideration, instead of a single standard, to think about the issue of positioning. For example, different standards are adopted to determine whether the supervision is rights-based or authority-based, external or internal, and pre-event or post-event. There will always be some overlap among different perspectives on the positioning, for instance, whether the perspective is authority-based, rights-based, or eclectic, external supervision may be a consensus. Logically speaking, a positioning description overlapping other descriptions is generally not fundamental and immanently determinate and thus cannot determine the nature of the people's supervisor system. External descriptions that correspond to different contexts are unable to be the core of positioning. Moreover, a positioning description that can be determined by other positioning is incapable of being the core of nature positioning. For instance, rights-based

[34] For example, some researchers contend that the people's supervisor system represents an institutional innovation that effectively fulfills citizens' right to supervision within the existing legal framework and it provides a kind of supervision exercised by the masses.

See Wen Shengtang, *Institutional Innovation in Civil Rights Supervision over Procuratorial Power: A Re-examination of the People's Supervisor System*;

Research Group on Theoretical Studies of the People's Supervisor System, *Theoretical Foundations and Legislative Issues of the People's Supervisor System (Part 1)*, Fangyuan Rule of Law Special Issue on People's Supervisors, 2006.

Likewise, some researchers argue that the supervision by people's supervisors constitutes citizen oversight, which belongs to the category of social supervision.

See Ding Haiyan, *A Discussion on the People's Supervisor System and Its Improvement*, Fangyuan Rule of Law Special Issue on People's Supervisors, 2008.

What's more, some researchers have specifically noted that the people's supervisor system is essentially a claim for social supervision.

See Xu Hanming, *An Economic Analysis of the Concept and Characteristics of the People's Supervisor System*, Fangyuan Rule of Law Special Issue on People's Supervisors, 2005.

[35] See Martin Loughlin, *Public Law and Political Theory*, translated by Zheng Ge, The Commercial Press, 2002, p. 55.

supervision, grounded in the principle of popular sovereignty, inherently possesses the nature of democratic supervision. Similarly, a positioning description that exerts no influence on other positioning cannot be the core of nature positioning either, as exemplified by pre-event or post-event supervision. According to the aforementioned triple exclusion criteria, the supervision based on authority or rights stands as the core of nature positioning of the people's supervisor system.

In the realm of legal science, we must position the nature of the people's supervisor system within the constitutional framework, as the general distinction between rights and authority holds little significance in positioning the nature of the system. Authority and rights are one of the most important and central pairs of categories in all social sciences that study human society. Sometimes the distinction between the two is not entirely clear-cut, like in *Black's Law Dictionary*, "rights" contains the interpretation of "a person's authority". Some scholars also believe that, in a certain sense, rights can be a type of authority. Authority signifies an effective binding force, whereas rights integrate the dual attributes of legitimacy and effectiveness, thus considered to be legitimate authority.[36] For a long time in history, rights and obligations have been seen as corresponding categories, while authority has consistently been neglected in legal studies. It was not until the bourgeois revolutions of the seventeenth and eighteenth centuries, particularly with the advent of modern constitutional nations, that the groundwork for the evolution of public law was established. As a result, civil rights and state power emerged as core categories in legal studies,[37] possessing opposing and distinguishable meanings. This is because neither slave-owning nor feudal states could ever give rise to a constitution, nor could they foster genuine rule of law. The emergence of a constitution serves as both a hallmark and a prerequisite for the establishment of modern rule of law. Adhering to the supremacy of the constitution is crucial for governing the country in accordance with the law and building a socialist country under the rule of law.[38] The key to building China into a socialist rule of law country also lies in the construction of socialist constitutionalism.[39] Therefore, we position the nature of the people's supervisor system within China's constitutional framework.

State power and civil rights are the core categories within the constitutional framework, so the core of nature positioning of the people's supervisor system is whether it should be regarded as a type of supervision based on state power, civil rights, or even fundamental rights. This is because power restraint is the timeless core essence of

---

[36] See Wang Lijun, *Dialectics of Power and Rights*, China Legal Publishing House, 2005, pp. 45–48.

[37] The law-power theory was among the first to prioritize power, breaking through the traditional framework of rights and obligations to establish a new one centered on rights and power. The rights and power highlighted in this theory actually correspond to the civil rights and state power that are now particularly valued in constitutional law.

For its representative views, see Tong Zhiwei, *Legal Rights and Constitutional Governance*, Shandong People's Publishing House, 2001.

[38] See Qin Qianhong, *Rule of Law and Constitutional Supremacy*, Modern Law Science, 1996.

[39] For details of the connotation, justification, and development vision of socialist constitutional governance within the Chinese context, see Qin Qianhong & Ye Haibo, *Research on Socialist Constitutional Governance*, Shandong People's Publishing House, 2008.

constitutionalism, and "constitutional limitations" are undoubtedly the oldest principle of constitutionalism, though not the most important part.[40] The civil rights in the constitution serve as the boundary for state power, and to safeguard these rights is to enforce the constitutional restrictions on state power. Consequently, restrictions on state power and its effective exercise, as well as the protection of civil rights, become the core of constitutional institutional arrangements. From a positivist standpoint, the constitution, as the foundational norm of a country's legal order,[41] has supreme legal force, shaping the country's legal order and establishing the ultimate benchmark that cannot be bypassed by any institutional design seeking legitimacy. Therefore, civil rights and state powers are bound to constitute the core of nature positioning of the people's supervisor system.

3.2.2 The Foundation for Positioning—Grounded in the Structural and Functional Disparities Between Civil Rights and State Power Within the Constitutional Framework

Based on the structural and functional distinctions between civil rights and state power within the constitutional framework, and considering the characteristics of the people's supervisor system agreed upon in its practical implementation, this book positions the people's supervisor system as a specific way to exercise basic civil rights. The constitutional theoretical framework of state power and civil rights is grounded in the theoretical presupposition of the classical liberal binary opposition between the state and the individual. As the third sector emerges in modern society, its theory has transcended the Western-originated polarized opposition model between the state and the individual. As an intermediate domain theory with a propensity for communication and collaboration, it resonates more deeply with China. As a result, the theoretical presupposition of the traditional binary structure has been challenged.[42] However, even the relationship of cooperation, communication, and negotiation between the subjects of state power and those of civil rights through the public sphere is necessarily on the premise of a certain degree of opposition and tension and thus not enough to undermine the status of the paradigm of state power and civil rights within constitutionalism.

---

[40] See McIlwain C. H., *Constitutionalism: Ancient and Modern*, translated by Zhai Xiaobo, Guizhou People's Publishing House, 2004.

[41] See Kelsen, *General Theory of Law and State*, translated by Shen Zongling, Encyclopedia of China Publishing House, 1996, pp. 130–149, 142–162.

[42] For example, what is the nature of the actions undertaken by the third sector? That is, do its internal governance and external participation in governance constitute an exercise of power or rights in the constitution? How will the social powers or rights of the third sector, with its nature defined as such, impact the clear demarcation between traditional state power and civil rights? Does this influence possess sufficient constitutional value to alter or transcend the existing research paradigm of constitutional law? Do regulations of the third sector reside within or beyond the legal normative system? That is, can they possess autonomous "legislative power" to operate outside the constitutional legal framework of a state, while simultaneously wielding legally binding force? These questions remain to be further studied.

Civil rights and state power exhibit both structural disparities and commonalities. Civil rights comprise five essential elements: interests, claims, entitlements, capacities, and freedoms.[43] They represent the entitlement and capacity of the subject to autonomously request others to act or refrain from acting, as well as the subject's own freedom to act or refrain from acting, in order to fulfill certain interest demands. State power refers to political coercive force and the authority to exercise control within defined jurisdictional reach. Firstly, regarding their origin, civil rights have been perceived at different historical stages as endowed by God, deemed essential for safeguarding human dignity or fostering comprehensive human development. Conversely, state power is viewed as established either through social contracts where individuals in a natural state alienate their God-given rights, or by the ruling class for the purpose of maintaining their own dominion. Rights possess primordiality and legitimacy, whereas state power is regarded as a necessary evil that requires vigilance and constraint. Secondly, regarding the subject, there are no particular restrictions on those who enjoy civil rights, aside from nationality or the capacity to actually exercise those rights. Conversely, due to the organizational nature of state power, its holders must be state organs legally established or organizations/individuals authorized by laws and regulations, typically subject to various substantive and formal restrictive conditions. Thirdly, in terms of content, civil rights encompass personal and freedom rights, political rights, social rights, among others. Meanwhile, state power can generally be divided into legislative, executive, judicial, military, head-of-state, and procuratorial powers. There is a distinct difference between the two. Fourthly, in terms of relativity, neither civil rights nor state powers are absolute and must be subject to certain restrictions. The legitimacy for restricting civil rights can solely originate from rights, such as public interests. In contrast, the limitation of state power can stem from the division or separation within the state power, while more fundamental constraints arise from basic civil rights that exist outside the realm of state power. Fifthly, in terms of effects, both civil rights and state power can generate a type of coercive force. The distinction lies in the fact that the binding force of civil rights depends on the people's collective recognition of such rights, otherwise they can only be enforced through the state's fulfillment of its protective and remedial obligations, while state power inherently possesses the resources, strength, and means to compel compliance from its subjects. Sixthly, in terms of normative form, the exercise of state power must be expressly granted by the constitution, laws, or legally binding normative instruments, or be delegated by competent authorities based on explicit authorization norms, all subject to the principles of legal reservation and legal supremacy. In contrast, whatever is not expressly prohibited by law constitutes a right.

There are also functional differences between civil rights and state power. The functional system of civil rights comprises: defensive fundamental rights enjoyed by citizens, stemming from their negative status, which afford them a sphere of freedom and action shielded from state intervention; rights of claim based on their positive

[43] See Xia Yong, *The Origins of the Concept of Human Rights*, China University of Political Science and Law Press, 2001, pp. 46–48.

status, through which citizens can request state power to assist, care for, or facilitate the pursuit of their interests; participation or influence rights derived from their proactive status as national "members," enabling them to engage actively in public affairs and impact or alter existing legal conditions; and fundamental rights that necessitate collective action for effectiveness, often requiring specific organizations or procedures for protection, thereby extending into the procedural dimension of fundamental rights.[44] State power serves two functions: firstly, to safeguard civil rights; secondly, to preserve the state's existence. Like civil rights, state power also has interest demands. However, preserving the state's existence is not its ultimate objective; rather, its ultimate aim lies in safeguarding the interests of the ruling class and, to some extent, those of the ruled class—civil rights. The function of state power in preserving the state's existence needs to be strictly limited, with the acquisition of national interests confined to what is sufficient to enable the state to fulfill its obligation of safeguarding civil rights. It is evident that the fulfillment of the functions of both civil rights and state power hinges on their interrelationship, with the realization of civil rights as their shared ultimate value pursuit.

We position the people's supervisor system as rights-based supervision due to the fact that: for one thing, it embodies the structural demands of civil rights. In terms of its origin, the people's supervisor system reflects democratic supervision over procuratorial power—a state power—by citizens outside the state power structure, thus possessing inherent democratic legitimacy. From the perspective of the subject, apart from the need to ensure supervision and judgment capabilities, there are no specific restrictive conditions for the subject enjoying rights. In terms of content, people's supervisors exercise the right to be informed, criticize and make suggestions, which falls within the category of political rights. In terms of effects, acts of rights also possess binding force, particularly the widely acknowledged binding force that basic civil rights in the constitution exert on state public power. The concern that positioning the people's supervisor system as a right might compromise the effectiveness of such supervision stems from a misconception about the effects of rights. In terms of normative form, while it is commonly held that "what is not explicitly forbidden by law is a right," rights that lack explicit constitutional and legal protection are vulnerable. In certain circumstances, it is actually the law that defines the scope of rights and has the capacity to restrict them. Rights lacking a clear constitutional and legal foundation are frequently the most susceptible to infringement by state power, and it is hard to secure judicial relief for such rights. Therefore, while the enjoyment of rights does not require legal or even constitutional provisions, rights have a natural aspiration to be safeguarded by the constitution and laws. Even if the people's supervisor system is positioned as rights-based supervision, it is necessary to strive to formalize it through official legal system. For another thing, the people's supervisor system possesses the functions of participation, influence, and procedural rights. By exercising their rights to criticize and make suggestions, supervisors can engage in the exercise of procuratorial power and rectify any errors that arise during

[44] For the theory of the subjective functional system of basic rights, see Li Jianliang, *The Conceptual Changes and Functional System of Basic Rights*, The Constitutional Era.

the process. These functions can only be fulfilled through organizational and procedural designs. We should not regard the people's supervisor system merely as an autonomous reform tool for the procuratorial power to get rid of doubts, nor should we assess its necessity on whether it conforms to the operational principles of the procuratorial power and whether it is beneficial to the exercise of the procuratorial power; at the very least, this should not be the sole criterion for evaluation. As rights-based supervision, the people's supervisor system has its own independent value function. Ultimately, the procuratorial power, as a state power, aims to safeguard civil rights.

3.3 The People's Supervisor System as a Specific Way to Exercise Basic Civil Rights

The people's supervisor system possesses the nature of rights-based supervision and serves as a specific way to exercise basic civil rights. Basic civil rights are significant and fundamental rights that individuals ought to enjoy, initially recognized and acknowledged by countries adhering to the rule of law, and constitute part of "human rights" that precede the establishment of the state. With the advent of modern constitution, civil rights that emerge subsequent to the establishment of the state, including political rights and social rights, which are based on the state's creation, have been incorporated into the category of basic rights. The provisions on basic rights in the constitutional text declare the actual commitment of the state to realizing these rights. Chapter II of current *Constitution* of China, "Fundamental Rights and Obligations of Citizens," provides the basic rights of Chinese citizens, but the provisions on basic civil rights are actually not limited to this chapter. The understanding of a basic civil right should not rely on any single article. Instead, it should be understood in combination with the relevant provisions in the General Provisions and those on the obligations of state organs.

Specifically, the supervision by people's supervisors over the discretionary power of procuratorial organs in the cases directly investigated by such organs is, in its nature, citizens' exercise of their right to criticize and make suggestions. The right of citizens to criticize and make suggestions is affirmed through the following constitutional norms: Firstly, Article 2 of the Constitution provides that all power in the People's Republic of China belongs to the people.... The people shall, in accordance with the provisions of law, manage state affairs, economic and cultural undertakings, and social affairs through various channels and in various ways. Secondly, Article 33 of the Constitution provides that the state shall respect and protect human rights. Lastly, Article 41 of the Constitution provides that citizens of the People's Republic of China shall have the right to criticize and make suggestions regarding any state organ or state employee, and have the right to file with relevant state organs complaints, charges or reports against any state organ or state employee for violations of the law or dereliction of duty... The state organ concerned must ascertain the facts concerning the complaints, charges or reports made by citizens and take responsibility for their handling. No one shall suppress such complaints, charges or reports or take retaliatory action.. Article 27 of the Constitution provides that all state organs and state employees must rely on the support of the people, stay engaged with them, listen to their opinions and suggestions, accept their oversight, and work hard to serve them.

There is a tension among the above-mentioned provisions in the constitutional text regarding citizens' right to criticize and make suggestions. For a long time, we have held the misconception that the codified constitution stands as a logically self-contained and self-consistent normative system. However, in reality, given that the essence of the constitution is "the concentrated manifestation of the comparing relation of various political forces during the establishment of a democratic state by the ruling class of a country",[45] self-containment and self-consistency are merely "fictions."[46] We briefly divide the above norms into three levels: At the first level, the provisions of Article 2 in the constitutional text serve as the logical basis for other provisions, but this article itself contains tensions. This article provides that "all power belongs to the people," but it also provides that the people shall, "in accordance with the provisions of law", manage state affairs. Here, the term "law," based on Article 5 in the constitutional text, which provides that "no law, administrative regulation or local regulation shall be in conflict with the Constitution," coupled with numerous provisions in the constitutional text that juxtapose "the Constitution and the law," can be interpreted systematically as referring to laws in a narrow sense, namely those enacted by the National People's Congress and its Standing Committee, which has resulted in the fact that it is the national legislature that determines the scope of the people's right to manage state affairs. At the second level, Article 33 in the constitutional text can serve as a general provision for constitutional rights. However, the term "human rights" within it may obviously give rise to a tension with "fundamental rights of citizens," because the expression of "human rights" carries an unavoidable classical liberal ideological backdrop, probably incompatible with the nationalist tendency that permeates the constitutional text. Therefore, beyond its declarative significance, the practical efficacy of this provision is limited. At the third level, Article 41 in the constitutional text is usually referred to as the provision on supervision, containing rights such as criticism, suggestion, complaint, accusation, and reporting. Article 41 also shows a way to participate in national governance, albeit without any legal restrictions on its exercise. Article 27 provides the obligation of state organs to listen to the opinions and suggestions of the people and accept their supervision, which can form a corresponding set of rights and obligations with the provisions of Article 41.

Therefore, we can take Article 41 and Article 27 in the constitutional text as the direct constitutional basis for the people's supervisor system, and position the nature of the system as the supervision by citizens exercising their right to criticize and make

---

[45] Zhou Yezhong ed., *Constitution*, Higher Education Press & Peking University Press, 2001, p. 44.

[46] Carl Schmitt: *Constitutional Theory*, translated by Liu Feng, Shanghai People's Publishing House, 2005, p. 13.

suggestions. Article 41 establishes the enjoyment of basic civil rights, and Article 27 defines the obligations of the state, equipping the basic civil rights in Article 41 with a rigid binding force. Meanwhile, the method of constitutional interpretation can be employed to take Article 2 and Article 33 in the constitutional text as its indirect basis. The phrase "in accordance with the law" in Article 2 should not be construed as a restriction on citizens' rights to manage state affairs, but rather as a requirement for the state's legislative power, that is, it has the obligation to enact various laws to guarantee the exercise of citizens' rights to manage state affairs. Besides, the term "human rights" in Article 33 can be understood in a positivist way and this article can be used as a general provision to integrate different basic rights and generate rights not listed in the constitution.

While our constitutional text includes provisions on the right to criticize and make suggestions, which can be exercised through specific channels like the petition system, this right has always been characterized by more criticism than suggestions in practice, with suggestions often going unheard. As a result, these provisions have not been effectively implemented. Although the constitutional fundamental rights are principled in nature and generally needs to be concretized in legal system for implementation, their enforcement is not solely contingent upon such concretization in branches of law. Once provided in the constitution, these rights acquire immediate normative effect.[47] However, its realization requires the manifestation of legal technical and judicial rationality, along with actions, plans, and even more refined legislative and judicial techniques,[48] so this approach is frequently overlooked in practice owing to the difficulty in its utilization. Moreover, China's constitution "has traditionally placed emphasis on the legislative safeguards of political organs, while somewhat neglecting judicial remedies for basic rights,"[49] resulting in the situation where constitutional fundamental rights in China can only be remedied and safeguarded in the form of legal rights. Therefore, the people's supervisor system proactively promoted by the procuratorial organs, as a specific way to realize basic civil rights, has a constitutional basis and also opens a channel for the direct implementation of constitutional fundamental rights. It can be optimistically anticipated that the practical value of the people's supervisor system will transcend mere supervision and restraint of the proper exercise of discretionary power in cases directly investigated by procuratorial organs. Rather, it will also serve as an institutional arrangement with direct binding force on state public power so as to supervise other state powers,[50] and

[47] See Han Dayuan ed., *Research on the Constitutional Foundations of China's Procuratorial System*, China Procuratorial Press, 2007, p. 397.

[48] See Zheng Xianjun, *Research on Fundamental Rights*, China Democracy and Legal System Publishing House, 2007, p. 510.

[49] *Ibid.*, p. 524.

[50] For example, some scholars suggest that China's police system could introduce a "people's supervisor" mechanism, drawing inspiration from the "people's assessor" system in people's courts, the recently implemented "people's supervisor" system in people's procuratorates, as well as the "police complaint council" system in Hong Kong Special Administrative Region.

See Liu Jie, *Constitutional Control of Police Power in China*, Journal of Beijing People's Police College, 2005.

offer an institutional model for the transformation of other constitutional fundamental rights from legal rights to actual rights.

3.4 A Comparative Study of the People's Supervisor System and the People's Assessor System

As one of the 12 breakthroughs in the judicial reform of the people's courts over the past decade, the improvement of the working mechanism of people's assessors has been hailed by the media as "the most democratic" reform.[51] The purpose and content of the people's supervisor system indicate that, like the assessor system of the people's courts, it is an effective form for citizens to participate in judicial affairs and reflects the requirements of litigation democracy, marking another major progress in China's judicial democratization following the people's assessor system.[52] Since both the people's supervisor system and the people's assessor system are institutional designs aimed at engaging the public in the exercise of state power, "there are many similarities between the two, primarily in the following three aspects: One similarity is their shared political significance. Both systems are a direct manifestation of the political rights of the people to be the masters of the country and their constitutional rights to participate in the management of state affairs under China's socialist system. Both systems enable ordinary citizens without legal professional backgrounds to participate in the country's judicial activities. This embodies the substantive reliance on the people in China's socialist judicial system, reinforces its essential democratic nature, and continuously deepens the public's sense of identification with judicial work. Second, the participants share the same identity. Both people's assessors and people's supervisors involved in these two systems are ordinary citizens from all sectors of society, embodying broad representativeness and strong public support. Both are capable of incorporating the public's cognitive perspectives, ethical standards, and values into judicial work, complementing the thinking of judges and procurators specializing in trials and prosecutions. This allows judicial organs to better embody the spirit of serving the people and upholding social fairness and justice, thus achieving the organic unity of social and legal effects in case handling, and fostering social harmony. Third, they serve the same function. Both systems contribute to enhancing judicial fairness. The implementation of the people's assessor system and the pilot operation of the people's supervisor system place China's judicial work under direct public supervision, effectively enhancing

[51] See Chen Fei & Yang Weihan, *People's Assessors: The "Most Democratic" Reform*, Xinhua Daily Telegraph, 2008, at 6.

[52] See Tong Jianming, Wan Chun & Gao Jingfeng, *A Proposal for Strengthening the Legal Supervision Functions of Procuratorial Organs in Judicial System Reform II*, People's Procuratorial Semimonthly, 2005.

the openness, transparency and social credibility of the judiciary, and strengthening the authority of judicial organs."[53]

The specific institutional arrangements in the normative documents regarding the people's supervisor system and its practical implementation by procuratorial organs across regions have borrowed insights from the people's assessor system. Some researchers, using the people's assessor system as a model, have made assumptions about the development of the people's supervisor system, with key viewpoints as follows: Viewpoint 1: evaluate the design of the people's supervisor system based on that of the people's assessor system, so as to justify the legitimacy of the people's supervisor system. Viewpoint 2: draw inspiration from the rigid binding force of the opinions of people's assessors in the people's assessor system, and grant rigid binding force to the opinions of people's supervisors. Viewpoint 3: learn from the specific institutional designs of the people's assessor system, including selection and appointment mechanism, content of rights, trial participation mechanism, as well as the people's courts' management and training modes for people's assessors, to improve the people's supervisor system. Viewpoint 4: draw upon the institutionalization path of the people's assessor system, which was established by a decision of the Standing Committee of the National People's Congress, with specific implementation measures formulated by the Supreme People's Court and subsequently codified in procedural law, to similarly institutionalize the people's supervisor system through legislation.[54] In fact, the extent to which the people's supervisor system can draw on the people's assessor system fundamentally depends on the difference in the nature positioning of the two systems, which determines their commonalities and discrepancies. The following is an analysis one by one:

3.4.1 Analysis of the Viewpoint that the People's Supervisor System Seeks Basis for Its Legitimacy from the People's Assessor System

The people's assessor system in China boasts a history of nearly 70 years, having established its unique operational patterns while also facing unresolved problems. Therefore, while the people's assessor system can offer valuable insights and readily available institutional resources to the people's supervisor system in multiple dimensions, bolstering confidence and minimizing costs in its design and implementation, it cannot yet be regarded as the basis for system design or legitimacy argumentation.

The different processes through which the two systems emerged dictate that the legitimacy of the people's supervisor system cannot be justified based on its similarity to the people's assessor system, nor can it be demonstrated by adopting the same methods used to justify the legitimacy of the latter. The jury system has a history

53 Zhong Liming, *A Comparative Study and Reflection on the People's Supervisor System and the People's Assessor System*, at http://essay.laweach.com/Essay_15529_8.html, last visited on August 30, 2008.

54 See Zhou Yongnian ed., *Introduction to the People's Supervisor System*, China Procuratorial Press, 2008, pp. 362–365.

of over a thousand years in the West, with two models: the jury system and the lay assessor system. The jury system was first put into practice in China in June 1930, when the Central Executive Committee of the Chinese Soviet Republic promulgated the *Provisional Regulations on the Organization and Adjudication of the Judicial Department*, which provided the system of jurors participating in trials. During the War of Resistance against Japanese Aggression and the War of Liberation, a system involving people's assessors in case trials was established and implemented in some anti-Japanese base areas and liberated areas. This people's assessor system played a crucial role in garnering the support and trust of the people towards the judicial system in these areas.[55] After the founding of the People's Republic of China, the people's assessor system was retained and explicitly incorporated into the 1954 Constitution, with further provisions in organic laws and procedural laws. Despite going through many twists and turns, in August 2004, the Standing Committee of the National People's Congress passed the *Decision of Improving the People's Assessor System*, bringing an end to the debate over its retention or abolition. The tradition and legal framework underlying the implementation of the people's assessor system constitute a crucial basis for its legitimacy. In contrast, the people's supervisor system is an independent institutional innovation of the procuratorial organs. It is a brand-new institutional design with completely Chinese characteristics that, unlike the people's assessor system, cannot find a solid basis from historical traditions. Meanwhile, given that its direct basis consists in normative documents within the procuratorial organs, it possesses binding force solely within these organs. In the absence of legally binding normative documents, such as the *Decision of Improving the People's Assessor System* and relevant articles in the three major procedural laws, as its direct basis, it is necessary to seek new ways for its legitimacy argumentation. The legitimacy of the people's supervisor system is primarily derived from both legal theory and practical needs. Its legitimacy argumentation can be conducted through its legal theoretical basis, including its alignment with constitutional ideals, its relationship with judicial democracy and due process of law, its value, its functions like institutional perfection, institutional optimization, and institutional legitimation, as well as its viability within the constitutional framework.

The people's assessor system itself faces unresolved problems similar to those of the people's supervisor system, and the latter also presents new problems absent in the former, so the people's assessor system is not a mature template for institutional design and cannot be copied without thinking. At the beginning of its implementation in China, the people's assessor system was primarily viewed as a political institution enabling citizens to exercise state power, with its role as a judicial democratic system coming second. The former aspect renders it indispensable and consistently highlighted and emphasized, while the latter often makes it face technical doubts and queries. Many problems remain unresolved, such as the imperfections in the specific

[55] See Liu Dexing, *The People's Assessor System: Its History, Current Status and Improvement*, Journal of Sichuan Normal University (Social Sciences Edition), 2008.

content of *Decision of Improving the People's Assessor System*,[56] the debate between elitism and populism in the selection and appointment mechanism of people's assessors, the conflict between a unitary lay assessor system and a plural system integrating lay assessors and jurors,[57] the question of equal rights but different responsibilities for people's assessors and judges, the guarantee of the independence of people's assessors and the shortening of their tenure, the scope of application of people's assessors and the subsequent judicial cost–benefit relationship, as well as the court's discretion in deciding whether to apply the people's assessor system. Many of these problems also arise in the design of the people's supervisor system, such as the debate between elitism and populism in selecting people's supervisors, and the management mechanism for people's supervisors, etc. The people's supervisor system also faces some brand-new problems, such as how people's supervisors can effectively and thoroughly engage with procuratorial power to exercise strong supervision and restraint over it, and whether they have the authority to directly meet with and interrogate suspects and their representatives to ensure informed and accurate decision-making. Therefore, while the people's assessor system is the most valuable model, it cannot be indiscriminately imitated; rather, an analysis based on specific circumstances is a must.

3.4.2 Analysis of the Viewpoint of Emulating the Rigid Binding Force

In accordance with the normative documents of the Supreme People's Procuratorate, the evaluations and suggestions of people's supervisors within the people's supervisor system lack substantive rigid binding force on procuratorial organs, with their effectiveness dependent on the acceptance of the chief procurator and the procuratorial committee. The supervision's lack of substantive rigid binding force significantly diminishes its effectiveness,[58] which has become a focal point of criticism regarding the people's supervisor system. In contrast, the opinions of the people's assessors carry the same weight as the decisions of the judges, with court verdicts rendered according to the majority rule. Once a verdict takes effect, it possesses immediate rigid binding force. Some researchers point out that it is necessary to learn from the people's assessor system and endow the supervision results of people's supervisors

[56] See Hu Zhiguo & Zhou Dongying, *Analyzing the People's Assessor System from a Legal Linguistic Perspective*, Tribune of Rule of Law, 2006.

[57] For example, some scholars suggest employing a model that combines both the jury system and the lay assessor system, with the former compensating for judges' lack of social experience and the latter supplementing their specialized knowledge.

See Li Zhengwei, *Solving the Inequality of the People's Assessor System*, Journal of Law Application, 2006.

[58] See Xu Guoping, *Three Improvements to the People's Supervisor System*, Procuratorial Practice, 2004.

with rigid binding force.[59] The specific proposal involves altering the current practice where, when a procuratorial organ declines to accept the supervision decision of people's supervisors, the superior procuratorate "may" initiate a review procedure, to one where the superior procuratorate "shall" initiate such a procedure. Furthermore, some scholars advocate for transforming the people's supervisor system from rights-based supervision to authority-based supervision.[60] The rationality of such viewpoints needs to be evaluated through a comparative analysis of the two systems.

In terms of nature positioning, both systems possess the attribute of rights and, in a certain sense, constitute a kind of social power capable of directly sharing a portion of state power. They must reject the infringement by state public power as rights do, and at the same time, they need to be regulated and the scope of the state power they share should be strictly limited, although this scope is gradually expanding. The difference lies in the fact that they represent distinct levels of rights, with varying degrees to which they, as social power, share state public power. The people's supervisor system is the second defense against the power with democratic legitimacy, while the people's assessor system embodies direct democracy. The people's assessors exercise the right of the people to participate in the management of state affairs directly based on the principle of people's sovereignty. It is a specific way to realize the constitutional right to participate in the management of state affairs and emphasizes direct participation in management through democratic means. The people's supervisor system is the way to exercise the right to criticize and make suggestions within the right of supervision, with a focus on the supervision of power through democratic means. While both the people's supervisor system and the people's assessor system possess functions and significance related to participation and power supervision, they differ in their focus and the extent to which they share state power, with the latter sharing much more state power than the former. This disparity is attributed to the inherent differences between judicial adjudication power and procuratorial power.

In terms of the targets of institutional influence, judicial adjudication power and procuratorial power have distinct operational patterns. The core power exercised by the court is the impartial adjudication power and people's assessors can participate in trial proceedings conducted by a collegiate panel. The collegiate panel offers an institutional setting for people's assessors to express their opinions independently and engage in communication and negotiation, and accords their opinions equal weight with those of the judges. The involvement of people's assessors does not impede the normal progression of trial proceedings. The verdict is rendered based on the majority rule, with no hierarchical relationship, which leads to a balance between the legal mindset of legal professionals and the common-sense reasoning of ordinary citizens, as well as between professional knowledge and public sentiment, on the foundation of discussion, communication, and independent judgment. By contrast, currently,

---

[59] See Ru Gongshan, *The Positioning of People's Supervisors*, Fangyuan Rule of Law Special Issue on People's Supervisors, 2008.

[60] See Chang Yan, *Research on People's Supervisor System*, Ph.D. Dissertation, Wuhan University, 2007.

people's supervisors solely exercise their right of supervision over cases directly investigated by procuratorial organs. Given the administrative nature of procuratorial organs' investigation power and the procurator-general responsibility system, the process of direct investigation by procuratorial organs has evolved into a tightly interconnected closed system where each participant fulfills their respective duties and responsibilities. It is improbable that such a system would offer an opportunity for people's supervisors to directly participate, as it would inevitably disrupt the proper functioning of the investigation process. For instance, the various deadlines established to safeguard the rights of criminal suspects may not meet the requirements of investigation due to the intervention of people's supervisors. Especially when the opinions of people's supervisors clash with those of the procuratorial organs, a conflict is bound to arise over whether to obey the opinions of the chief procurator or procuratorial committee at the same or higher level or to follow the opinions of people's supervisors, which will significantly impact the independent and efficient exercise of procuratorial power.

The proposal to shift from "may" to "shall" in initiating a review procedure by a superior procuratorate when procuratorial organs decline to accept the supervision decision of people's supervisors actually denies these supervisors' right to choose and exhibits redundancy with subsequent provisions. Article 26 of the *Provisions of the Supreme People's Procuratorate on the Implementation of the People's Supervisor System (Trial)* provides: "If a majority of people's supervisors participating in the supervision process disagree with the decision of the procuratorial committee, they may request a review by the people's procuratorate at the higher level… The people's procuratorate at the higher level shall conduct the review promptly and communicate the results. The decision of the higher-level people's procuratorate shall be implemented by the subordinate people's procuratorate." In terms of textual interpretation, this regulation carries three distinct layers of meaning: firstly, only when a majority of people's supervisors involved raise objections can a review be requested. This regulation is rational, adopting democratic mechanisms to guarantee the utmost correctness in decision-making. Secondly, people's supervisors "may" or "may not" raise objections. This grants people's supervisors the right to choose. The shift from "may" to "shall" would make it an obligation and actually deprive them of their right to choose. Finally, the people's procuratorate at the higher level "shall" conduct the review promptly and communicate the results, which makes the review an inevitable outcome with procedural rigid binding force. By reference to Article 70 of the *Criminal Procedure Law of the People's Republic of China*, which provides the public security organs' right to request a review and reconsideration of the people's procuratorate's decision to disapprove an arrest,[61] it can be deemed that

[61] Article 70 reads in full: "If a public security organ considers a people's procuratorate's decision to disapprove an arrest to be erroneous, it may request reconsideration, provided that the detained person shall be released immediately. Where the objection is not sustained, the organ may apply to the people's procuratorate at the higher level for review. The superior people's procuratorate shall conduct the review without delay, make a decision on whether to modify the original decision, and notify the subordinate people's procuratorate and public security organ for implementation." The article uses "may" for public security organs' requests for reconsideration and review and

Article 26 mentioned above has fully granted the supervision conclusion of people's supervisors procedural binding force on procuratorial organs. The aspect requiring improvement lies in clearly specifying the time limit for the review process and defining the form and procedure for communicating the results.

The viewpoint of adopting rigid binding force by transforming the people's supervisor system into authority-based supervision or by granting substantive binding force to the supervision results lacks feasibility. The operational characteristics of the procuratorial power determine that people's supervisors can only be external to the procuratorial organs and supervise the exercise of their power, but cannot have direct substantive binding force. Through the design of supervision procedure, the supervision results can become criticism and suggestions that procuratorial organs must carefully consider, aiding them in making accurate judgments or rectifying their errors, and it's necessary to have punitive measures in place for those who refuse to accept or cooperate with supervision. To advance this system, it is imperative to uphold the independent status of the people's procuratorates, as established by the constitution. Efforts should be made to refrain from reshaping the people's supervisor system into a rigid form of authority-based supervision and from transforming the right to criticize and make suggestions into a decisive power that overrides procuratorial power.[62] The issue that needs to be addressed is that, despite the procedural rigid binding force imposed on supervision results, the ultimate decision-making power, according to existing normative documents, remains with the procuratorial organs. Consequently, the effectiveness of the people's supervisor system, as an external oversight mechanism, depends entirely on whether the procuratorial organs take it seriously, making it susceptible to being perceived or misunderstood by the public as something "for show." Essentially, this issue poses a bottleneck in the design of the people's supervisor system.

Thus, the question of how to address the situation where the majority of people's supervisors involved in the supervision still disagree with the review results of the superior procuratorial organs cannot be overlooked. This question is fundamentally a manifestation of the tension between the principle of democracy and the principle of constitutional rule of law. Specifically in the field of criminal procedure law, it is manifested as the tension between Article 6 of the *Criminal Procedure Law of the People's Republic of China* on relying on the mass and taking the law as the criterion, as well as Article 7 on the responsibilities of ensuring correct and effective enforcement of law. The respective strengths and drawbacks of democracy and constitutional rule of law have been thoroughly rethought, summarized, and compared. In practice, efforts should be made to find an optimal balance between

"shall" for procuratorates' review, precisely mirroring the linguistic pattern found in Article 26 of the *Provisions of the Supreme People's Procuratorate on the Implementation of the People's Supervisor System (Trial)*. Given that both procuratorial organs and public security organs, as state power-exercising entities, maintain a relationship characterized by division of labor, cooperation, and mutual restraint, it is believed that Article 26 also carries the significance of imparting rigid binding force to supervision decisions.

[62] See Han Dayuan ed., *Research on the Constitutional Foundations of China's Procuratorial System*, China Procuratorial Press, 2007, p. 424.

the two, maximizing their strengths while overcoming their drawbacks. In modern society, democratic participation and respect for minority opinions have become inherent aspects of democracy. Substantive rule of law transcends formal rule of law, and by the early twentieth century, as Western liberal democratic constitutionalism evolved, it began to incorporate substantive constitutionalism to address the shortcomings of formal constitutionalism. The distinction between socialist constitutionalism and Western constitutionalism lies in the fact that the former has always prioritized the realization of substantive constitutionalism. The substantive value of contemporary Chinese constitutionalism is to safeguard personal dignity and facilitate comprehensive human development.[63] Since modern nations must uphold the principle of popular sovereignty through a representative system, a separation arises between those who possess sovereignty and those who exercise it. The will of the people represented by the law may diverge from the opinions of individuals in real life. Furthermore, owing to the inherent limitations of the law, disagreement may emerge in interpreting the law and objections may be raised against the legal provisions themselves in certain circumstances. The supervision opinions of people's supervisors that raise objections to procuratorial organs may stem from different interpretations of the law or may align with "human sentiment" yet contravene legal provisions. In such scenarios, a screening mechanism is needed. Discrepancies in legal interpretation can be addressed by seeking authoritative clarification. As for the conflict between "human sentiment" and "the law," the authority of the constitution and the law must not be compromised for the sake of the so-called social effect. Instead, the issue should be addressed in strict accordance with the law, with subsequent political avenues explored to incorporate public opinions by amending the law and the constitution.

There are two institutional design options. Option 1: when the opinions of people's supervisors diverge from the decisions proposed by the procuratorial organs, a three-tier procedural mechanism is established to deliberate and decide on these different opinions, comprising a review by the chief procurator, a discussion by the procuratorial committee, and a further review by the superior procuratorate. If the supervision opinions are still not accepted by the superior procuratorial organs, they ought to convince more than half of people's supervisors with compelling reasons. Should they fail to do so, more than half of the supervisors have the "right to disclose," enabling them to disclose the case to the Standing Committee of the People's Congress at the same level, who will then make a decision, thus transforming flexible supervision into a more rigid one.[64] Article 3 of the *Organic Law of the People's Procuratorates* provides: people's procuratorates at all levels shall each set up a procuratorial committee. The procuratorial committee shall apply the system of democratic centralism and, under the direction of the chief procurator, hold discussions and make

---

[63] See Qin Qianhong & Ye Haibo, *Research on Socialist Constitutional Governance*, Shandong People's Publishing House, 2008, pp. 42–77.

[64] See Wang Jianghua & Li Xin, *Investigation Power of Procuratorial Organs over Duty-Related Crimes and Its Supervisory Constraints*, Journal of Yunnan University (Law Edition), 2006.

decisions on important cases and other major issues. in the case of the chief procurator disagreeing with the majority's opinion over a decision on an important issue, the matter may be reported to the standing committee of the people's congress at the corresponding level for final decision. This indicates that, under certain circumstances, the standing committee of the people's congress may directly decide on controversial matters. The objections are raised by people's supervisors either to legal interpretations or to the law itself, so it's a rational choice to refer these matters to the people's congress for a decision. Option 2: the issue of objection can be referred to the court for a decision via judicial review. This primarily draws inspiration from the criminal procedure law, which grants victims the right to challenge in court the procuratorate's decision not to prosecute. The current people's supervisor system supervises three types of cases and five types of situations in procuratorial organs, spanning the entire exercise of procuratorial power and extending beyond the discretionary power of public prosecution. In addition, given the characteristics of cases directly investigated by procuratorial organs, not all cases involve clear victims, so alternative avenues are necessary to bring disputes to the court for examination. The court, characterized by its neutrality and professionalism, serves as the ultimate judicial remedy, so it is also reasonable to entrust it with resolving disputes, and to allow the investigation or trial process to proceed based on its rulings. It should be noted that this is merely a preliminary concept, and its feasibility requires further consideration and argumentation within the framework of constitutionalism, taking into account factors such as constitutional and legal basis, institutional costs, and so on.

3.4.3 Analysis of the Viewpoint of Emulating the Specific Systems

Since the adoption of the *Decision of Improving the People's Assessor System* by the Standing Committee of the National People's Congress on August 28, 2004, the *Supreme People's Court and the Ministry of Justice on Issuing the Opinions on the Work of Appointing, Training and Appraising People's Assessors* promulgated by the Supreme People's court and Ministry of Justice on December 13, 2004, the *Measures of the Supreme People's Court for the Management of the People's Assessors (Trial)* promulgated by the Supreme People's Court and the *Circular of the Relevant Issues Concerning the Administration of Expenses for the People's Assessors* jointly formulated by the Ministry of Finance and the Supreme People's Court, the selection and appointment mechanism, rights and obligations, management mechanism, trial participation mechanism, and safeguard mechanism for people's assessors have been established with clear regulations. These regulations, coupled with rich experience accumulated in practice, have provided valuable insights for the specific design of the people's supervisor system.

i. On the Selection and Appointment Mechanism

The selection and appointment mechanism for people's supervisors is a highly debated issue in practice, with two representative models currently in existence. One is the model of appointment by the Standing Committee of the People's Congress at the same level. Here is a good example: the Standing Committee of the People's Congress of Hanyang District, Wuhan City, approved the *Implementation Measures for the Work of People's Supervisors in Hanyang District, Wuhan City (Trial)* and *Rules for the Appointment and Removal of People's Supervisors in Hanyang District, Wuhan City (Trial)* to specify the procedures for announcement, recommendation, registration, review, candidate selection, public notification, and appointment. Its distinctive feature lies in the establishment of a working group tasked with selecting and appointing people's supervisors and composed of personnel from the Personnel Appointment and Removal Committee of the Standing Committee of the District People's Congress, the Internal and Judicial Affairs Committee, the District Procuratorate, the District Judicial Bureau, and other relevant departments. This working group is responsible for carrying out the procedures, and ultimately, the Standing Committee of the District People's Congress convenes a meeting to formally appoint people's supervisors and issue appointment letters. The other is the model of approval by procuratorial organs. A typical example is the *Measures for the Selection and Appointment of People's Supervisors by Shanghai Procuratorial Organs (Trial)*. According to its provisions, the Municipal People's Procuratorate and its branches shall determine the number of people's supervisors to be selected. Candidates shall be recommended by government agencies, public organizations, enterprises, public institutions, and grassroots entities, subject to the individual's consent. Upon approval by the respective chief procurators, the official candidates shall be confirmed, and the Municipal People's Procuratorate shall issue them with the people's supervisor certificate and people's supervisor ID card.

In both models, the candidates for people's supervisors are generated through recommendation. However, the model of appointment by the people's congress at the same level offers better safeguards for the independence of people's supervisors from procuratorial organs. This model adopts the practice of the people's assessor system, where candidates are determined through consultation between the people's court and judicial administrative department and then approved by the Standing Committee of the People's Congress. Meanwhile, internal bodies of the Standing Committee are involved in the consultation process, enhancing the power of the people's congress in selecting and appointing people's supervisors and also establishing specific and feasible procedures. Compared to the model of approval by procuratorial organs, this model is more neutral and inclusive. However, this appointment method also faces two doubts. Firstly, while the people's congress and its standing committee are empowered by law or decisions of the NPC Standing Committee with legal effect to elect or approve personnel, there is no a direct legal basis for people's supervisors, raising the question of whether the NPC Standing Committee's appointment of people's supervisors exceed its authority? Secondly, the appointment of people's supervisors by the Standing Committee of the People's Congress may turn them into instruments for the supervision of individual cases by the People's Congress. We consider these two doubts to be untenable, as according to Article 44, Paragraph 1 of the *Organic Law of the Local People's Congresses and Local People's Governments of the People's Republic of China*, the standing committee of a local people's congress at or above the county level shall ensure, in its administrative area, the observance and execution of the Constitution, laws, administrative regulations and the resolutions of the people's congresses and their standing committees at higher levels. The people's supervisor system is a specific way to exercise the constitutional right to criticize and make suggestions, and by appointing people's supervisors, the Standing Committee of the People's Congress exercises its authority to ensure the observance and execution of the Constitution and laws. Although appointed by the Standing Committee of the People's Congress at the same level, people's supervisors exercise their right of supervision independently, relying on their own judgments. No hierarchical or subordinate relationship exists between them. Additionally, given that the People's Congress and its Standing Committee only supervise the work performance of procuratorial organs, the people's supervisor system can be a valuable complement to the supervision by the People's Congress.

The institutional design aimed at improving the selection and appointment mechanism for people's supervisors builds upon the model by the people's congress at the same level, while also learning from the mechanism of self-recommendation for people's assessors within the people's assessor system and the mechanism for the election of people's assessors by grassroots people's courts.

First, both the right to participate in the management of state affairs and the right of supervision are functionally citizens' right to participate based on their proactive status. Therefore, the mechanism of self-recommendation for people's assessors within the people's assessor system should be drawn upon. The current people's supervisor system is still in its nascent stage and not well known to the public, so it's reasonable now to adopt a recommendation-based approach. Nonetheless, greater efforts should be exerted to enhance the publicity of the system. Upon the system's maturation, self-recommendation ought to be prioritized, with recommendation as a secondary means. Only when citizens participate with a sense of ownership can the effective implementation of the system be ensured and the lack of transparency and openness in the recommendation process be made up for.

Second, in practice, procuratorial organs at every level appoint people's supervisors. However, there exists controversy over whether they are appointed through the "same-level supervision model", or the "higher-level supervision model" by the municipal people's procuratorate or its branches, or the "centralized supervision model" by the provincial people's procuratorate.[65] Researchers have the following misconceptions when discussing the advantages of these models:

The notion that the higher-level supervision model and the centralized supervision model can overcome the drawbacks of judicial regionalization lacks persuasiveness,

[65] For example, Article 3 of the *Shanghai People's Procuratorate's Implementation Opinions on the People's Supervisor System (Trial)* provides that people's supervisors shall be selected and appointed by the Municipal Procuratorate or its branches, and shall perform their supervisory duties uniformly under the title of "People's Supervisors of Shanghai Procuratorial Organs." For a comparative analysis of the advantages and disadvantages of appointment by municipal procuratorate or its branches, provincial procuratorate, or same-level organs.

See Zhou Yongnian, ed., *Introduction to the People's Supervisor System,* China Procuratorial Press, 2008, pp. 188–195.

because people's supervisors appointed through these models are still from various regions. Moreover, it is only with broad representativeness that these supervisors align with the original intent of judicial democracy. It is impossible to find people's supervisors who have no ties to any region. By contrast, the appointment of people's supervisors by grassroots people's procuratorates is the closest and most easily accessible to the general public, which is actually more conducive to their selection, management, and participation in supervision. The people's supervisor system inherently possesses the function of institutional legitimation and does not necessarily have an adversarial relationship with procuratorial organs. People's supervisors and procuratorial organs share common value pursuit. Even from a supportive stance, people's supervisors can provide valuable criticism and suggestions to facilitate better exercise and fulfillment of procuratorial functions and powers. The recognition of procuratorial organs by people's supervisors, which is then communicated to the general public, represents the optimal outcome of this system's effective functioning.

The notion that the higher-level supervision model and the centralized supervision model offer a new approach for higher-level procuratorates to supervise and guide the work of their lower-level counterparts, despite being well-intentioned, would lead to the merging of internal and external supervision approaches into a single one, making the people's supervisor system reliant on the authority of higher-level procuratorates for implementation, so that it ends up losing its independence or even existing in name only. The people's supervisor system has its value of independent existence. The management system of the procuratorial organs must not be imposed onto the people's supervisor system featuring rights-based supervision, nor should people's supervisors serve as proxies for higher-level procuratorates and share their authority. In fact, the essential binding force of people's supervisors' stems from the demands of the ordinary people they represent for judicial justice and their alignment with the constitutional principle of popular sovereignty, rather than from which level of procuratorial organs they are appointed by.

Therefore, we propose learning from the people's assessor system to let grassroots procuratorates elect people's supervisors and establish a unified provincial roster of people's supervisors. Procuratorates above the grassroots level will no longer appoint additional people's supervisors. When supervision by people's supervisors is required, suitable supervisors may be randomly drawn from this roster in accordance with the principles of guaranteed independent supervision, cross-region supervision, and actual needs.[66] This approach incorporates the strengths of the higher-level supervision model and the centralized supervision model, including resource integration, judicial cost reduction,[67] and unified regulation of organizational coordination for people's supervisors. And it also embraces the merits of the same-level supervision model, which demonstrates well the supervision results, facilitates the participation

[66] *Ibid.*, pp.193–195.

[67] It should be noted that the costs of the people's supervisor system extend beyond appointment expenses, encompassing also time, effort, and financial resources invested in communication, transportation, organization, management, etc. during the work process. The issue of costs requires comprehensive consideration and is not solely determined by the number of supervisors appointed.

of people's supervisors in the supervision process, and seamlessly interfaces with relevant systems.

ii. On the Management Mechanism

People's assessors are subject to centralized and unified management jointly exercised by grassroots people's courts and judicial administrative departments at the same level. Emulating the practice of people's courts in managing people's assessors, many regions have adopted a centralized approach for procuratorial organs to manage people's supervisors. However, the appropriateness of such emulation remains debatable. For one thing, the two operate on different mechanisms. People's assessors restrict judges' abuse of power by sharing the adjudication power and cannot exist independently without the adjudication power. The opinions expressed by people's assessors during collegiate panel trials carry substantial weight in case adjudication. In contrast, people's supervisors are external to procuratorial organs. With what they know about the procuratorial organs' case handling, they offer supervisory opinions on the exercise of procuratorial power according to their own judgment. For another thing, people's supervisors and people's assessors exercise their rights in different capacities. When serving on a collegiate panel, people's assessors become de facto judges, jointly exercising adjudication power with judges. By contrast, when exercising their right of supervision, people's supervisors engage in supervision in their capacity as ordinary citizens, maintaining their independence without participating in case handling. Therefore, people's assessors should follow the professional ethics of judges and undertake judges' responsibilities. The people's courts must adopt centralized and unified management, establishing supporting systems such as training, assessment, rewards and penalties, and accountability for misjudged cases, so as to mitigate or prevent the risks in their performance of duties. Unified management by both courts and judicial administrative organs is a prerequisite for people's assessors to exercise their rights. People's supervisors, instead, must uphold their identity as ordinary citizens and maintain independence from procuratorial organs. The procuratorial organs' management of people's supervisors should be regarded as an expedient during the pilot phase of the people's supervisor system. Ultimately, it is necessary to eliminate the procuratorial organs' substantive management authorities that could impact the exercise of people's supervisors' rights, including appointment and removal, rewards and penalties, and assessment.

The corresponding issue is the establishment of the people's supervisor office. Some researchers propose locating the people's supervisor office within the standing committees of local people's congresses, making it a working department of these committees. The recommendation and appointment of people's supervisors would be handled by the standing committees of the people's congresses.[68] Meanwhile, the people's supervisor office originally set up within the people's procuratorates would be renamed the "liaison office of the people's supervisor." In practice, there are also instances where management is conducted by the relevant working committees of

[68] See Liu Jie, *Constitutional Control of Police Power in China*, Journal of Beijing People's Police College, 2005.

the standing committee of local people's congress. This proposal remains open to discussion, due to the fact that, on the one hand, many procuratorates have established a people's supervisor office in practice. As a coordination service agency for people's supervisors to exercise their right, this office possesses professional expertise and is well-versed in case handling procedures. Furthermore, being internal to the procuratorial organs, it has a better grasp of case handling information within these organs, playing a crucial role in facilitating the exercise of people's supervisors' right of supervision. It offers advantages unmatched by any external organization, and has developed a relatively mature set of operational procedures in practice,[69] significantly enhancing supervision efficiency. If it is hastily abolished and then re-established or replaced with an entirely new structure, this would inevitably lead to a waste of institutional resources and disrupt the functioning of the people's supervisor system. On the other hand, locating the people's supervisor office within the standing committees of local people's congresses as one of their working departments could easily turn people's supervisors into instruments for the supervision of individual cases by the people's congress considering that people's supervisors are appointed by these committees. This would blur the intended positioning of the people's supervisor system as rights-based supervision and social supervision, making it part of authority-based supervision of the people's congress. Consequently, the people's supervisor system would lose its raison d'être as an innovative system.

Building upon existing institutional resources, the people's supervisor office within procuratorial organs should further strengthen its functions of communication, service and procedural "management", including maintaining the roster of people's supervisors, archiving files of the cases subject to supervision, documenting and compiling statistics on supervisory activities, and other service-oriented administrative duties that do not impede people's supervisors' exercise of their right. The office should strengthen the individual independence of people's supervisors and adopt a "loose" management approach, that is, formulate relevant measures for the performance of duties by people's supervisors and allow self-management through people's supervisor meetings. The people's supervisor plenary sessions are convened only once or twice annually, with participation by representatives from procuratorial organs, relevant working committees of the standing committee of the people's congress, judicial administrative organs, and communities (grassroots organizations). People's supervisors should report their own performance of duties. The retention or dismissal of those deemed unsuitable to continue serving as people's supervisors should be determined by voting, and the results should be reported to the procuratorial organs for submission to the standing committee of the people's congress for appointment or removal in accordance with the procedures. The training of people's supervisors can draw on the practice of the people's assessor system, with procuratorial organs or judicial administrative organs conducting the training either separately or jointly. The training content should include a comprehensive understanding of

[69] For example, the People's Procuratorate of Hubei Province formulated the *Working Regulations for the People's Supervisor Office of Hubei Procuratorial Organs (Trial)*, which contains detailed and actionable provisions on quality standards and operational procedures for the office's work.

the procuratorial organs' case-handling procedures, foundational legal knowledge, and enhancement of the people's supervisors' senses of responsibility, mission, and honor.[70]

iii. On the Right to Investigate and Collect Evidence

As an external supervision mechanism, people's supervisors must keep a certain degree of distance from procuratorial organs. According to relevant regulatory documents, people's supervisors acquire information through briefings given by case handlers at procuratorial organs and their responses to the supervisors' inquiries, reports from the public, observation mechanism, and statements from relevant parties. The information acquired through these channels is asymmetrical to that obtained by procuratorial organs in directly investigating cases through the exercise of their investigation power. Various challenges arise in practice for people's supervisors to observe interrogations, hear statements from relevant parties, and obtain the opinions of the lawyers involved, owing to factors such as the limitation on the investigation period, the requirement for approval from the chief procurator, and restrictions imposed by related systems like detention facility regulations. Consequently, this results in a conflict between suffering from information asymmetry and giving accurate and valuable supervision opinions. For this reason, procuratorial organs across the country are not only analyzing the existing problems concerning the protection of the right to know for people's supervisors within the current system, but also actively exploring ways to safeguard this right.[71] In practice, apart from efforts to establish periodic reporting mechanism, supervisory rights notification mechanism, liaison channels between people's supervisors and procurators, strengthen and standardize the procedures for case handlers' briefings and Q&A sessions during supervision, and broaden information channels, the issue of whether the people's supervisor system can adopt the investigation power granted to people's assessors within the people's assessor system has sparked considerable debate both in practice and in theory.

We hold the view that people's supervisors should not possess investigation power, because granting such power to people's supervisors would actually amount to sharing the substantive procuratorial power. This would not only violate the provisions of the criminal procedure law and its associated regulations concerning procuratorial power and the rights of litigation participants in the stages of case filing, investigation, arrest, and prosecution, but also inevitably raise doubts about its legality,

---

[70] See Zhong Liming, *A Comparative Study and Reflection on the People's Supervisor System and the People's Assessor System*, at http://essay.laweach.com/Essay_15529_8.html, last visited on August 30, 2008.

[71] See He Qiming, Xu Degao & Tang Xiaowei, *Smoothing Information Channels to Ensure Effective Supervision: Procuratorial Organs in Nantong City Safeguard People's Supervisors' Right to Know Through Four Links*, Fangyuan Rule of Law Special Issue on People's Supervisors, 2006.

Shen Zhanqun, *Mechanism Conception for Safeguarding People's Supervisors' Right to Know*, Fangyuan Rule of Law Special Issue on People's Supervisors, 2006.

Chen Wenhua, *Ensuring People's Supervisors' Right to Know with Information Interaction as the Focus*, Fangyuan Rule of Law Special Issue on People's Supervisors, 2006.

Zhang Linbiao, *Issues in Safeguarding the Right to Know In the "Five Types of Situations"*, Fangyuan Rule of Law Special Issue on People's Supervisors, 2006.

legitimacy, and evidentiary weight within the existing legal framework. Moreover, the investigation power granted to people's supervisors naturally lacks the efficacy of professional procuratorial organs' exercise of procuratorial power, thus making it uncertain whether they can arrive at more accurate conclusions and even causing new problems, namely, by sharing substantive procuratorial power, people's supervisors lose their original impartial stance, and the pernicious nature of power gives rise to a circular dilemma: who should supervise the supervision of the "people's supervisors"?

In this regard, we can draw inspiration from the problems encountered in the design of the people's assessor system. The people's assessor system was once overly burdened with expectations, but placing all hopes on the refinement of this system to solve the main problems causing judicial injustice and corruption in the judicial field today has undoubtedly become its unbearable weight.[72] The legislation itself has already bestowed a series of crucial functions and values upon this system. The attempt to give it additional functions would only lead to more contradictions in its operation, accompanied by disappointment and dissatisfaction stemming from unfulfilled hopes, ultimately undermining its inherent value. Similarly, the people's supervisor system inherently involves public participation in supervising procuratorial power, utilizing ordinary citizens' common sense, emotional understanding, and specialized knowledge to help procuratorial organs identify mistakes, rectify mistakes, and better exercise procuratorial power. If we were to entrust people's supervisors with the duties of investigating crimes and safeguarding human rights that should be shouldered by procuratorial organs and demand that they make professional, accurate, and impartial legal judgments, then, as a necessary consequence, they would have to be granted the same powers possessed by procuratorial organs and actually become a new kind of "procurators" out of uniform. In fact, we can exercise restraint over procuratorial organs by drawing upon other systems like the lawyer system with lawyers' professional expertise and leveraging legal rights to conduct interviews, review case files, and investigate, without the need to place undue demands or excessive value expectations on the people's supervisor system. Compared to granting it new powers, it is of greater importance to improve the existing system to ensure its operability, and to establish corresponding sanction mechanisms for procuratorial organs' failure to fulfill their obligation to accept and cooperate with supervision and their duty of disclosure.

iv. Analysis of the Viewpoint of Learning from the Institutionalization Path of the People's Assessor System

Although the enjoyment of rights is not contingent upon the provisions in laws or even the constitution, rights possess an innate claim to constitutional and legal protection. Even if the people's supervisor system is positioned as rights-based supervision, it remains necessary to strive for its institutionalization through established legal frameworks. The institutionalization of the people's supervisor system has

[72] Liu Zhibin, *The Unbearable Weight of the People's Assessor System*, China Society Periodical, 2005.

emerged as a consensus and an urgent concern for both practical departments and theoretical researchers, but there remains controversy over which path to adopt. Some researchers believe that the institutionalization of the people's assessor system serves as a model for legislative path, advocating for the adoption of a similar approach as the people's assessor system. In their opinion, there is no need to incorporate provisions related to the people's supervisor system into the *Constitution*, but to add principled provisions in the *Criminal Procedure Law* and the *Organic Law of the People's Procuratorates*. They propose that The Standing Committee of the National People's Congress should enact the *Decision of the Implementation of the People's Supervisor System*, while the Supreme People's Procuratorate, in conjunction with the Ministry of Justice, should devise detailed regulations for its implementation. The Ministry of Justice should also formulate specific rules concerning the selection, assessment, commendation, and removal of people's supervisors. Additionally, the Ministry of Justice, in collaboration with the Ministry of Finance, should establish provisions for the financial support of people's supervisors.[73]

We deem this proposal the most appropriate approach at present. The Standing Committee of the National People's Congress has established a path dependence for legal institutionalization by adopting decisions for matters that require legal regulation but remain immature or lack conditions for separate legislation or legal interpretation. This approach offers greater flexibility compared to formal legal enactment, and, as it does not require strict compliance with the formal requirements of legal norms, it encounters less resistance and incurs lower costs than the drafting of formal legal texts. Compared to the people's assessor system, the people's supervisor system faces greater legitimacy controversy and lacks maturity, making it more viable to adopt the form of decision. Standalone legislation will be enacted upon the system's maturation and refinement. The most feasible and optimal approach currently is to amend and enact laws at the central level, followed by the formulation of specific judicial interpretations or implementing rules.

In practice, the legal effect of the existing normative documents concerning the people's supervisor system issued by local people's congresses at all levels requires prudent assessment. As people's supervisors' right of supervision also serves as a social power, it shares a certain degree of state power and involves the national litigation system which, in accordance with the *Legislation Law of the People's Republic of China*, is subject to legal reservation and can only be provided by law. However, in practice, almost local people's congresses all levels have issued normative documents on the people's supervisor system, among which some even have the authority to enact local regulations. These normative documents play a significant and positive role in promoting and standardizing the people's supervisor system. However, there also exist inconsistencies and even wide discrepancies among normative documents issued by various regions, which actually results in suspects in different regions being treated differently and afforded varying levels of protection during criminal proceedings.

[73] For a systematic discussion, see Zhou Yongnian, ed., *Introduction to the People's Supervisor System*, China Procuratorial Press, 2008, pp. 354–367.

We believe that the provisions on the legal reservation of the litigation system in the Legislation Law are open to debate. For one thing, they exhibit a degree of tension with China's constitutional system. In China, people's courts and people's procuratorates are established by, responsible to, and subject to the supervision of the people's congresses at the same level, so the people's congresses should have decision-making authority over significant matters of the courts and procuratorates at the same level, and correspondingly, the authority to formulate normative documents. For another thing, they diverge from the practical implementation of China's judicial system reform. Local people's congresses at all levels have played a proactive role in the process of judicial system reform. At a stage where the system is still in its infancy and requires regulation, it is impossible for the National People's Congress and its Standing Committee to enact unified legal norms nationwide. The experimental legislation and normative document formulation endeavors undertaken by local people's congresses at all levels not only provide rules for various reform measures but also serve as a valuable source of experience for central legislation. Therefore, it is inappropriate to completely deny the authority of local people's congresses at all levels to enact normative documents on the litigation system that adhere to the spirit of the Constitution and laws. Besides, they should enhance their expertise in formulating such norms. However, in the absence of revisions to the Legislation Law, normative documents formulated by local people's congresses at all levels can only serve as a source of experience for central legislation and should not be encouraged. Unified regulations at the central level should be introduced promptly, then local people's congresses at all levels can revise or re-enact their existing normative documents in accordance with the legal norms established at the central level.

3.5 The Influence of the Nature Positioning of the People's Supervisor System on Its Development

The nature positioning of the people's supervisor system discussed in this book is primarily based on an ideal consideration aligned with the principles of the rule of law and constitutional governance, rather than a factual description of the existing practices of the people's supervisor system. There always is a certain tension between the current social situation and the pursuit of ideal values. Legal norms, therefore, must strive to find a balance between these two, by institutionalizing designs and behavioral rules that reflect the current social situation without compromising the pursuit of ideal values, and enforcing them through the coercive power of the state. Based on the separation, integration, and tension among the ideal, normative, and factual levels, this book aims to leverage the principles of the rule of law and constitutional governance to define an ideal nature positioning for the people's supervisor system. Then, by examining the practical implementation of the people's supervisor system according to this ideal nature positioning, the book seeks to offer feasible suggestions for the enhancement and development of the system, ultimately giving birth to a normative system design.

The people's supervisor system, positioned as rights-based supervision in nature, is developing with a greater emphasis on voluntary public participation, democracy, procedural integrity, and external supervision. It is worth highlighting that the primary consideration behind positioning this system as authority-based supervision lies in its ability to impart rigid binding force to the supervision results of people's supervisors, thus safeguarding the effectiveness of their supervision. In fact, on the one hand, the people's supervision system, as a specific way to exercise citizens' basic rights, does not undermine the effectiveness of their supervision. Corresponding to state obligations, civil rights exert binding force on the state through the fulfillment of these obligations. The constitutional norms grant citizens the right to supervise, while also providing the state's obligation to accept such supervision. The right of people's supervisors to supervise procuratorial power requires procuratorial organs to fulfill their obligation to accept supervision, but the supervision results of people's supervisors possess only procedural binding force, lacking substantive binding force. Their supervision results can only attain rigid binding force upon acceptance by the procuratorial organs. However, this does not imply that procuratorial organs can decide at will whether to accept the supervision results. With the aid of their internal procedural designs, democratic mechanisms, the professional judgment of the chief procurator, and the authority-based supervision by superior procuratorial organs, it is believed that accurate judgments can be achieved to the fullest extent possible. On the other hand, if the supervision results of people's supervisors have rigid binding force on procuratorial organs, the supervisors would definitely interfere with the independent exercise of procuratorial power. Moreover, their supervision, due to its share of procuratorial power, assumes the nature of authority and thus becomes subject to supervision, which would inevitably recreate a dilemma of who is to supervise the supervisors and a cycle of supervision. Besides, based on the structural features of state power, if people's supervisors are to exercise state power, they must adhere to the requirements of state power entities, so they would actually turn into "procurators" out of uniform, which goes against the original intent of the system's design. Some researchers propose learning from the people's assessor system, granting people's supervisors rigid binding force in their supervision results. However, the people's supervisor system cannot become another "people's assessor system." The extent to which the people's supervisor system can learn from the people's assessor system is limited, given the distinctions between judicial adjudication power and procuratorial power, which operate according to different principles. The people's assessor system had a direct constitutional basis at the beginning of the founding of the People's Republic of China, with a solid foundation and supporting institutional design. It has also possessed a direct legal basis since January 1, 2005. In contrast, the people's supervisor system is completely an institutional innovation, and an overly radical implementation would exert considerable impact on the existing legal system. People's assessors collaborate with judges in exercising judicial functions, striking a balance between professional legal judgments and common-sense assessments through deliberation, within a clearly defined legal scope of implementation.

In contrast, people's supervisors exercise their rights independently of procuratorial organs. Their supervision results, despite being not infallible, are of great value because they are presented in the form of criticism and suggestions which, through their rigid procedural binding force, oblige procuratorial organs to rethink, thus aiding such organs in arriving at accurate judgments or rectifying their errors.

Chapter 2
Demonstrating the Legitimacy of the People's Supervisor System

A system's survivability and development prospects will be decided by the system's legitimacy. It is of vital importance to demonstrate the legitimacy of the people's supervisor system, which is an institutional self-innovation pioneered by the procuratorial organs. Because of this, the legitimacy, validity and theoretical basis have emerged as hotspots of discussion of researchers since the trial implementation of the people's supervisor system. Opinions in favor of the system abound: for example, some researchers noted directly that the legitimacy of the people's supervisor system is derived from the basic requirements of the principles of democracy and the rule of law, and as such the system is the institutional expression of the basic principles in current Constitution of China. Those researchers also noted that the establishment, existence and functioning of the people's supervisor system are permitted and subject to the constitutional review under the current Constitution of China. Therefore, though the people's supervisor system is not textually provided by the Constitution or the Organic Law, its institutional legitimacy is backed directly by the Constitution, in particular the essence of the democratic principle, which states that "the power must be supervised and checked" and the principle of rule of law.[1] Some researchers believed that the people's supervisor system is an effective path toward achieving people's constitutional rights and the requirement of achieving procedural justice, judicial justice and the goal of efficient value, contributing to people's proactive participation in legal processes and the cultivation of people's legal awareness.[2] As an important practice of the principle of popular sovereignty, the people's supervisor system is a crucial step in building law-based governance and an essential choice to prevent judicial corruption and ensure the correct use of procuratorial power contributing to achieve the organic unity of substantive justice

[1] See Mo Jihong, *The Justifiability of People's Superviosr System*, Journal of National Prosecutors College, 2009.

[2] See Jia Zhaoyang, *Studying People's Supervisor System*, Journal of National Prosecutors College, 2005.

Q. Qin, *Legislative Research on the People's Supervisor System*,
https://doi.org/10.1007/978-981-95-7972-3_2

and procedural justice.[3] Some scholars believed that the balance theory and the information right theory are also the theoretical basis of the people's supervisor system.[4] Voices doubting the system's legitimacy, in comparison, are much fewer, represented by Professor Zhou Anping's research results, *Critique of the People's Supervisor System*. The article pointed out that the supervision objects of the people's supervisor system are specific judicial operations of the people's procuratorates, and if we strengthen the system, we will be in the quagmire of supervision of individual cases. Under the current institutional arrangement, people's supervisors are in fact "procuratorial advisers", and thus the significance of this reform is merely political. The legitimacy of people's democracy could not illustrate the legitimacy of the people's supervisor system. Even though the people's supervisor system is strengthened, it does not improve supervision efficiency due to procedural arrangements. Furthermore, it is clear that the people's supervisor system is not in alignment with the requirement of the rule of law[5] considering the fact that the establishment of the people's supervisor system is based on the moral self-discipline of people's supervisors and results in the new problem of "who supervises the supervisors".

In general, researchers in favor of the people's supervisor system mainly demonstrate the legitimacy of this system from the relationships among this system and constitutionalism, democracy, rule of law, human rights protection, power restraint, procedural justice, judicial justice, and efficiency. Professor Zhou Anping, a legal researcher and a people's supervisor, witnessed the launch of the people's supervisor system and participated in its operation. It is worthy of attention that his clear viewpoints and reasons that the people's supervisor system does not conform to the spirit and requirements of the rule of law. In author's opinion, the previous researches do not always share the same theoretical basis and subjects of discussion in demonstrating or doubting the legitimacy of the people's supervisor system, which is a major reason causing the different opinions.

In terms of theoretical basis, many researchers, while demonstrating the legitimacy of the system, do not have a clear idea of the relations among constitutionalism, democracy, rule of law, human rights protection, power restraint, procedural justice, judicial justice, and efficiency. Moreover, purposes and rules differ among constitutionalism, democracy and the rule of law, and there are tensions among procedural justice, human rights protection and power restraint, as well as between justice and efficiency. Many researchers deal with them by simply listing and respectively demonstrating, which is inevitably superficial and repetitive. Given that the very understandings of the meaning of constitutionalism and the principles of the rule of law diverge among the researchers, it is no wonder that they are very likely to arrive at different views on the people's supervisor system. In terms of the subject of

[3] See Qin Guang, *On People's Supervisor System*, Journal of Guangxi University (Philosophy and Social Science), 2007.

[4] See Bai Gantao, *Rational Reflections on the Implementation of the People's Supervisor System by the Procuratorial Organs*, Journal of Heilongjiang Administrative Cadre College of Political Science and Law, 2005.

[5] See Zhou Anping, *Critique of the People's Supervisors System*, Journal of Nanjing Normal University (Social Science Edition), 2007.

discussion, the people's supervisor system itself has different dimensions including values, norms and practices. Views from the pursuit of ought-to-be value tend to favor the people's supervisor system, and views from solely the existing norms or practice easily discover its many inadequacies and imperfections, leading to doubts over its legitimacy. For example, based on the system design of the "internal supervision" in the current normative documents, it usually leads to conclusions that the people's supervisor system, as a label used by the procuratorial powers to seek natural legitimacy, lacks effectiveness, authority, and binding power, thus doubting its legitimacy.[6] That is why so many differing opinions all appear to be reasonable.

Hence, this research, with respect to the theoretical basis and research subject, takes the following into account: The people's supervisor system is an institutional innovation without historical and traditional support and direct legal basis, so its legitimacy originates mainly from jurisprudence and practical needs. The legitimacy of the people's supervisor system could be demonstrated from its jurisprudential basis, which includes the unity between the people's supervisor system and constitutionalism, the people's supervisor system and judicial democracy, the relations between the people's supervisor system and the due process of law, the functional values of the people's supervisor system (namely, the function and value of institutional improvement, institutional refinement and institutional recognition), and the living space of the people's supervisor system under the framework of constitutionalism, provided a clear picture of their relations is present. Considering the constant changes and development of the people's supervisor system in practice in the absence of solid legal basis, which leaves room for further institutional growth and construction, this book discusses the institutional legitimacy from an institutional ought-to-be perspective, with appropriate comparisons to existing institutional norms and practices based on the nature positioning of "the people's supervisor system as a specific way for exercising fundamental rights of citizens".

1 Jurisprudential Basis of the People's Supervisor System

1.1 Correspondence of the People's Supervisor System with the Concept of Socialist Constitutionalism

From the classical Greek period, when the term "constitution" in its original sense merely referred to the general nature and structure of things,[7] to the Roman constitution bearing the core principle "the people are the only source of law",[8] to the

[6] See Wu Jun, *The "Extra-institutional" Model and the "Intra-institutional" Path of the People's Supervisors System*, Nomocracy Forum.

[7] See McIlwain, C. H., *Constitutionalism: Ancient and Modern*, translated by Zhai Xiaobo, Guizhou People's Publishing House, 2004, p. 29.

[8] *Ibid.*, pp. 52–53.

constitutional revolutions of the Middle Ages that aimed to build modern constitutionalism marked by long-running, desperate, immense blood and staggering costs,[9] to the eventual solid establishment and unprecedented recognition of constitutional system in modern and contemporary society. Constitutionalism has, throughout the successive historical stages, an immutable core nature: it is the legal restriction on the government, the opposition to autocracy. Its opposite is arbitrariness, the rule by will rather than by law. In contemporary times, people's representatives added to constitutionalism the connotation of "political responsibility" by winning initiative on the discretion of national policies. However, the oldest, firmest and most persisting nature of true constitutionalism remains the same from the beginning: the legal restriction on the government. Seeking to minimize the chances of the government harming the people and maximize the restrictions on state power has been traditionally the most prominent topic of classical constitutionalism. Neo-constitutionalists argue that the contents and core of constitutionalism lie not only in restricting government power and preventing autocratic rule, but also in transcending the traditional theory focused on restricting the arbitrary exercise of state power. Moreover, through constitutional design and the functioning of the constitution, constitutionalism should also ensure the exercise of state power, thus achieving economic efficiency, democratic management, and other social values. The goal is to unify the restriction and preservation of power, and to best safeguard the rights of the people through a political power system that is both restrained and efficient.[10]

The constant exploration and pursuit of power restraint under constitutionalism aim at the protection of human rights ultimately. It is said that the constitutionalism, which is one of the institutional designs by humans for a better life, has been filled with humanistic caring in the first place of its emergence. Whether it is the control or the correction of the expansive nature of state power or the "dark consciousness" of humanity, the ultimate concern is the people's survival and development in both "this world" and "other world". In fact, "Tis evident, that all the sciences have a relation, greater or less, to human nature; and that however wide any of them may seem to run from it, they still return back by one passage or another."[11] Human rights may take on three forms. The first is the ought-to-be form of moral rights, which have been enjoyed by humans ever since the day human came to this world and existed before nations, serving as the logistic precondition of nations and the ultimate goal of value of nations. The second is the textual form of legal rights, which confirms and protects various human rights by the form of law and is the minimum the protection of human rights. The third is the actual form that is being enjoyed, which is the rights actually enjoyed by every individual in the society. These three forms differ from one another, and the optimal scenario is where all ought-to-be rights could convert into the form of legal rights and become the actual rights of everyone. Yet, under

---

[9] *Ibid.*, pp. 56–79.

[10] See Li Long & Wang Xigen, *On the Laws of Constitutionalism*, Collected Works of Li Long, Wuhan University Press, 2006, p. 409.

[11] Hume, *A Treatise of Human Nature*, translated by Guan Wenyun, The Commercial Press, 1980, p. 6.

the fundamental limitation of the human development level of productivity, there are large gaps among these three forms of human rights. The differences among the value pursuit, textual expression and practice of constitutionalism in a nation is the most accurate and concise epitome of the difference among these three forms of human rights, though it does not prevent the protection of human rights from becoming the core concept of the constitution.

What needs clarification is that constitutionalism as a proper system in the contemporary era, which was born out of the bourgeois revolutions in the West. Such a system is deeply rooted in Western culture, and is itself a complex form of culture created in the long-term historical evolution of the West.[12] For China, constitutionalism is derived from the West, and is one of the many tools gathered in a haste to seek prosperity for the nation and defend against foreign invaders. Only when people gradually realize that constitutionalism is not merely a tool for a certain purpose and that it has its own value of purpose, will constitutionalism be truly recognized and become the goal of pursuit. Currently, building a country of constitutionalism under rule of law has become a proactive choice to achieve the common sense, and power restraint and protection of power efficient operation, both of which come from the west, and the core concept of human rights protection, which is the universal value of constitutionalism, have all been accepted by the academic and practice communities. However, building constitutionalism under the socialist context of China naturally has its unique aspects different from Western constitutionalism. Some researchers who investigated the compatibility between socialism and constitutionalism pointed out that there are strong internal relations between the two systems, and that it could be said that there will be no socialism without the successful building of constitutionalism, and constitutionalism oriented toward substantive justice can only be accomplished in socialist countries.[13] Socialist constitutionalism is a kind of substantive constitutionalism as it not only guards against illegal infringement but also eliminates legal infringement, and formal constitutionalism is a natural requirement for socialist constitutionalism.[14] The core concept of socialist constitutionalism is to restrict state power both in form and in substance, and to ensure efficient operation of state power to achieve equal, free and all-around development of human.

---

[12] See Wang Renbo, *The Chinese Path to Constitutionalism*, Shandong People's Publishing House, 2003, p. 1.

[13] See Qin Qianhong & Ye Haibo, *Studies on Socialist Constitutionalism*, Shandong People's Publishing House, 2008, p. 44.

[14] The distinction between formal constitutionalism and substantive constitutionalism lies in the fact that the former, while aiming to eliminate unlawful infringements in the process of constitutional development, carefully preserves lawful infringements and pursues only formal justice. In contrast, the latter seeks not only to eliminate unlawful infringements but also to eradicate lawful infringements, achieving substantive justice.

Ibid., pp. 61–70.

1.1.1 The People's Supervisor System: A Mechanism Using Power to Restrain Power in Both Form and Substance

The people's supervisor system serves as an external supervision mechanism over the powers exercised by procuratorial organs in handling duty-related cases, including the power to investigate duty-related crimes, the power to prosecute, the power to supervise litigation, and the power to supervise enforcement. By initiating supervisory procedures and conducting evaluations in cases where criminal suspects object to arrest, or where the procuratorate intends to withdraw a case or decide not to prosecute, the system restrains the procuratorial organs' power to decide on arrests of the power to investigate duty-related crimes, and the discretionary power of the power to prosecute. Through supervising actions in violation of laws or disciplines, including failing to file when necessary, filing when unnecessary, extended detention, illegal searches, seizures and freezes, failing to confirm or execute decisions of criminal compensation when necessary, and procuratorial personnel's bending laws for personal gains, accepting bribes, extorting confessions by torture and obtaining evidence by violence, the system effectively places under supervision every action of the procuratorial organs using their powers during the course of case self-investigation, and it supervises both the legitimacy of the procedure of power operation and the justice of the result of power operation. Through exercising their constitutional rights of raising criticism and suggestions by commenting independently, giving opinions and suggestions directly, and making their results of commenting procedurally rigid, people's supervisors exposed the otherwise almost closed processes and outcomes of self-investigating cases by procuratorial organs to their scrutiny outside of the procuratorial system, in particular processes involving case withdrawals and decisions not to prosecute. If, with the development of the system, mechanisms such as the public disclosure of supervisory outcomes or the establishment of impartial authoritative institutions (such as the Standing Committee of the National People's Congress or the people's courts) to make final decisions are introduced, the people's supervisor system will undoubtedly constitute a powerful external restraint and deterrent on the exercise of procuratorial power, which, in turn, would help prevent and curb the abuse of prosecutorial power in self-investigating cases. This makes the people's supervisor system correspond to the concept of socialist constitutionalism to restrain state power both in form and substance.

1.1.2 The People's Supervisor System: A Specific Way and an Institutional Safeguard of Exercising Fundamental Constitutional Rights

The people's supervisor system is a specific way for the people to exercise the right of criticism and suggestion, which is a constitutional right. Articles 2, 33, and 41 of the *Constitution* provide the people the rights to participate in the administration of state affairs and to raise criticisms and suggestions regarding state organs and their personnel. However, these rights have been difficult to effectively realize in practice for a long time, the constitutional provisions are abstract and there is a lack of legal mechanisms that are practical. The people's supervisor system provides specific ways to exercise such rights. For a start, the system offers an institutional platform on which people can participate in the administration of state affairs and exercise the right to raise criticism and suggestions. The system confirms that the supervisory objects are the "three types of cases" in the self-investigating cases of the procuratorial organs, and ensures that people have the rights to raise criticism and suggestions over "five types of situations" and "one type of situation". The system also provides institutional protection and a platform of operation for the launch of the supervision procedure of people's supervisors by establishing the People's Supervisor Office as the organ for communication and service supervision, and a legally rigid mechanism for transferring the written opinions of cases and related materials. In addition, the system guarantees a precondition for people to participate in the operation of procuratorial powers and exercise the rights of criticism and suggestions: the right to know. The people's supervisors' right to know is minimally guaranteed through procedures such as case introduction and explanations provided by procuratorial personnel, their responses to questions raised by people's supervisors, attendance at interrogations of criminal suspects and witnesses by case handlers, listening to statements from involved parties, hearing the opinions of the lawyers, and participating in procuratorial law enforcement inspections. Moreover, as the people's supervisor system continues to develop and improve, this right to know will be further protected, thus maximizing information symmetry. This, in turn, ensures that criticisms and suggestions are more targeted, accurate, scientific, and constructive.

The people's supervisor system also serves as a way of protection and remedy for the basic constitutional rights of the criminal suspects and the victims. In the designation, the system absorbs the supervision view of people's supervisor or the basic constitutional rights of people's supervisor that could voice opinions and suggestions on mostly affairs related to criminal suspects, and the original purpose of the system design is to prevent the procuratorial organs from harming the rights of the criminal suspects. Procuratorial organs' unnecessary case filings in self-investigating cases will place innocent people under criminal prosecution or people in violation of laws under inappropriate prosecution, which may lead to infringement on their dignity, personal liberty and the right of property. Illegal arrests, extended detention, and illegal searches, seizures and freezes of property may infringe upon the criminal suspect's dignity, personal liberty, right to inviolability of residence, freedom and confidentiality of communication, as well as the right to private property. Extorting confessions by torture and obtaining evidence by violence infringe a criminal suspect's right to personal dignity, freedom of expression, bodily safety, and even the right to life. Failure to confirm or enforce decisions on criminal compensation, where such compensation is necessary, violates people's right to obtain state compensation. Moreover, discretionary non-prosecution and non-prosecution due to insufficient evidence by procuratorial organs may inflict harms to the personal dignity of innocent suspects. These rights are fundamental rights enshrined in the Constitution as well as in the International Covenants on Human Rights to which China is a party and pertain to the individual's self-preservation, freedom, and comprehensive development. The protection of these rights constitutes the ultimate value pursuit of constitutionalism. The supervision by people's supervisors over such matters and actions serves as a safeguard for the rights of criminal suspects. At the same time, it provides an additional opportunity and way for suspects to seek proper remedies when their rights are infringed.

Moreover, it should not be forgotten that criminal actions undermine the established social order, and infringe the fundamental constitutional rights of the victims. Especially, in the duty-related cases, though there may not be specific victims, the interest of the people is infringed eventually. Therefore, while protecting the interests of suspects, the interests of the victim and the public must as well be protected. Professor Fletcher noted in summarizing the concepts of criminal laws of the twentieth century, and envisioning their development in the twenty-first century, "We have begun to view criminal law as one among many disciplines that serve the fundamental values that safeguard public security. It declares a moral denunciation of wrongful conducts" and "(the criminal law) seeks the just balance among the claims of victims, the interests of society, and fairness toward criminal suspects.[15]" Viewing from the current mechanism design of the people's supervisor system, it is of great significance for a number of aspects, such as supervising planned withdrawal cases and planned non-prosecution cases, the right to raise opinions or suggestions on failures to file cases that should be filed, acts of favoritism for personal gains, corruption, and actions violating laws and regulations by procuratorial personnel, safeguarding the rights of criminal suspects to a just and impartial trial, the rights of victims and the people to access judicial remedies, and the protection of people's rights to personal dignity, equality, and other fundamental rights. Also, the system will provide a new way for accessing at least procedural remedies for the acquisition of rights, if supervisory opinions disagreeing with the case outcomes and other opinions and suggestions are accepted and implemented by the procuratorial organs. This is also the important direction in which the people's supervisor system can be further developed and improved. For example, there are initial researches in the academia into whether the scope of supervision of the system includes the victim's disagreement with the procuratorial organ's decision not to arrest,[16] and some regions begin to integrate this into the specific ways of operation of supervision in practice.[17]

[15] George Fletcher, *Rethinking Criminal Law in the 20th Century*, translated by Jiang Suo, Peking University Press, 2006, p. 499.

[16] See Guo Wanyong & Li Jingbao, *A Preliminary Study on the Feasibility of Including Cases in Which Victims Object to the Non-arrest Decision in Criminal Proceedings within the Supervision Scope of the People's Supervisors System*, Legal System and Society, 2009.

[17] For example, the People's Procuratorate in Changshu, Jiangsu Province once decided not to approve the arrest of two out of six suspects in an intentional injury case. The victim's family expressed dissatisfaction with this decision. The case was subsequently brought into the people's supervisors' supervision procedure, where the supervisors unanimously agreed with the decision made by the procuratorate. In the end, the victim's family came to understand and accept the procuratorial decision.

1.1.3 The People's Supervisor System Facilitates the Efficient Operation of Procuratorial Powers

Distrust and restraint of state power are the core concepts of constitutionalism, and people's freedom from state interference has always been protected and cherished by liberal constitutionalism. However, as human-nature relations grow tenser in contemporary days, the strength of an individual is increasingly dwarfed by the rise of social powers and the establishment of welfare states. Individuals become more and more reliant on state power, and the achievement of many traditional rights of freedom depends on not only the passive non-interference from the state, but also on the active operation of state power. To achieve the value pursuit of protection of rights, it is necessary to, while restraining state power, ensure the effective operation of it, and strike a proper balance between the two. The relation between individuals and the state is more than just adversarial as in the traditional binary country-society structure; it is more of a cooperative one featuring interdependence. For this, some researchers have emphasized the need to base the design and planning of the relationship between state power and citizens' rights on China's specific national conditions during this period of transition, and the need to establish a healthy and balanced structure between state power and citizens' rights that achieves a mutually interactive, symbiotic, and mutually reinforcing win–win framework.[18] The people's supervisor system is not merely a restraint mechanism on the power of procuratorial organs in their self-investigation cases, but also a booster that helps the effective operation of the procuratorial power, as "supervision should not be interpreted solely as a form of restraint; it should also encompass the meanings of support and assistance."[19] The system facilitates the operation of procuratorial power by supervising the "three types of cases", raising opinions for the "five types of situations" and raising both suggestions and opinions for the "one type of situation". The benefits include, firstly, ordinary people may express their desires and needs from the angle of general ethics and their social experience, and people's supervisors with expertise in all walks of life may provide intellectual support, such as professional opinions and suggestions. The procuratorial organs seriously consider and respond to those opinions and suggestions, thus regulating their law-enforcement activities, improving the quality of law enforcement and case handling, and ensuring judicial justice. Secondly, by participating in and familiarizing themselves with the process that the procuratorial organs use in self-investigating cases, people may recognize and understand the process more easily, reducing obstacles in law enforcement. Finally, the introduction of the external supervision from people's supervisors helps procuratorial organs to resist external disruptions and stay independent, thereby enabling the procuratorial power

---

See Zhang Huanming & Zhang Xuesong, *Braving the Waves in Experimental Reform: Changshu's Pilot Implementation of the "3 + 2" Supervision Model for People's Supervisor*, Jiangsu Legal Daily, 2009, p. 5.

[18] See Zhao Xiumin, *The Relationship between Power and Rights in the Perspective of Constitutionalism*, Journal of Gansu Political Science and Law Institute, 2004.

[19] Xu Chongde, *On Studying and Discussing the Constitution*, Law Press China, 2000, p. 243.

to exercise autonomy and initiative, and to better fulfill its constitutional and legal duty of upholding the authority and dignity of the Constitution and the law through legal supervision.

1.2 The People's Supervisor System and Judicial Democracy

The balance between law and will remains the core problem of political system practice, just like all the bygone eras,[20] and the tension and balance between constitutionalism and people's rights are its concentrated embodiment in contemporary days. As Mao Zedong noted in as early as 1940, "constitutionalism is democratic politics", the view that directly defines constitutionalism from the perspective of democracy or regards democracy as one of the main factors of constitutionalism has remained dominant in the field of constitutional studies for a long time. However, "there is a significant difference between constitutionalism and democracy, as the latter refers to the ownership of power, and the former refers to the restraints on power."[21] If popular sovereignty is seen as the primary source of governmental legitimacy, it will demonstrate that any argument advocating for substantive restraints on the government apart from the will of the people is flawed. However, when the masses demand for democracy without scruples, it ultimately leads to anarchism or democratic tyranny. It is thus necessary to admit that "constitutionalism embodies a minimum level of universality and absolute value, which means that the *Constitution* is used to delineate and limit political power, and to safeguard the freedom of the people."[22] This book, based precisely on this definition, does not incorporate judicial democracy as a theoretical branch of democracy into the concept of constitutionalism for discussion.

Besides, it is necessary to admit that, in countries where the belief in democracy is weak or absent, the constitution is practically non-existent, as it would be violated and forgotten in no time.[23] This is because that, wise as the framers were, they were necessarily limited by their profound ignorance.[24] For constitutional texts to possess vitality, they must be interpreted and applied within the concrete context of the era's development. Specifically, this can be achieved through adopting the democratic political processes to formulate amendments to constitution and laws that concretize constitutional provisions without conflicting with the constitution and through adopting the constitutional interpretation which is in the process of judicial

---

[20] See McIlwain, C. H., *Constitutionalism: Ancient and Modern*, translated by Zhai Xiaobo, Guizhou People's Publishing House, 2004, p. 122.

[21] Liu Junning, *Republicanism, Democracy, and Constitutionalism: A study of Liberal Thought*, SDX Joint Publishing Company, 1998, p. 126.

[22] See Qin Qianhong & Ye Haibo, *Studies on Socialist Constitutionalism*, Shandong People's Publishing House, 2008, p. 61.

[23] Robert Dahl, *The Undiscovered Country*, translated by Tong Dezhi, Jiangsu People's Publishing House, 2008, p. 51.

[24] *Ibid.*, pp. 39–51.

review or constitutional court deciding. The latter, as a non-democratic institutional design, has long been questioned. However, some researchers have attempted to argue that this counter-majoritarian mechanism protects certain important rights that are closely related to democracy itself,[25] and is thus legitimate. In fact, the inspiration of democracy is so intense and deeply ingrained in the public consciousness that contemporary theories of constitutionalism struggle to fully evaluate the trajectory of state and societal development shaped by the will of the people. If the constitutionalism theory is still to remain a dynamic cause, it cannot afford to sever itself from the power of democracy. The involvement of democracy in the judicial field is not only the prerequisite of the development of constitutionalism, but also a crucial way of reconciling the tension between constitutionalism and democracy.

1.2.1 Democratic Pursuit in the Operation of the Procuratorial Power

Democracy can be interpreted in multi-meaning. It could be regarded as an "method that individuals acquire the power to decide by means of a competitive struggle for the people's vote,"[26] and the process and outcome where autonomous and equal individuals exercise their rights to participate in and manage state affairs in order to realize public autonomy. In terms of the process, it requires democratic majority decision-making; in terms of the outcome, it demands that every member of the community, who stands on equal footing, is equally respected and noticed, and that a binding consensus among community members should be formed on the basis of fully communication and deliberation. The framework of power and distribution of rights of a country are legitimate when they are agreed upon by the people or their deputies who can represent their will, which is the well-known core of the principle of popular sovereignty. However, the critical question is how to obtain or be regarded as having obtained the people's agreement, and how to recognize a decision is the expression of "public will" not the interest of certain individuals or groups. This means that, for one thing, the operation of state power is legitimate only when it is founded on democracy, which makes it easily get supports and be agreed upon by the people, and that, for another thing, the realization form of democracy is multiple and flexible.

The democratic foundation of China's current procuratorial system mainly lies in several aspects. Firstly, prosecutors are elected, appointed and removal by organs that

[25] For details, see Jeremy Waldron, *Judicial Review and the Conditions of Democracy*, translated by Tong Dezhi, Jiangsu People's Publishing House, 2008, pp. 244–248.

[26] Joseph Schumpeter, *Capitalism, Socialism and Democracy*, translated by Wu Liangjian, The Commercial Press, 1999, p. 395.

represent the people's will.[27] The Supreme People's Procuratorate shall be responsible to the National People's Congress and the National People's Congress Standing Committee. Local people's procuratorates at all levels shall be responsible to the state organs of power that created them and to the people's procuratorates at higher levels. Secondly, the procuratorial power is organized in accordance with the *Constitution* and laws, which are democratic legitimate, and it must operate in accordance with the Constitution and laws. Finally, the Constitution clearly provides that the people's procuratorates of the People's Republic of China are the legal supervision organs of the state and have a constitutional duty to uphold the sanctity of the Constitution and laws and ensure the unity and correct compliance of legal system.[28] That being said, "Trust established on the foundation which lacks of general concern and participation by the people is superficial," and when the procuratorial power "needs to fight the powerful state or political power and protect its unique value, it struggles to

---

[27] According to the current *Constitution* and the *Organic Law of the People's Procuratorates of the People's Republic of China*, the procurator general of the Supreme People's Procuratorate is elected and dismissed by the National People's Congress; the deputy procurator generals, members of the Procuratorial Committee, and procurators of the Supreme People's Procuratorate are appointed and removed by the Standing Committee of the National People's Congress upon the recommendation of the procurator general of the Supreme People's Procuratorate; the procurator generals of the people's procuratorates at the provincial, autonomous region, and directly governed municipality levels are elected and dismissed by the corresponding people's congresses; the deputy procurator generals, members of the procuratorial committees, and procurators are appointed and removed by the standing committees of the corresponding people's congresses upon the recommendation of the provincial-level procurator generals; the appointment and removal of procurator generals at the provincial, autonomous region, and directly governed municipality levels must be submitted to the procurator general of the Supreme People's Procuratorate for approval by the Standing Committee of the National People's Congress; the procurator generals of the autonomous prefectures, provincial cities, counties, cities, and urban districts are elected and dismissed by their respective people's congresses; the deputy procurator generals, procuratorial committee members, and procurators are appointed and removed by the standing committees of the corresponding people's congresses upon the recommendation of their procurator generals; the appointment and removal of procurator generals at these levels must be submitted to the procurator general of the higher-level procuratorate for approval by the standing committee of the corresponding people's congress; at the provincial and county levels, the people's procuratorates established for industrial and mining areas, state farms, and forest districts have procurator generals, deputy procurator generals, procuratorial committee members, and procurators who are appointed and removed by the standing committees of the people's congresses at their level upon the recommendation of the procurator generals of the dispatched people's procuratorates; the standing committees of the national, provincial, autonomous region, and directly governed municipality people's congresses may remove procurator generals, deputy procurator generals, and procuratorial committee members of lower-level procuratorates based on recommendations from their own procurator generals.

[28] Some researchers have summarized the core values underpinning the existence and development of the modern procuratorial system as law protection, rights protection, and supervision. Among these, the system of public prosecution plays a key role in safeguarding the law by enhancing the professionalism and efficiency of criminal prosecution, upholding national interests and social order, and ensuring the uniform and correct implementation of state laws.

See Chen Zhengyun, *Legal Supervision and the Reform of Procuratorial Functions*, Chinese Journal of Law, 2008.

obtain a democratic social foundation that supports this kind of endeavor."[29] In the face of widespread public skepticism regarding the procuratorial organs' authority to investigate duty-related crimes, as well as the internal confusion about their own institutional positioning, the procuratorial power needs to seek broader public recognition and support. Public participation in the exercise of procuratorial power thus becomes a key component of its democratic pursuit.

Public participation in the procuratorial power is of great constitutionalism significance and value in that it affects and restrains the process, operation and outcome of the procuratorial power. For one thing, public participation in the procuratorial power operation reinforces the democratic legitimacy of the procuratorial power. "Democratic legal systems tend to uphold the interest of the majority, as it comes from the majority of the citizens."[30] The current democratic foundation of the procuratorial power mostly comes from the operation of the representative system, which reflects the will and interest of the "majority" more in an abstract sense. Due to the inherent flaws of the representative democracy system, the expression of this kind of will and interest of the "majority" may be distorted or even usurped. In the operation process of the procuratorial power in accordance with the constitution and laws, it has important constitutionalism value as a means of taking in people's opinions and soft-supervision on legislation to introduce supervision and participation by the general public who are not law makers and enforcers, directly understand, observe and raise opinions and suggestions as the "minority" or representatives of the people in individual cases and raise criticism and suggestions on laws created by democratic political decisions or law enforcement by the procuratorial power. For another thing, public participation is of realistic value to the procuratorial power in obtaining greater recognition by the people and legitimacy. In China, the operation mode of the procuratorial power is strongly administrative and exclusive. Given the complex and covert nature of duty-related crimes, the procuratorial organs' process of handling such crimes is also highly professional, technical, covert and unified, which means that it is difficult for the general public to approach and comprehend the handling process, which in turn may give rise to public misunderstanding and distrust of the process. The procuratorial organs can only earn solid trust and recognition from the people and thus obtain the foundation for more extensive legitimacy when they face people's skepticism and dissatisfaction with an open altitude, and give people a chance to understand and participate in the operation of the procuratorial power, which is in itself a chance for the procuratorial organs to clarify and defend themselves.

---

[29] Tanase Takao, *Dispute Resolution and the Judicial System*, translated by Wang Yaxin, China University of Political Science and Law Press, 2004, pp. 247–248.

[30] Tocqueville, *Democracy in America (I)*, translated by Dong Guoliang, The Commercial Press, 1988, p. 264.

1.2.2 The People's Supervisor System: A Way for Procuratorial Work to Participate in Democracy

Evaluating the participation of people's supervisors and the institutional design of the supervisory procuratorial power from the perspective of democracy, researchers have two opposing opinions. One holds a positive view on the democracy of the people's supervisor system, believing that "the meaning of the people's supervisor system lies not only in its improvement of the supervisory procedure in people's procuratorates' direct investigation into duty-related crimes and thus filling a gap in the restraint mechanism for the procuratorial system, but also, more profoundly, in allowing for the first time the public to directly participate in and involve in the law enforcement activities of the procuratorial organs."[31] "The people's supervisor system is in fact a system for reflecting public will, and by standardizing the means of reflecting public will, it increases the democratization degree in the decision-making mechanism of the procuratorial organs in investigating duty-related crimes, which effectively reduces the arbitrariness in the process," and "is an advanced democratic political system that aligns with the prevailing trends of contemporary rule of law culture."[32] The other opinion holds a negative view instead, believing that the judiciary system itself is a product of the democratic system, and people's supervisors are not necessarily more democratic than the prosecutors. Popular sovereignty is expressed by the democratic pursuit in the institutional design, rather than people's direct participation in the judicial process. Moreover, judicial activities are highly professional, and people's direct participation in them is tantamount to denying their professionalism.[33]

The author believes that the people's supervisor system is a way for procuratorial work to participate in democracy, a channel and means of exploring the connection between the procuratorial organs and the public from system and in practice. It allows the people to participate in the administration of state affairs, and places the operation of the procuratorial power under public supervision. The system is significant in many aspects. Firstly, it demonstrates that the legitimacy of the procuratorial power is based on public will, and the people could both realize their will through the people's congresses at all levels and realize democracy in other ways. Secondly, the system provides rules and references for the rationalization of other decisions. Thirdly, the system allows people in other walks of life to conditionally participate in procuratorial work, and play the role of restraining the procuratorial power. Fourthly, the system gives the democratic value a chance and a means to self-correct.[34] The democracy of people's supervisors does not equal to their representativeness. People's supervisors, who are ordinary people, supervise and participate

[31] Liu Tieying, *Thoughts on the Socialization of Law Enforcement by Procuratorial Organs*, Journal of National Prosecutors College, 2005.

[32] Wen Shengtang, *A Study on the Theoretical Foundation and Legislative Issues of the People's Supervisor System (I)*, Fangyuan Rule of Law Special Issue on People's Supervisors, 2007.

[33] See Zhou Anping, *Critique of the People's Supervisors System*, Journal of Nanjing Normal University (Social Science Edition), 2007.

[34] See Han Dayuan & Wang Xiaobin, *A Constitutional Perspective on the People's Supervisor System*, Journal of National Prosecutors College, 2005.

in the process of procuratorial organs' investigations into duty-related crimes, which in itself gives the system direct democratic significance. The state political power is achieved by individuals enjoying some autonomous right to decision,[35] and the direct participation by people's supervisors holds strong significance, which is an improvement of and a soft restraint on the representative democracy.

The negative opinion, which regards that people's supervisors are not necessarily more democratic than prosecutors, and the design of institutional democracy already meets the requirements of popular sovereignty and does not need the democratic form of direct participation as the reason of objection, actually confuses the relation between the democracy and the representativeness of people's supervisors, and fails to comprehend the various ways of the realization of democracy. In fact, the current normative documents of the Supreme People's Procuratorate adopt a democratic recommendation mechanism for the selection of people's supervisors, but from the perspective of long-term institutional development, this selection and appointment mechanism has already undergone a breakthrough. There are supports both in the academic circle and in practice for the selection and appointment mechanism of people's supervisors, which requires self-recommendation and random selection. When the database of people's supervisors is open and their selection is governed by "principled criteria", the regular "appointment" of people's supervisors will render the concept of "the people" more concrete within the system, and the extension of the "people", who specifically and probably participate in individual-case supervision, will continue to expand. In this way, direct judicial democracy, while supervising the clean and fair operation of justice, will become a specific way of China's progressive democracy and rule of law. The people's supervisor system may be the actual beginning of China's direct democratic system, as the choice lies in public opinion, the operation in the judicial system, the reflection in politics, and the significance in the rule of law.[36]

The people's supervisor system is also an institutional design for the orderly democratic participation in procuratorial power, having distinct advantages over other forms of participation. Democratic participation of people's supervisors, which is an orderly and standardized mechanism of participation, has the dedicated platform, procedure, and protection. With the deepening of pilot programs, a relatively mature and stable participation mechanism has been formed and has been voluntarily accepted and recognized by procuratorial organs. In modern society, with technological advancement and the spread of the Internet media, an increasing number of ordinary people are expressing their views on judicial activities in numerous ways, even if a judicial process has nothing to do with their own interests. Such a spontaneous and random form of public will expression does reflect the actual public will to some extent. However, due to information asymmetry and media commercial hype, those remarks tend to be irrational, whose effect could be infinitely enlarged

[35] See Yan Hailiang, *An Interpretation of the Democratic Significance of "The State Respects and Protects Human Rights"*, Study & Exploration, 2007.

[36] See Wu Jun, *The "Extra-institutional" Model and the "Intra-institutional" Path of the People's Supervisors System*, Nomocracy Forum.

by the Internet or media. Gustave Le Bon noted that "Crowds, doubtless, are always unconscious, but this very unconsciousness is perhaps one of the secrets of their strength."[37] The passive response from the procuratorial organs will certainly lead to pressure on the independence and fair operation of the procuratorial power. Therefore, guiding the people to orderly participate in judicial activities and understanding the true public will become the inevitable choice, which is met by the people's supervisor system. Finally, it is necessary to emphasize that "a democratic organization does not necessarily provide the best guarantee of the legitimacy or fidelity of execution; the most effective guarantee of the legitimacy of a given function lies in the personal responsibility of the officials in that organ."[38] The democracy of the people's supervisor system certainly is the reason for its legitimacy; however, the key lies in submitting the divergences between the evaluation decisions of people's supervisors and the procuratorial authorities to an authoritative body for adjudication or making it public to exert broader social pressure through public supervision.

1.3 The People's Supervisor System and the Due Process of Law

Due process of law, since its creation, has served the function of limiting the arbitrary exercise of power and preventing the arbitrary deprivation and infringement of rights. It is not only a constitutional principle, but also a fundamental principle in criminal law. According to Professor Orth's research, the UK was the first to express the requirement of "due process of law", yet they failed to preserve the vitality of this important phrase. In contrast, the constitutions of the states and the federal government in the United States explicitly promise the protection of "due process of law", thus maintaining its vitality. In the United States, with respect to procedural due process, the principle prohibiting one from being "a judge in one's own case" was recognized from the very beginning. Although it is now rarely mentioned, due process will always prohibit unjust procedures. Corrupt, unfair, or terrible decision-makers are not permitted to conduct trials. Other forms of procedural abuse include the absence of a hearing or insufficient time granted to the parties for preparation. In addition to safeguarding liberty rights, procedural due process also has the "potential power to shake power structures". An example of this is the requirement for a hearing before depriving citizens of their welfare rights (social rights). Regarding substantive due process, the paradigm of "depriving Party A to grant Party B" has been replaced by the paradigm of "depriving Party A". In this context, "what is deprived and who benefits is less important than the nature of the deprivation itself". This protection

---

[37] Gustave Le Bon, *The Crowd: A Study of the Popular Mind*, translated by Feng Keli, Central Compilation & Translation Press, 2005, p. 4.

[38] Kelsen, *General Theory of Law and State*, translated by Shen Zongling, Encyclopedia of China Publishing House, 1996, p. 331.

extends not only to personal rights listed in the constitution but also to unenumerated rights such as the right to privacy.[39] The focus of due process of law protection has shifted from property to contracts, then from contracts to civil rights. It can be anticipated that new rights (including those not enumerated in the Constitution) will continually seek to obtain protection from due process of law.

In this sense, although the Constitution of China does not explicitly include a due process of law clause, its orientation toward due process of law can be deduced from the fundamental rights function system. The textual expression of fundamental rights regulation in the Constitution does not specifically highlight the defense against infringements by state power but instead universally for all subjects of infringement. However, by utilizing the clauses such as "the state shall respect and protect human rights" and "the personal dignity of citizens shall not be violated", it is relatively easy to derive the functional orientation of the right to defense against state power. As substantive fundamental rights, the individual freedoms provided in the constitutional texts, such as personal freedom, the inviolability of homes of citizens, freedom and confidentiality of correspondence, personal dignity, all actually encompass an aspect of connotation that demands procedural justice. Constitutional fundamental rights also encompass the function of right to benefit, which includes the interpretation of the right to obtain fair judicial remedies. However, "the payment dimension of fundamental rights inevitably encounters a significant dilemma in practical application, which is the confirmation of the fundamental rights for constitutional payments, and means that it shall greatly restrict the legislative body's freedom of action and potentially impose an excessive burden on state finances, thus risking a crowding-out effect on other fundamental rights of the people. On this basis, the contemporary constitutional academic community generally adopts a cautious attitude toward the existence of so-called "social fundamental rights" and even "the right to claims for payment" under the Constitution.[40] Its binding force is far inferior to that of the right to defense. Constitution of China only provides that citizens have the right to "file charges", actually, the fact that this right is formed and limited by legislation serves as an example. In addition to the above-mentioned functions related to the right to defense and the right to benefit, German public law scholars came up with the concept of "procedural identity" to improve the connotation of Jellinek's theory and regarded it as "the extension of fundamental rights" based on the view of Jellinek that procedural rights is classified the as the payment of positive status, and its connotation is limited to fundamental judicial rights, particularly the right to claim judicial relief, and does not extend to other procedural rights or organizational safeguard rights.[41] Scholars in the Taiwan Province of China directly extended the procedural function dimension of fundamental rights based on the facts that fundamental rights can be safeguarded through specific organizations and procedures and procedures

[39] See John V. Orth, *Due Process of Law: A Brief History*, The Commercial Press, 2006.

[40] Li Jianliang, *The Conceptual Evolution and Functional System of Fundamental Rights: Starting from Jellinek's "Status Theory" (II)*, Constitutionalism Era, p. 184.

[41] See Häberle, Grundrechte im Leistungsstaat, in: VVDStRL, 30 (1972), S.86ff.
Ibid., p. 160.

and organizations are essential conditions for the realization of fundamental rights.[42] If the theory regarding the organizational and procedural safeguard of constitutional fundamental rights is correct, it will undoubtedly provide a direct path for deriving the requirement of due process of law from the fundamental rights regulations in Constitution of China.

1.3.1 The Due Process of Law that the Procuratorial Organs Should Follow in Investigating Duty-Related Crimes

The requirement of due process of law in the fundamental rights regulations of Constitution of China should primarily focus on procedural justice. This is because fair procedures remain at the core of due process in contemporary days.[43] The due process of law principle at the constitutional level should provide protection for all fundamental rights of constitution, among which those most closely related to criminal law are the rights with strong moral value—such as personal dignity, privacy, personal rights, and property rights. The due process of law principle mainly and initially restrains the administrative power and the judiciary power, which is undeniable. Yet, it is worth emphasizing that the respect of procedural justice to the legal procedure is not merely limited to the exercise of power "in accordance with the procedures provided by law"; it is more important that exercising the rights in accordance with "due" legal process.[44] The due process of law principle at the constitutional level has a particular value that lies in its restraint on legislative power. The organizational and procedural norms related to fundamental rights may, in themselves, interfere with or violate constitutional fundamental rights and shall therefore also be subject to restraints. As Justice John Marshall Harlan stated, "if due process is merely the guardian of procedure, then in cases where life, liberty, or property are taken by legislation, the procedural guarantee would be powerless to protect. Therefore, despite the fact that the protection of due process is rooted in the procedural safeguard that is regarded as the objection of arbitrary seizure by the executive and tyranny 'in accordance with law' in *Magna Carta*, in this country it has now 'become a bulwark against arbitrary legislation'."[45] Certainly, it should also be recognized that, though constitutionalism has a counter-majoritarian effect, it is still regarded as a supplementary principle to majoritarianism rather than a denial of it.[46] The interventionist nature of organizational or procedural regulations shall not be equated with provisions that directly restrict or intervene in the fundamental rights of the people. Therefore, when conducting constitutional reviews of procedural and organic laws, moderation and reservation should be exercised; otherwise, the legislative body's

---

[42] *Ibid.*, pp. 186–188.

[43] See John V. Orth, *Due Process of Law: A Brief History*, The Commercial Press, 2006, p. 7.

[44] See Xu Yawen, *On Procedural Justice*, Shandong People's Publishing House, 2004, p. 269.

[45] See John V. Orth, *Due Process of Law: A Brief History*, The Commercial Press, 2006, p. 55.

[46] See Joseph Weiler, *The Worlds of European Constitutionalism*, translated by Cheng Weidong et al., China Social Sciences Press, 2004, p. 103.

freedom in formulating procedural and organic laws will be subject to improper intervention by the constitutional review authority.[47] It can merely require that legislation does not violate a minimum degree of procedural justice. The specific procedural details and the extent of procedural completion belong to legislative political freedom of formation.

If such a standard is applied in measuring the power and procedure provided by Chinese laws on the self-investigating cases of the procuratorial organs, it is obvious that the requirements of due process of law are yet to be met. One of the main grounds used to doubt the self-investigation power of the procuratorial organs is that the power violates the idea of due process of law. For example, some scholars believe that the necessary neutrality and transcendence of fair legal supervision cannot be maintained, since the procuratorial organs are tasked with both investigating duty-related crimes and supervising the investigation, which means that they have simultaneously two opposing powers—the power of legal supervision and criminal prosecution.[48] Some scholars even propose that the direct investigative power of the procuratorial organs should be completely revoked.[49] Japanese scholars point out that the concept of "due process", as a fundamental principle of criminal procedure law, refers to the due process regarding the overall rights of defendants and criminal suspects. Although Japan highly respects the idea of due process, it is not always easy to implement this principle in practice. This is because, while punishment of offenders and due process can sometimes coexist, at times they may even be in opposition to each other. In Japan, there is a clear sense of resistance when offenders are exempted from punishment on procedural grounds. Closely tied to Japan's concept of precise justice, the verification of factual truth is a central concern of people—not only for criminal justice professionals such as judges and prosecutors, but for the defendants themselves, who are also eager to pursue the truth.[50] The situation in China is even more obvious. In terms of the design philosophy of criminal justice procedures, China has long prioritized the discovery of substantive truth as the paramount objective. For substantive truth, human rights protection and adherence to due process of law have generally been regarded as incidental requirements that are "considered alongside" the pursuit of truth. Scholars often trace the philosophical basis of the concept of substantive truth back to the "correspondence theory".[51] It is only in recent years,

---

[47] Li Jianliang, *The Conceptual Evolution and Functional System of Fundamental Rights: Starting from Jellinek's "Status Theory" (II)*, Constitutionalism Era, p. 188.

[48] See Chen Ruihua, *The Nature of Judicial Power*, Chinese Journal of Law, 2000.

[49] See Cai Dingjian, *The Transformation of Procuratorial Functions in the Course of Judicial Reform*, Political Science and Law, 1999.

[50] See Hiroya Matsuo, *Japanese Criminal Procedure Law (II)*, China Renmin University Press, 2005, p. 370.

[51] The Scholastic philosopher Thomas von Aquin developed a formulation for the correspondence theory: truth is the conformity of thought and reality. However, this only provided a criterion for "truth" and did not resolve the question of how the content of subjective cognition could correspond to objective reality. Kant's transcendental epistemology offered an answer to this by proposing that the subject constructs the experience of the object through the application of a priori reason and understanding—a theoretical evolution of the concept.

with growing emphasis on human rights protection, reflection on the diminishing efficacy of traditional judicial practices and growing public dissatisfaction, those efforts have begun to embrace and implement the principles of due process.

In fact, if we extrapolate from the insights of Nietzsche and Foucault, interpret the meaning of "adversarial relations", and regard truth in criminal justice as a strategic relationship shaped by the conflict of desires and power, then, the emergence of any conception of truth is the result of warfare, confrontation, and struggle among power, politics, and perspectives of experience.[52] Such a procedural interpretation thus reveals the necessity of incorporating due process into the pursuit of substantive truth in criminal judicial procedure. Setting aside periods of extreme social disorder, in times of relative peace and stability, the soundness of criminal justice should not be evaluated by the number of offenders apprehended, but rather by the extent to which due process is faithfully observed.[53] In the operation of the procuratorial power in China, in particular in the realm of duty-related crime investigation, where there is a lack of due process of law, observing the due process of law principle is a basic requirement of protecting fundamental constitutional rights.

1.3.2 The Due Process of Law Dimension of the People's Supervisor System

The fundamental requirements of the principle of procedural due process of law are essentially: "No one shall be the judge in their own case", and "Parties have the right to state and to be heard."[54] The former aims to eliminate bias. Hobbes once pointed out the reason why no one shall be the judge in their own case, stating: "Since we assume that everything a person does is for their own interests, it is therefore inappropriate for anyone to serve as an arbiter in a dispute involving themselves."[55] Rawls offered a solution to the problem, stating that "judges must be independent and impartial, and they must not adjudicate their own cases. Trials of all kinds must be fair and open, and must not be influenced by public clamor. The principles of natural justice are meant to ensure that the legal order is maintained justly and according to rules."[56] The latter requires that, when deciding to punish that affects a party's vital interests, a fair opportunity must be given for that party to defend itself, which includes notification, explanation of reasons, and the right to be heard,

---

See Xu Hengda, *The Epistemological Formation and Conceptual Archaeology of "Substantive Truth-finding Doctrine": Focusing on the Development of German Criminal Procedure from the Middle Ages to the Early Modern Period*, National Chengchi University Law Review, 2008, pp. 145–148.

[52] *Ibid.*, pp. 150–154.

[53] See Hiroya Matsuo, *Japanese Criminal Procedure Law (II)*, China Renmin University Press, 2005, pp. 370–371.

[54] See Xu Yawen, *On Procedural Justice*, Shandong People's Publishing House, 2004, pp. 10–27.

[55] Hobbes, *Leviathan*, translated by Li Sifu et al., The Commercial Press, 1996, p. 119.

[56] Rawls, *A Theory of Justice*, translated by He Huaihong et al., China Social Sciences Press, 1988, p. 229.

and requires that the party concerned be able to participate in the handling of duty-related criminal cases by the procuratorial organs in a peaceful, voluntary, meaningful manner, through a fair and comprehensible procedure.[57]

Following the aforementioned standards, the due process dimension of people's supervisor mainly lies in the following points. First, in situations where criminal suspects object to arrest, or in supervisory procedures where the procuratorial organs intend not to prosecute or to withdraw a duty-related crime case, people's supervisors play the role of neutral third-party overseers. Although people's supervisors are not the final decision-makers, their involvement can lead to procedural reconsideration. When a criminal suspect or victim disagrees with a decision made or intended to be made by the procuratorial organs and a dispute arises, the presence of people's supervisors offers the procuratorial organs an opportunity to be heard by a neutral third party. As the right to information of people's supervisors is guaranteed, criminal suspects and victims may also gain the opportunity to be heard by a neutral third party. Through this act of hearing, the function of absorbing discontent within the process can be realized, thereby resolving the dispute. In practice, efforts have been made to introduce a hearing system for people's supervisors,[58] and the introduction of such a system would highlight the due process dimension of the people's supervisor system. Second, people's supervisors can raise opinions on cases of favoritism for personal gains, corruption, and violations of law in the handling of procuratorial personnel's duty-related crimes, and offer suggestions and opinions on other violations of laws and discipline. This way, they are able to safeguard the neutrality of the procuratorial organs in handling cases and prevent bias arising from money, personal interests, relatives, organizations, hostility, and other factors. In fact, even if the procuratorial organs can avoid bias in handling duty-related crimes, however, due to the fact that they undertake all stages of handling including case filing, investigation, arrest, and prosecution, the internal mechanisms for mutual restriction among these stages under the system leading by the procurator generals and the procuratorial committees are difficult to truly function. Justice is also not realized in a way that the public "can see". The involvement of people's supervisors is invaluable for increasing the transparency and acceptability of these procedures. Finally, the design of the people's supervisor system, which includes the notification system for the supervisory right of people's supervisors, the random selection or ranking system for people's supervisors, the recusal system, the independent evaluation system and more, can meet the requirements of due process of law.

[57] Professor Michael D. Bayles proposed seven value standards of litigation procedures, including the principles of peace, voluntariness, participation, fairness, comprehensibility, timeliness, and finality. He argued that the intrinsic value of procedure lies not in its dependence on the outcome of a judgment, but in the qualities inherent in the procedure itself – those aspects that bring a sense of satisfaction to the participants.

See Michael D. Bayles, *Principles of Law: A Normative Analysis*, translated by Zhang Wenxian et al., Encyclopedia of China Publishing House, 1996, p. 32, 34–37.

[58] See Sun Shengyu and Fan Jifang, *Yunlong, Xuzhou Launches the People's Supervisor Hearing System*, at http://news.jcrb.com/jiancha/jcdt/200807/t20080823_39929.html, last visited on August 1, 2008.

2 The Functions and Value of the People's Supervisor System

From the perspective of the ought-to-be value pursuit of the people's supervisor system, the people's supervisor system serves as a reinforcement of the power supervision mechanism over the procuratorial organs in handling duty-related crimes. Besides its institutional improvement function, it also improves the system for handling such cases by the procuratorial organs, enhances the people's recognition of the procuratorial organs' authority in handling duty-related crime cases, promotes fair and efficient handling of self-investigating cases by the procuratorial organs, and realizes the dual values of social control and human rights protection. The functions of institutional improvement, institutional refinement, and institutional recognition together constitute a closely connected functional system. Only when these functions are realized together can they ultimately promote the value pursuits of fairness, efficiency, social control, and human rights protection, and enable the maximum harmonious coexistence and realization of these interacting value demands. The setting of functions and values at the ought-to-be level of the people's supervisor system holds significant importance for the legitimacy of the system. Overemphasizing a single function or value, or neglecting any of them, can lead to negative consequences and affect the recognition of the system's legitimacy. In practice, the people's supervisor system has realized these functions and values to varying degrees.[59]

2.1 The Institutional Improvement Function: Supplying and Improving Structural Gaps and Enhancing Coexisting of Mechanisms

The existing mechanism for handling duty-related crimes within the procuratorial organs has inadequacies in terms of institutional design. In accordance with the provisions of the *Criminal Procedure Law*, the procuratorial organs enjoy legislative power, investigative power, prosecutorial power, and the power to withdraw cases in handling duty-related crimes. These powers are distributed among different departments within the procuratorial organs, implementing a system of divided supervision by the procurator generals, while strengthening the supervision of lower-level procuratorial organs by the Supreme People's Procuratorate and higher procuratorial organs, to maximize the assurance of quality and fairness in handling duty-related crime cases through internal restriction mechanism. In addition, there are general supervisions from state power organs, the Party committees at the same level, and public opinions. In duty-related crime cases where public prosecution is initiated,

[59] The achievements scored in the practice of the People's Supervisor System are discussed in detail in Chapter III and omitted here.

the procuratorial organs are also subject to the restriction of the criminal adjudicative power exercised by the People's Courts, which are neutral. These supervisory measures, especially the individual-case adjudication by the People's Courts, can to some extent effectively restrain and supervise the exercise of power by the procuratorial organs in handling duty-related crimes, thus preventing the abuse of procuratorial power. However, when the procuratorial organs decide not to file a case, to withdraw a case, or not to initiate a public prosecution, the current legal framework provides no opportunity for court intervention and supervision. Aside from the internal checks under the responsibility system of the procurator general and the procuratorial committee, who belong to the same organ or system, there is a lack of strong external supervisory and restraining mechanisms. However, the internal check mechanism of the procuratorial organs risks "becoming the judge in their own cases", which inevitably triggers doubts among the people on procedural fairness. The power to decide on arrests is an important power within the procuratorial organs' investigative powers over duty-related crimes. It is a form of criminal force measure that deprives criminal suspects of their personal freedom. Unlike the institutional design of criminal arrest approval power, where the procuratorial organs supervise the investigative powers of public security organs, or the institutional design in other countries where the arrest approval power lies with the courts, in the investigation of duty-related crime cases, the power to approve arrests is generally exercised by the same procuratorate. In cases that are serious or complex, the final decision rests with the procurator general or the Procuratorial Committee. Since the power of the procurator general and the procuratorial committee extends to all stages of the case-handling process, their role in making final decisions undermines the checks and separations among internal departments, which may result in violations of due process of law.

The existing external supervision mechanisms for the procuratorial organs' handling of duty-related crimes have functional and efficacy limitations. As for external supervision by the people's congresses at the same level, it cannot take the means of individual-case supervision, but rather operates on a macro level through general case-type supervision or work supervision. As a result, it is difficult to identify specific issues within individual cases handled by the procuratorial organs, making it hard to achieve substantive and timely supervisory effects. Supervisions by Party committees at the same level and by public opinion are not a formal institutional arrangement with legal effects. Even though such forms of supervision may play a positive role and yield direct and obvious effects in certain situations, they do not constitute long-term and orderly institutional design. As a result, these supervisory mechanisms are not well-developed, their channels of expression are limited, and their ultimate effectiveness lacks the safeguard of law. Therefore, the decisions not to file a case, to withdraw a case, or not to prosecute in self-investigating cases have become "blind spots" for external supervision, and are also the stages where the procuratorial organs are most prone to problems and where public dissatisfaction is most concentrated. In addition, although lawyers of criminal suspects can serve as an effective check on the procuratorial organs by virtue of their professional knowledge and skills, the protection of lawyers' rights is currently insufficient. Their involvement in duty-related crime cases comes relatively late, which greatly limits their ability to function as a counterbalance. Moreover, in practice, lawyers usually act from the standpoint of the criminal suspect and work to protect the suspect's interests, thus placing them in an adversarial position to the procuratorial organs rather than a neutral one.

For one thing, the introduction of the people's supervisor system serves as a reinforcement of the existing supervisory mechanisms. Firstly, the people's supervisor system functions as an external right supervisory mechanism, and its introduction fills a gap in the current system of supervision. Unlike the procuratorial organs and the lawyers of criminal suspects, the people's supervisor system can take a relatively neutral position and supervise decisions to withdraw or not prosecute a case in terms of individual cases, offering opinions on situations where a case is not filed when filing is necessary, or vice versa. Secondly, as the exercise of their supervisory power follows a designated procedure with procedural rigidity and binding force, the opinions and suggestions and especially the supervisory decisions of people's supervisors, being distinct from those within the procuratorial system, become external views that the procuratorial organs must take seriously and consider carefully. This serves as a reinforcement of the existing supervisory mechanisms over the procuratorial organs' powers of case initiation and prosecution in duty-related crimes. Finally, by including cases where criminal suspects object to arrest decisions within the supervisory scope of the people's supervisor system, a neutral third party is established to oversee the exercise of power by the procuratorial organs. This creates an opportunity to introduce a hearing mechanism, thus improving the original institutional design and, at the same time, strengthening the remedies available to protect the rights of criminal suspects. For another thing, the introduction of the people's supervisor system does not interfere with and substantially conflict with the existing system.[60] Due to its procedural nature, the rigidity of its procedural effectiveness, and its case-specific nature, as well as its role as a right supervisory mechanism, it can serve as a supplement to the supervision mechanism of the people's congresses. At the same time, it constitutes an important concrete embodiment and reinforcement of social supervision, therefore providing supports for the effective functioning of the existing mechanisms.

2.2 The Institutional Refinement Function: Mutual Support of Justice and Efficiency

The people's supervisor system can promote the realization of judicial justice. First, as ordinary citizens, people's supervisors can provide intellectual support through supervision and offering opinions and suggestions, breaking the prosecutorial organs'

[60] The institutional living space of the people's supervisor system under the constitutionalism framework will be discussed in dedicated sections later in the book, and is omitted here.

professional fixed mindset. From the perspective of ordinary citizens' ethics, moral concepts, life norms, and common sense, people's supervisors can examine the behavior of criminal suspects, helping the procuratorial organs understand and characterize the suspects' motives and the nature of their actions. At the same time, they enable the procuratorial organs to grasp the real social impact of the behavior. People's supervisors who possess professional knowledge and skills (both legal and non-legal) can also provide specialized intellectual support, assisting the procuratorial organs in solving technical difficulties encountered during case handling. In addition to understanding the facts of a case, people's supervisors can also comprehend legal norms from the perspective of ordinary citizens, enabling the procuratorial organs to timely identify gaps between the legal norms and reality, to understand areas where the public is prone to misunderstand the law, to make more accurate legal characterizations of the suspects' behavior, and thereby to make case handling more humane, which is conducive to the realization of substantive justice and the protection of human rights. Moreover, the people's supervisor system serves as a mechanism for the supervision and restraint of power through rights. Supervision is a mechanism that corresponds to democratic power, it is not a form of regular power, but rather a force that keeps power rational. It controls power, compelling it to remain vigilant, to review, and to correct itself, thus redeeming power.[61] The supervision by people's supervisors over the "five types of situations" is closely aligned with the four key areas of rectification outlined in the special rectification work plan of the Supreme People's Procuratorate: bending the law for personal gains and trading power for money, reckless law enforcement, handling cases in violation of laws and regulations, neglect of duty and inaction in law enforcement, and failure to exercise procuratorial powers independently and in accordance with the law. The implementation of the people's supervisor system addresses the most prominent issues raised by the public and responds to their most pressing demands, aiming to resolve the problems that hinder judicial fairness in the procuratorial organs.[62] Finally, the people's supervisor system can, through procedural mechanisms, effectively prevent potential arbitrariness resulting from the centralized exercise of procuratorial power. When a simple majority opinion of people's supervisors is vetoed by the procurator general, who holds a relatively superior position in the exercise of procuratorial power, such veto does not take immediate effect; instead, the procurator general must exercise the right to submit the matter to the procuratorial committee for deliberation. The exercise of this procedural, social supervisory right, though increasing the costs of submission for deliberation, coordination, and implementation, and weakening the rigidity and relative advantage of the procurator general's authority, can nevertheless

---

[61] See Song Yuansheng, *On Social Supervision over Investigative Actions: From the Perspective of Specialization*, Journal of Henan Administrative Institute of Politics and Law, 2008.

[62] See Zhou Yongnian ed., *Introduction to the People's Supervisor System*, China Procuratorial Press, 2008, p. 42.

prevent or delay the potential abuse of discretionary power, investigative supervision power, and prosecutorial power by the procurator general.[63]

The people's supervisor system can contribute to the realization of judicial justice with its functions of intellectual support, power restraint, and procedural control. At the same time, it also plays a positive role in improving judicial efficiency. First, the people's supervisor system as an external supervision mechanism sets a barrier to the independent exercise of procuratorial power, helping the procuratorial organs resist improper external interference and thereby improving the efficiency of procuratorial operations. Second, the existence of the people's supervisor system as a procedurally rigid external supervision mechanism, along with the intellectual support provided through the opinions and suggestions offered by people's supervisors, can prompt internal reflection and correction within the procuratorial power structure. This helps reduce internal friction within the system, enabling errors to be prevented before they occur and corrected promptly when they do. As a result, the possibility of final errors is reduced, and so is the cost of relying on other power mechanisms for correction and remedy. On the above basis, the procuratorial organs will naturally gain greater trust and support from the public, which in turn will further promote the sound operation of the system and lead to the overall optimization of the mechanism for handling duty-related crimes by the procuratorial organs.

2.3 *The Institutional Recognition Function: The Combination of Public Participation and Due Process of Law*

Since the establishment of the procuratorial system on the European continent, prosecutors have found themselves in the "valley zone" between the two forces of judges and the police. Caught between these two distinct and powerful groups, they have struggled to explore and clear their own positions. For one thing, prosecutors are unwilling to be regarded as inferior "dwarf judges"; for another thing, they are also reluctant to become senior "judicial police officers".[64] Accurately identifying their proper role has always been a difficult challenge for prosecutors. In this context, the power of procuratorial organs to handle self-investigating cases inevitably falls into an even deeper quagmire of being questioned. In such a predicament, even the legitimacy of prosecutorial power itself requires justification. Discontent and skepticism toward the system are often expressed through disorganized channels, which can significantly undermine the efficiency of institutional operation. For the procuratorial organs, in a certain sense, it cannot be denied that their actual intention of independently establishing the people's supervisor system is to try to absorb and

---

[63] Xu Hanming, *An Economic Analysis of the Concept and Characteristics of the People's Supervisor System*, Fangyuan Rule of Law Special Issue on People's Supervisors, 2005.

[64] Cited from Long Zongzhi, *On the Positioning of Public Prosecutors*, People's Procuratorial Semimonthly, 1999.

alleviate the public disappointment and dissatisfaction with the current judicial situation of the procuratorate through the implementation of the system. This strategy is still largely based on political considerations.[65] The research findings of research group on the theory of the people's supervisor system under the Supreme People's Procuratorate directly point out that the people's supervisor system is essentially a system reflecting social conditions and public opinions, an effective approach to advancing the democratization of prosecutorial decision-making, and an advanced democratic political system in line with the trend of contemporary rule of law civilization.[66] As Professor Robert Dahl pointed out, democracy, as an existing or real-world entity, is conceived in various ways as a unique political system and practice, a special set of rights, a social and economic order that guarantees certain consensus outcomes, or the only process capable of making collective and binding decisions. In China, democracy has always been regarded as an important constitutional principle and even the primary value of constitutionalism, serving as the foundation for the existence and development of the entire legal system. This means that if a system possesses democratic legitimacy, it can maximize the public recognition. As a procuratorial participation democratic system, the people's supervisor system naturally has this function of institutional recognition, which also helps the procuratorial organs' mechanism for handling duty-related crimes gain greater recognition.

In fact, the people's supervisor system not only embodies the democratic function and value of public participation, but also has the value of due process of law. For people's supervisors, the process of participation in supervision is the process of expressing their will and accepting legal education. It also is the process for the procuratorial organs to clarify misunderstandings and provide explanations, as well as the process of communication between the procuratorial organs and the public. Through this process, both the public and the procuratorial organs have found an institutionalized mechanism for being heard. "Once people participate in the process, it becomes difficult for them to resist the consequences that the process entails. In these processes, individuals are brought under control, or at the very least, their arbitrariness is under control".[67] On this basis, consensus and mutual recognition are more easily achieved. The procuratorial organs gain a better understanding of public opinion, which also means they are better positioned to meet public expectations. For parties involved in a case and for the general public, the presence of people's supervisors as a neutral third party embodies the due process values that "no one shall be the judge in their own case" and that "all parties have the right to state and be heard."[68] The institutionalized and standardized operation of this system in itself helps enhance the acceptability of judicial outcomes, thus facilitating the timely

---

[65] See Zhou Anping, *Critique of the People's Supervisors System*, Journal of Nanjing Normal University (Social Science Edition), 2007.

[66] See Theoretical Research Team on the People's Supervisor System, *Theoretical Foundations and Legislative Issues of the People's Supervisor System (I)*, Fangyuan Rule of Law Special Issue on People's Supervisors, 2007.

[67] Lü Shilun ed., *Study on the Contemporary Western Theoretical Jurisprudence*, China Renmin University Press, 1997, p. 237.

[68] See Xu Yawen, *On Procedural Justice*, Shandong People's Publishing House, 2004, pp. 10–27.

resolution of disputes, reducing judicial costs. In practice, the people's supervisor system may encounter situations where, due to the high quality of case handling by the procuratorial organs, there are few or no cases requiring supervision, which in turn leads to doubts about the system. In author's opinion, the legitimacy of the system should not be measured by the number of supervised cases, and the very existence of the people's supervisor system is significant in terms of institutional recognition. The key lies in designing a system that not only ensures effective supervision but also minimizes operational costs, or explores ways to expand the scope of the system's application.

If the people's supervisor system embodies only the democratic value of public participation but lacks the value of due process of law, then it cannot be distinguished from other mechanisms of public participation which are defined in a broad sense, and would lose its unique significance of existence. It is precisely because the people's supervisor system, for one thing, is a concrete means for people to exercise their fundamental constitutional rights, allowing ordinary citizens to participate in the relatively closed process of handling duty-related crimes by the procuratorial organs, and because only a limited and non-specific group of people can participate through the way which is legally procedural, that the system embodies and practices the spirit of natural justice. It achieves a dialectical balance between the minority and the majority, avoids disorderly and ineffective participation, and gains its own unique existential value and legitimacy. The complementary relationship between public participation and the function and value of due process of law can better safeguard human rights and will inevitably enhance public recognition of the procedures and outcomes in the handling of duty-related crimes by the procuratorial organs. It is important to be aware of the fact that the procuratorial organs have their own value positioning, and in the reform of procuratorial functions, they should neither be designed merely as case-handling bodies or "prosecution zealots", nor be viewed as purely charitable institutions or "spokespersons" for human rights, as either extreme would lead to a distortion of their function as legal supervisors.[69] The people's supervisor system occupies a neutral position. It not only focuses on safeguarding the rights and interests of criminal suspects, victims, and the state, but also pays attention to the positive functioning of procuratorial power. Through procedural supervision and the procedure of the submission of opinions and suggestions from the people's supervisor system, both human rights protection and the protection of the interests of society and the state can be considered. This aligns with the goals and direction of the reform of procuratorial functions, and it also means that in these aspects of the exercise of procuratorial power, greater understanding and recognition can be achieved through the participation of people's supervisors.

---

[69] See Chen Zhengyun, *Legal Supervision and the Reform of Procuratorial Functions*, Chinese Journal of Law, 2008.

3 The Living Space of the People's Supervisor System Within the Constitutional Framework

The people's supervisor system possesses a solid jurisprudential basis due to its alignment with concept of constitutionalism, its role as a means of realization of prosecutorial participation in democracy, and its adherence to the principles of due process. Furthermore, its functions and values, such as institutional improvement, optimization, and public recognition, enable it to meet practical needs, thereby adequately approving its legitimacy both in terms of value concept and practical significance. However, for the people's supervisor system to operate positively in practice, it is essential to demonstrate its institutional living space within the constitutional framework. As a product of human behavior, a system comprises a set of established rules, compliance procedures, and ethical norms. It is a comprehensive system of rules and implementation mechanisms,[70] interwoven with formal rules rooted in the Constitution, laws, and regulations, as well as informal rules embodied in customs, traditions, and conventions. It represents the interactive process through which different social groups negotiate survival and resource distribution. The people's supervisor system shall not only find its basis or institutional exit within the formal rules of constitutionalism as outlined in constitutional and legal texts but must also consider whether it aligns with the policies of the Party and the state. Additionally, the feasibility of its integration with the internal operational rules of procuratorial power must be examined. Although the policies of the Party and the state are not formal rules with direct legal effect and are more subjective and mutable compared to formal rules, they reflect the will and interests of the people and embody the dominant value propositions of an era. In certain sense, they can be seen as precursors and guides to the formation of formal constitutional and legal rules, with the potential to ascend to the status of formal constitutional rules. Their significance and strength in national development cannot be overlooked. Similarly, many procuratorial business systems lack external legal effect and are often governed by informal rules, such as internal operational documents issued by the Supreme People's Procuratorate. Nevertheless, these systems form the practical basis for the exercise of procuratorial power and constitute the institutional environment in which the people's supervisor system operates. Thus, procuratorial business systems represent an indispensable institutional background when discussing the living space of the people's supervisor system.

It should be noted that although these formal and informal rules collectively form the institutional background for the people's supervisor system in practice, tensions exist among these rules, sometimes even leading to conflicts and inconsistencies. Under the constitutionalism of rule of law, no law shall be in conflict with the constitutional provisions, no internal prosecutorial document shall be in conflict with the Constitution and laws, and Party and state policies shall be legally effective when reflecting legal and constitutional rules. Therefore, when discussing the living space

[70] See Douglass C. North., *Structure and Change in Economic History*, translated by Chen Yu et al., Shanghai Joint Publishing, Shanghai People's Publishing House, 1994, pp. 225–226.

of the people's supervisor system, a systematic approach must be adopted within the constitutional framework, that is, using constitutional texts as the supreme authority, subjecting relevant laws, regulations, and internal normative documents of prosecutorial organs to constitutional scrutiny, and interpreting Party and state policies in a manner that aligns with constitutional intent rather than conducting fragmented, isolated comparisons. For example, *the Provisions on the Requirement for People's Procuratorates Below the Provincial Level to Report to the People's Procuratorate at the Next Level up for Approval of Decisions to Withdraw Cases or Not to Prosecute in Directly Investigated Cases (for Trial Implementation)*, This normative document provides that procuratorates below the provincial level shall obtain approval from the people's procuratorate at the next level up when deciding to withdraw a case or not to prosecute. The original intent of this system was to strengthen the leadership and supervisory constraints of higher-level people's procuratorates over lower-level ones in handling directly investigated cases, thereby improving the quality of decisions to withdraw cases or not to prosecute. While this approval system does not conflict with provisions of *Constitution* and *Organic Law of People's Procuratorates*, which provide a leadership relationship between higher and lower procuratorates, its implementation, primarily through written reviews without granting suspects and other interested parties the right to debate or be heard, may undermine the interests related to prosecutorial hierarchy provided in the Criminal Procedure Law. Specifically, it weakens the rights of victims to appeal to higher people's procuratorates against non-prosecution decisions and of the non-accused to challenge such decisions, concentrating power in the hands of procurator general, Procuratorial Committees, and higher-level procuratorates. While this enhances uniformity and authority in case handling, it also increases the risk of power abuse and reduces opportunities for error correction. Under the people's supervisor system, the procedural rigidity of supervisors' oversight over proposed case withdrawals and non-prosecutions is reflected in the requirement that, when the Procuratorial Committee's decision contradicts the supervisors' dissenting vote and a majority of participating supervisors have different opinions over the decision, they may request review by people's procuratorate at the next level up, which must promptly conduct the review and provide feedback. However, the mandatory approval process under *the Provisions on the Requirement for People's Procuratorates Below the Provincial Level to Report to the People's Procuratorate at the Next Level up for Approval of Decisions to Withdraw Cases or Not to Prosecute in Directly Investigated Cases (for Trial Implementation)* renders this procedural rigidity of binding force meaningless. Furthermore, while *Provisions of the Supreme People's Procuratorate on the Implementation of the People's Supervisor System (Trial)* lacks clear time requirements for supervisory procedures, *the Provisions on the Requirement for People's Procuratorates Below the Provincial Level to Report to the People's Procuratorate at the Next Level up for Approval of Decisions to Withdraw Cases or Not to Prosecute in Directly Investigated Cases (for Trial Implementation* imposes specific deadlines for submitting materials to procuratorates at the next level up, including the supervisors' opinions, creating procedural conflicts. In such cases, it is necessary to evaluate not only the rationality of the people's supervisor system's design but also whether the prosecutorial organs' internal systems comply with constitutional and legal basis and have rationality.

3.1 Constitutional Basis and Legal System Interface of the People's Supervisor System

3.1.1 Constitutional Textual Basis of the People's Supervisor System

Any institutional form devoid of constitutional normative support and lacking the fundamental constitutional essence shall be inherently unsustainable. From a constitutional textual perspective, while no express provision in constitutional norms directly corresponds to the people's supervisor system, normative validity may nevertheless be conferred upon it through constitutional interpretation. Furthermore, from the fundamental constitutional spirit, the transformation of constitutional rights provided on paper into substantive and exercisable rights for citizens in practice necessitates constitutional implementation. The effective restraint and supervision of various public powers to safeguard citizens' fundamental rights have garnered increasing attention. Article 41 of the *Constitution*, often referred to as the "supervision rights clause" encompasses right to criticize, right to make suggestions, right to file complaints, right to file charges, and right to file reports. This article also represents an approach of participating in state management, without being subject to restrictions based on law. Article 27 provides the obligation of state organs to listen to people's opinions and suggestions, accept their oversight, forming a corresponding relationship of rights and obligations with Article 41. Articles 41 and 27 of the *Constitution* can thus serve as direct constitutional foundations for the people's supervisor system. Article 41 provides citizens' fundamental rights, while Article 27 provides the state's corresponding obligations, endowing the rights under Article 41 with rigidity of binding force. Additionally, the methodology of constitutional interpretation may be invoked to designate Articles 2 and 33 of the *Constitution* as indirect foundations. The stipulation "in accordance with the law" in Article 2 shall not be construed as imposing restrictions upon citizens' right to manage state affairs, but rather as prescribing an affirmative obligation upon the legislative power of the State to enact requisite legislation guaranteeing the exercise of such right. With respect to the "human rights" formulation in Article 33, a positivistic interpretation may properly be adopted, whereby this provision shall operate as an omnibus clause for both systematizing diverse fundamental rights and giving rise to unenumerated constitutional rights.

The people's supervisor system further demonstrates its constitutional conformity through its safeguarding of fundamental rights for suspects, defendants, and victims in duty-related criminal cases. The existing Constitution expressly provides that citizens' fundamental rights shall not be violated, including personal freedom and personal dignity. This is, in a substantive sense, the paramount constitutional foundation for evaluating the normative validity of the people's supervisor system. From the original intent of constitutional regulation of state-citizen relations, it is incumbent upon the State to perfect relevant legislation to guarantee the aforementioned fundamental rights of citizens. Meanwhile, citizens shall be entitled to seek supervision and remedy through diverse modalities and channels against any infringement of their fundamental rights by public power. The establishment of the people's supervisor system may be recognized as an institutional innovation in the protection of citizens' fundamental rights. Furthermore, victims in cases investigated by procuratorial organs themselves may, through the people's supervisor system, state their opinions and file complaints, charges and reports against unlawful, criminal, or infringements. Such actions constitute concrete means of citizens exercising their fundamental rights of supervision and petition as constitutionally provided (modes of exercising such fundamental rights may carry particular significance), while potentially obtaining remedies through the implementation of the people's supervisor system.

3.1.2 Legal Basis of the People's Supervisor System

After the Constitution has demonstrated that the people's supervisor system embodies citizens' rights of supervision and suggestion while possessing value rationality, the constitutional provision proclaiming that "the people shall, in accordance with the provisions of law, manage state affairs" must also have corresponding legal norms to realize its effect. The fundamental rights of citizens to supervise procuratorial power are primarily guaranteed by the *Criminal Procedure Law of the People's Republic of China* (hereinafter referred to as the *Criminal Procedure Law*), the *Organic Law of People's Procuratorates of the People's Republic of China* (hereinafter referred to as the *Organic Law of People's Procuratorates*), and the *Procurators Law of the People's Republic of China* (hereinafter referred to as the *Procurators Law*) as specialized legislation governing the exercise of prosecutorial authority. Among these, the *Criminal Procedure Law*, as the fundamental law regulating criminal proceedings, should establish overarching principles for supervising procuratorial power. The *Organic Law of People's Procuratorates*, which serves as the fundamental law for the establishment and operation of procuratorates, and the *Procurators Law*, which regulates the authority, appointment and removal of prosecutors, mutually correspond with the *Criminal Procedure Law*.

The existing *Organic Law of People's Procuratorates* and the *Procurators Law* both expressly provide the principle of "accepting supervision by the masses (the people)", providing both the doctrinal basis and institutional interface for its legalization.[71] Article 6 of the *Criminal Procedure Law* provides that "in conducting criminal proceedings, the people's courts, the people's procuratorates and the public security

[71] See Chen Han, *Legalization, Socialization, and Proceduralization: Prospects for the Development of the People's Supervisor System*, Journal of Guangdong Ocean University, 2007.

organs must rely on the masses, base themselves on facts and take law as the criterion", while Article 3 of the Procurators Law provides that "procurators shall observe the Constitution and laws, and be devoted to serving the people". These provisions constitute abstract normative prescriptions governing the relationship between the prosecutorial organs and citizens' rights during the exercise of prosecutorial power. Although bearing declaratory characteristics, they establish the legal basis for public participation in the exercise of prosecutorial power, with their essential purport being to ensure the intrinsic connection between prosecutorial power and citizens' rights. However, Article 7 of the *Organic Law of People's Procuratorates*, which provides that "people's procuratorates must, in executing their work, persistently seek truth from facts, follow the mass line, heed the opinions of the masses and subject themselves to the supervision by the masses", not only corresponds to the relevant provisions in the *Criminal Procedure Law* and *Procurators Law*, but also stresses that the foundation of the exercise of prosecutorial power, which must rely on the people, lies in the unification of supervision by the people.

Meanwhile, the principle of independently exercising of prosecutorial power provided by the Constitution and laws establishes boundaries for the people's supervisor system. Article 131 of the *Constitution* provides: "the people's courts shall, in accordance with the provisions of law, independently exercise adjudicatory power, and shall not be subject to interference from any administrative organ, social organization or individual." Article 9 of the *Organic Law of People's Procuratorates* provides: "the people's procuratorates shall exercise procuratorial power independently, in accordance with the provisions of law, and shall not be subject to interference by any administrative organ, public organization or individual." Article 9 of the *Procurators Law* provides: "public procurators, when performing their functions and duties according to law, shall be protected by law and not be subject to interference by administrative organs, public organizations or individuals." A literal interpretation of constitutional and statutory provisions confirms that both procuratorial organs and individual prosecutors enjoy legally guaranteed immunity from interference by administrative organs, social groups, or individuals. This fundamental principle delineates the operational parameters for the people's supervisor system, requiring that its supervisory activities and actions of making opinions and suggestion must not constitute improper interference with the independent functioning of prosecutorial power. Correspondingly, people's supervisors themselves must observe defined limits and responsibilities in exercising their rights.

3.2 *The Party and State Policy Basis of the People's Supervisor System*

The people's supervisor system aligns with the governing party's political criteria and adheres to its fundamental political orientation. The Report to the 17th National Congress of the CPC clearly pointed out that: "We need improve the mechanism of restraint and oversight and ensure that power entrusted by the people is always exercised in their interests. Power must be exercised in the sunshine to ensure that it is exercised correctly." The Report further calls to "deepen the reform of the judiciary system, optimize the distribution of judicial functions and powers, standardize judicial practices, and build a fair, efficient, and authoritative socialist judiciary system." The fundamental approach is to "improve institutions for democracy, diversify its forms and expand its channels, and we need to carry out democratic election, decision-making, administration and oversight in accordance with the law to guarantee the people's rights to be informed, to participate, to be heard, and to oversee." The fundamental political direction set forth in Report to the 17th National Congress, along with the goals of democratic political system reform guided by the Scientific Outlook on Development, is to establish more standardized and effective supervision over state power. This supervision fundamentally relies on public participation and transparent power operation, emphasizing the active exercise of citizens' rights to advance the development of democratic institutions and the protection of human rights. In particular, it highlights expanding democratic participation in the functioning of judicial power and enhancing transparency in judicial work. This represents an extension and deepening of the concept stated in the Report to the 16th National Congress: "We should form a sound judicial system featuring clearly specified powers and responsibilities, mutual coordination and restraint, and highly efficient operation."

The establishment and subsequent development of the people's supervisor system constitutes a constructive institutional innovation in supervising the exercise of prosecutorial power in self-investigating cases by procuratorial organs. By introducing societal oversight mechanisms over prosecutorial power, this reform not only aligns with the fundamental principles of democratic political development but also corresponds with the current trajectory of political reform. It represents a significant breakthrough in judicial reform under the leadership of the governing party.

3.3 The Interface Between the People's Supervisor System and Relevant Institutional Frameworks

Within the existing supervisory mechanism, people's congresses at all levels constitute the primary state organs exercising oversight over procuratorial work, their supervisory status and authority having been unequivocally established by law. A critical issue warranting deliberation is how the people's supervisor system may institutionally articulate with the NPC supervision under the settled framework, so as to ensure coordinated interaction between these two distinct supervisory modalities.

The implementation of the people's supervisor system has revealed substantive institutional conflicts with existing procuratorial work mechanisms, manifesting primarily as "systemic incongruities with the case-filing supervision system, duty-related crime investigation system, investigatory supervision system, public prosecution system, and accusation and complaint procuratorial system."[72] These conflicts, which occur both in procedural timelines and authorities, directly impair the operational efficacy of both systems while generating non-negligible adverse impacts on the pilot implementation of the people's supervisor system.

Consequently, ensuring the organic integration of the people's supervisor system with the NPC supervision mechanism and procuratorial work systems holds pivotal significance for enhancing the operational efficacy of the people's supervisor system. Regarding this issue, primary consideration must be given to the fundamental principles governing institutional coordination, so as to regulate the essential pathways and modalities of such integration.

3.3.1 Basic Norms for Institutional Articulation

(i) Principle of Legality

The current normative framework of the people's supervisor system derives solely from regulatory documents issued by the Supreme People's Procuratorate and local procuratorates, as well as local people's congresses. In terms of legal nature, these documents can only be classified as internal working regulations of procuratorial organs. In stark contrast, the modalities and statutory authority of NPC supervision over procuratorial organs are expressly provided in laws including the *Law of the People's Republic of China on Deputies to the National People's Congress and to the Local People's Congresses at Various Levels* and the *Organic Law of People's Procuratorates of the People's Republic of China.* As for procuratorial work mechanisms, their normative basis is more extensive, encompassing not only statutory laws but also judicial interpretations promulgated by the Supreme People's Procuratorate and internal regulations adopted by procuratorates at all levels.

Therefore, in coordinating with relevant systems, the people's supervisor system must fundamentally adhere to the principle of legality and shall not use its pilot status as justification for violating existing legal provisions and fundamental principles. As noted in legal scholarship, "While society may initially tolerate experimental systems operating beyond established legal frameworks during their formative stages, the indefinite continuation of extra-legal practices is inconceivable, as it inevitably undermines public confidence in legal rules and expectations of the rule of law."[73] Specifically, the following essential tenets must guide this coordination: First, regarding matters expressly provided by written laws, such as supervisory authority, case-handling timelines, and procedures, the people's supervisor system must strictly comply with relevant laws and regulations without creating conflicts. Second, during the coordination process, the hierarchical order of legal norms must

[72] Chen Fukuan, *Application and Rules of the People's Supervisor System*, Law Science, 2008.

[73] Xu Weilin, *Rational Reflections on the Legalization of the People's Supervisor System*, Hubei Social Sciences, 2007.

be respected to ensure proper application of relevant regulations. Third, where clear normative guidance is difficult to match, the system must adhere to the fundamental principles of relevant laws and shall not violate their purposive intent or basic value judgments.

(ii) Principle of Efficiency

The fundamental purpose of institutional coordination lies in resolving inter-system conflicts, reducing operational costs of the people's supervisor system, clarifying its procedural mechanisms, and optimizing its implementation outcomes. Taking the coordination between the people's supervisor system and procuratorial work mechanisms as an example, given that "procuratorial organs are the sole state institutions participating in the entire criminal procedure, encompassing case filing, investigation, prosecution, trial, and execution. The relevant mechanisms related to the people's supervisor system include the case-filing supervision system, duty-related crime investigation system, investigatory supervision system, public prosecution system, and accusation and complaint procuratorial work system",[74] the coordination process between these two institutional frameworks shall prioritize enhancing the operational effectiveness of the people's supervisor system and better achieving its foundational objectives when addressing interface issues.

(iii) Principle of Coordination

The principle of coordination refers to that during institutional interfacing, the people's supervisor system and procuratorial work mechanisms shall, in accordance with their respective functions, mutually complement and coordinate with each other by addressing their differing operational emphases and functional characteristics, thereby enhancing the precision of oversight.

Specifically, in this coordination process, "procuratorial organs shall provide necessary working conditions for people's supervisors to perform their duties, so as to facilitate the full realization of the System's intended effects."[75] Meanwhile, the design of the people's supervisor system shall specifically address the deficiencies and gaps in procuratorial work mechanisms. Where existing systems provide comprehensive regulations, the people's supervisor system may limit or avoid overlapping coverage; whereas for areas lacking systematic regulation or remaining unregulated, the System shall prioritize its supervisory focus.

3.3.2 The Interface Between the People's Supervisor System and NPC Supervision Mechanism

From legitimacy, both the people's supervisor system and the NPC supervision mechanism originate from the doctrines of popular sovereignty and power restriction, aligning with the fundamental value propositions of socialist rule of law. However,

---

[74] Chen Fukuan, *Application and Rules of the People's Supervisor System*, Law Science, 2008.

[75] *Ibid.*

compared to the supervisory modalities of people's supervisors, NPC supervision demonstrates distinct characteristics. In terms of efficacy origin, NPC supervision constitutes statutory oversight expressly provided by constitution and legislative provisions. In terms of supervision methods, it represents macro-level supervision primarily conducted through reviewing procuratorial work reports and employing routine measures such as inspections, inquiries, and oversight activities, without involvement in specific procuratorial operations. In terms of the supervision nature, NPC supervision constitutes power-based oversight that "represents the highest level of supervision embodying state will and gives concrete expression to China's fundamental system",[76] characterized by legally binding force and normative rigidity.

The supervision conducted by people's supervisors and NPC supervision share fundamental philosophical commonalities while exhibiting distinct methodological and effectual differences, thereby regulating the normative exercise of prosecutorial power at micro and macro levels respectively. As noted in legal scholarship, "their shared attributes constitute the prerequisite for establishing coordination mechanisms, while their differential characteristics and functional complementarity provide both necessity and feasibility for such institutional interface".[77] To further improve the people's supervisor system, enhanced institutional articulation between people's supervisor and NPC supervision shall be developed.

(i) The Coordination in Selection and Appointment Procedures

The prevalent practice in selecting people's supervisors across various regions involves recommendations from government agencies, social groups, and relevant enterprises and institutions to procuratorial organs, with final appointments made through certification by procurator generals. However, this selection and appointment approach risks compromising the neutrality and public credibility of people's supervisors, thereby potentially diminishing public trust in the oversight outcomes. To address this, institutional mechanisms should be established for standing committees of people's congresses at all levels to oversee the selection and dismissal processes of people's supervisors. While some scholars advocate that "the selection and appointment of people's supervisors should be jointly administered by people's congresses and procuratorates, considering both professional expertise and potential candidates from among deputies to people's congresses at same level".[78] It must be emphasized that "NPC deputies already exercise statutory supervisory powers through established legal mechanisms for procuratorial oversight, including but not limited to inspection rights and joint inquiry submission procedures. Conferring upon them the concurrent status of people's supervisors would result in creating unnecessary institutional

[76] Zhou Yongnian, ed., *Introduction to the People's Supervisor System*, China Procuratorial Press, 2008, p. 96.

[77] Chen Xinsheng, *Complementarity and Connection between People's Supervisor Supervision and NPC Supervision*, People's Congress Studying, 2008.

[78] Qinggeletu & Wuyunbateer, *Proposal for Connecting the People's Supervisor System with NPC Supervision*, People's Procuratorial Semimonthly, 2005.

redundancy, thereby potentially compromising operational efficiency".[79] Therefore, while entrusting people's congresses with the selection and appointment responsibility is advisable, this should not involve selecting and appointing from NPC deputies; instead, the process should emulate the breadth and representativeness characteristic of deputy elections, with neutral people's congress organs conducting cross-sectoral recruitment from all segments of society, thereby enhancing the representativeness, inclusiveness and fundamental neutrality of people's supervisors.

(ii) The Coordination in Supervision Mechanisms

The legal status of NPC supervision, endowed by the Constitution, possesses permanence and supremacy. While the people's supervisor system demonstrates normative legitimacy in its establishment, such legitimacy must nevertheless operate within defined legal parameters. Accordingly, to achieve institutional coordination, statutory provisions may require that people's supervisors or the office of people's supervisors submit detailed reports to people's congresses concerning procuratorial organs' compliance with supervision, specifically encompassing case types, supervisory matters, as well as the legal effect and results of such supervision, thus diversifying the means and channels by which people's congresses access information about procuratorial activities.[80] This reporting mechanism would enhance the precision with which people's congresses exercise their statutory supervisory power while simultaneously improving the efficiency of other NPC supervision mechanisms over procuratorial organs.

The coordination process must further account for the constitutional status of people's congresses, which encompasses not only the power to administer and oversee the supervisory activities of people's supervisors, but also the obligation to provide guidance and safeguards for such supervision. For instance, to fully guarantee people's supervisors' right to know, a regular reporting system may be established whereby procuratorial organs periodically brief people's supervisors on their work, drawing upon the supervisory methodologies of people's congresses. Additionally, during researching activities and law enforcement inspections conducted by people's congresses, procuratorial organs may proactively invite people's supervisors to participate in such activities. Furthermore, provisions may provide that when people's supervisors disagree with review decisions made by higher-level procuratorates regarding lower-level procuratorates' determinations, they shall have the right to petition people's congresses to initiate statutory oversight procedures.[81]

---

[79] Zuo Weimin & Wu Weijun, *People's Supervisors: Deepening and Developing the Concept and System*, People's Procuratorial Semimonthly, 2005.

[80] Zhou Yongnian, ed., *Introduction to the People's Supervisor System,* China Procuratorial Press, 2008, p. 99.

[81] Under current regulations, when a higher-level procuratorate upholds the review decision made by the procuratorial committee of a lower-level procuratorate, and a majority of the people's supervisors still disagree with the review outcome, no further remedial mechanisms are provided.

For details, see Chen Xinsheng, *The Complementarity and Connection between People's Supervisors' Supervision and NPC Supervision*, People's Congress Studying, 2008.

3.3.3 The Interface Between the People's Supervisor System and Procuratorial Work Mechanisms

(i) The Coordination with the Case-Filing Supervision System

Within the existing criminal procedure legal system, case-filing supervision refers to the legal supervision by procuratorial organs over whether criminal case registration authorities fail to file a case that should be filed or improperly file a case without grounds, as well as the overall legality of criminal case registration activities. Given that supervision over public security organs' case-filing activities falls exclusively within the statutory supervisory purview of procuratorial organs, leaving no substantive overlap with the people's supervisor system, the institutional coordination under discussion primarily concerns the interface between the people's supervisor system and the self-investigation departments' case-filing supervision mechanisms within procuratorial organs themselves.

The people's supervisor system and the case-filing supervision system exhibit multiple points of institutional conflict, necessitating the establishment of a scientifically sound coordination mechanism. In terms of supervisory scope, the existing case-filing supervision system primarily focuses on self-investigation departments' failures to file a case that should be filed[82] while lacking provisions for addressing improper filings without legal grounds by these departments, consequently creating an operational void for people's supervisors' supervision in such circumstances. In terms of responsible supervisory departments, according to the *Provisions of the Supreme People's Procuratorate on Implementing the People's Supervisor System (Trial)*, supervision of both fails to file a case that should be filed or improperly files a case without grounds under the purview of investigation supervision departments. The case-filing supervision system vests prosecution review departments with specific supervisory power, thereby creating regulatory inconsistencies that may precipitate jurisdictional uncertainties in the course of people's supervisors' case supervision activities. In terms of procedural mechanisms, people's supervisors principally depend on autonomous "discovery" processes, including independent information collection, report evaluations, and petition handling, to identify cases requiring supervision. In contrast, "the case-filing supervision system mainly relies on either self-initiated discoveries by procuratorial organs or petitions submitted by supervisory and administrative organs and victims to commence review procedures".[83] These divergent mechanisms may generate conflicts, such as when procuratorial organs exercise ex officio supervision while people's supervisors have not yet

[82] Article 379 of the *Rules of Criminal Procedure for the People's Procuratorates* provides: If the arrest review department or prosecution review department of a people's procuratorate discovers that the investigation department of the same procuratorate has failed to request case registration for a matter that should be criminally investigated, it shall recommend that the investigation department submit such request; if the recommendation is not adopted, the matter shall be reported to the chief procurator for decision.

[83] Zhang Shaolin & Du Minxia, *Reasonable Connection Between the People's Supervisor System and Criminal Procuratorial Work*, Law Science, 2008.

"actively discovered" the case, raising questions about whether to initiate people's supervisor procedures. Although the system's original design envisions procuratorial organs notifying people's supervisors to commence supervision, the non-mandatory nature of such notifications inevitably raises concerns about excessive reliance on discretionary human factors in system operation.

To address the institutional dissonance between the people's supervisor system and the case-filing supervision mechanism while establishing their operational interface, the following coordinated measures may be implemented. Firstly, concerning situations where only the people's supervisor system provides external supervision over improper case filings by procuratorial organs' self-investigation departments, an internal supervisory mechanism operated by designated oversight departments within procuratorial organs could be instituted. Secondly, to resolve potential jurisdictional conflicts between procuratorial departments, clear functional delineations should be established whereby investigation supervision departments serve as substantive review bodies for reconsideration cases, the accusation and complaint departments act as procedural reception and response units, and the office of people's supervisors operates as the implementing body for supervisory procedures. Thirdly, regarding procedures for the initiation, when victims or administrative law enforcement agencies petition for reconsideration of non-filing decisions, procuratorial organs should mandatorily subject such cases to prior review by people's supervisors, thereby positioning the People's Supervisor review as a prerequisite procedure for reconsideration determinations.[84]

(ii) The Coordination between the People's Supervisor System and the Duty-Related Crime Investigation System

The conflicts between the people's supervisor system and the duty-related crime investigation system primarily manifest in three aspects.

First, procedural deficiencies exist in the supervision mechanism. The people's supervisors' supervision of the "three types of cases" relies passively on materials submitted by relevant authorities, while supervision over the "five types of situations" and "one type of situation" requires active discovery. After submitting supervisory opinions to procuratorial organs, the lack of independent investigative right renders the oversight outcomes rigidity of binding force. Furthermore, the supervision process predominantly involves unilateral case briefings by handling prosecutors, depriving supervisors of direct case exposure. Even when permitted to observe witness examinations, their inability to directly pose questions inevitably diminishes supervision efficacy.

Second, temporal conflicts arise between case dismissal supervision periods and criminal procedure timelines. Current regulations provide a seven-day supervision period for people's supervisors (extendable to fifteen days for complex cases), whereas the *Criminal Procedure Law* provides the criminal suspect of the dismissed case is under arrest, he/she shall be released immediately. Consequently, "the supervision duration must be rationally coordinated with investigation periods, avoiding both

---

84 *Ibid.*

insufficient supervision time due to rigid procedural compliance and investigation period overruns caused by accommodating supervision needs".[85]

Third, institutional contradictions emerge between the case dismissal approval system and the people's supervisor system. Pursuant to Supreme People's Procuratorate regulations, the procuratorates below the provincial level (including provincial-level) shall obtain approval from the people's procuratorate at the next level up when deciding to withdraw a case while deal with the direct-accepted case.[86] However, before reporting to withdraw a case, the procuratorates at lower-level shall initiate people's supervisor procedures and unresolved issues persist regarding whether the procuratorate at the next level up may modify or revoke decisions already reviewed by lower-level people's supervisors, and if so, how such alterations interact with the original supervisory opinions' validity.[87]

Therefore, to institutionally improve the interface between the people's supervisor system and investigative systems, the following measures may be implemented.

First, the proactive efficacy of people's supervisors' supervision shall be enhanced regarding the "three types of cases". Where people's supervisors identify cases meeting supervisory criteria, the office of people's supervisors shall provide support and, upon approval by the procurator general, initiate supervisory procedures. Concurrently, procedural timelines must be coordinated, investigative departments shall complete all preparatory work for accepting supervision before proposing case dismissal decisions, ensuring adequate time for supervisory review.

Second, people's supervisors shall be empowered to hear opinions from suspects or their representatives and exercise direct questioning rights. Additionally, people's supervisors shall be permitted to accompany procuratorial personnel to care settings for joint interrogation of detained suspects, defendants, or prisoners related to their supervised cases.

Finally, the interface between the case dismissal approval system and the people's supervisor system requires standardization. For cases where procuratorial organs propose dismissal subject to higher-level approval, the following procedures are recommended: First, in cases where people's supervisors' voting approves proposed dismissals, and such opinions are adopted by either the procurator general or Procuratorial Committee after review, the dismissal proposal shall be submitted to the procuratorate at the next level up with the supervisors' voting records incorporated. Second, when the procurator general or procuratorial committee rejects the business departments' proposal and the people's supervisors' endorsement post-review,

---

[85] Wang Yanxiang & Liu Zheng, *Connection between the People's Supervisor System and the Duty Crime Investigation System*, Law Science, 2008.

[86] See Article 3 of *the Provisions on the Requirement for People's Procuratorates Below the Provincial Level to Report to the People's Procuratorate at the Next Level up for Approval of Decisions to Withdraw Cases or Not to Prosecute in Directly Investigated Cases (for Trial Implementation)* formulated by Supreme People's Procuratorate.

[87] Wang Yanxiang & Liu Zheng, *Connection vetween the People's Supervisor System and the Duty Crime Investigation System*, Law Science, 2008.

the procuratorial committee shall issue a prosecution decision. A majority objection by participating people's supervisors triggers mandatory review by the procuratorate at the next level up. Third, where people's supervisors vote against dismissal while demanding alternative dispositions (continued investigation, non-prosecution or prosecution), but the procurator general or procuratorial committee confirms the dismissal's legality, the committee shall formally resolve to propose dismissal, submitting it for higher-level approval with documented Supervisor objections.[88]

(iii) The Coordination between the People's Supervisor System and Public Prosecution Mechanism

The intersection between the people's supervisor system and the public prosecution system primarily concerns the "planned not to prosecute" category within the "three types of cases". Where public prosecution departments intend not to prosecute cases transferred by investigative departments, they must submit case materials to the office of people's supervisors for supervision prior to final decision-making. However, pursuant to the *the Provisions on the Requirement for People's Procuratorates Below the Provincial Level to Report to the People's Procuratorate at the Next Level up for Approval of Decisions to Withdraw Cases or Not to Prosecute in Directly Investigated Cases (for Trial Implementation)*, such planned not to prosecute decisions shall obtain approval from procuratorates at the next level up. In terms of legal nature, the people's supervisors' supervision of planned not to prosecute cases represents external rights-based supervision, with final outcomes subject to procuratorial committee decisions or higher-level procuratorate review. Meanwhile, higher-level procuratorates' examination of non-prosecution proposals constitutes internal professional review that carries mandatory binding force under the *Constitution* and the *Organic Law of the People's Procuratorates* governing inter-procuratorial relations. This dual-system framework creates coordination challenges. For example, when people's supervisors complete their supervision with procurator general approval, which normally would not require procuratorial committee deliberation, but higher-level procuratorates raise objections during the approval process, questions arise regarding their power to modify or revoke decisions already validated through people's supervisor procedures. These circumstances necessitate urgent attention to establish proper procedures ensuring higher-level procuratorates' review processes adequately protect the validity of people's supervisors' voting opinions during non-prosecution approvals.

Regarding this matter, it is recommended that procuratorial organs adopt differentiated approaches based on specific circumstances.

Where people's supervisors' voting endorses proposed non-prosecution and the same-level procuratorate concurs, the supervisory opinion shall be submitted together with the approval request to the higher-level procuratorate. If the higher-level procuratorate agree, the case shall be approved per reporting procedures. Disagreement

[88] The main ideas mentioned here see Zhou Yongnian, ed., *Introduction to the People's Supervisor System*, China Procuratorial Press, 2008, pp. 300–301.

by the higher-level procuratorate raises the issue of reconciling conflicting determinations between people's supervisors' supervision and superior procuratorial decisions. Some scholars propose that "when procuratorates at the next level up deem prosecution or case withdrawal appropriate for cases where subordinate procuratorates propose non-prosecution, they should initiate their own people's supervisor procedures. During such supervision, procuratorates at the next level up should present both the subordinate procuratorate's supervisory opinions and their own review conclusions to their procurator general or procuratorial committee for final determination."[89] While this approach aims to enhance proper application of non-prosecution decisions, practical challenges emerge as people's supervisors of higher-level procuratorates lack mechanisms to access first-hand case materials or directly interact with handling personnel and parties. Moreover, current regulations contain no provisions for people's supervisors of Procuratorates at the next level up directly overseeing subordinate procuratorates' cases, necessitating substantial modifications to supervisory methods and scope that require further study. Under the existing legal framework, priority may be given to higher-level procuratorates' authority over subordinate procuratorates' supervisory outcomes, permitting direct resolution of approval requests. For cases where people's supervisors endorse non-prosecution but same-level procuratorates object, standard review procedures may apply: people's supervisors petition higher-level procuratorates for review, with the higher-level procuratorate combining the review and approval processes into a single determination.

Where people's supervisor votes against proposed non-prosecution decisions and procuratorial organs decline to adopt such opinions, the institutional coordination proves relatively straightforward. In such cases, the standard review procedures shall apply, whereby people's supervisors may petition the higher-level people's procuratorate for reconsideration, with the superior procuratorate rendering a consolidated determination on the matter.

(iv) The Coordination between the People's Supervisor System and the Procuratorial Committee Mechanism

Under current regulations, when people's supervisors disagree with procuratorial organs' handling opinions during case supervision, the matter must be submitted to the Procuratorial Committee for discussion and decision when necessary. This makes the proper coordination between the Procuratorial Committee and people's supervisors particularly crucial.

Within the existing people's supervisor system framework, procuratorial organs must undergo people's supervisor supervision before making final decisions on "three types of cases" and "five types of situations" cases. This means the people's supervisors' supervision serves as a mandatory prerequisite procedure before the procurator general or procuratorial committee makes final rulings. Case-handling departments cannot submit cases to the chief procurator for approval or to the procuratorial

[89] *Ibid.*, p. 316.

committee for discussion and decision before undergoing people's supervisor supervision. However, in current procuratorial practice, when handling self-investigating cases, handling departments generally lack independent decision-making power and must obtain approval or decisions from either the procurator general or procuratorial committee. This process involves multiple procedures such as case-filing approval, detention decisions, and arrest decisions. If every case and every litigation stage requires procuratorial committee discussion and decisions, this would not only contradict the fundamental purpose of establishing procuratorial committees but could also completely distort the people's supervisor system into a mere appendage of prosecutorial power, thereby losing the system's independent character.

To ensure proper coordination between the people's supervisor system and the procuratorial committee's case deliberation mechanism while enhancing the committee's operational efficiency, the following considerations should be implemented.

Regarding the interface between the supervision system for the "three types of cases" and the procuratorial committee mechanism, taking cases involving proposed maintenance of original arrest decisions as an example, it is imperative to formally establish people's supervisors' supervision as a mandatory prerequisite procedure. This means no case may be submitted to the Procuratorial committee for discussion and decision without first undergoing this supervisory process, thereby strengthening its rigidity of binding effect. This approach prevents scenarios where the procuratorial committee reaches preliminary conclusions through prior deliberations before submitting cases to people's supervisors, which would render both the supervision process and outcomes merely perfunctory. Similar procedures should apply to cases involving proposed case withdrawals or non-prosecutions, which must likewise undergo prior people's supervisor supervision. For cases where the procuratorial committee has already conducted deliberations and made preliminary decisions (whether to maintain original arrests, withdraw cases, or not prosecute) before initiating people's supervisor procedures, such cases must be resubmitted to the procuratorial committee for reconsideration following the supervisors' vote. This ensures the Committee makes final determinations after hearing arguments from both case-handling departments and People's Supervisors.[90]

The same mandatory supervision principle should extend to cases involving the "five types of situations" requiring people's supervisor supervision as an indispensable procedural step in case disposition.

It must be emphasized that as both an exercise mechanism and safeguard for citizens' fundamental constitutional rights, the people's supervisor system maintains intrinsic connections with criminal procedures. While the system itself possesses legitimate foundations, its legalization remains crucial for ensuring sound operation.

---

[90] See Chen Weigang, *Connection between the People's Supervisor System and the Procuratorial Committee System*, at http://fy.jcrb.com/shownews1.aspx?newsid=986, last visited on June 19, 2009.

Chapter 3
Legislative Basis of the People's Supervisor System

1 Analyzing of the Theoretical Preparations for the Legislation of the People's Supervisor System—Consensus and Lacks

From the origin of the system, the people's supervisor system possesses the value legitimacy and fits the general rule of constitutional development. However, from the perspective of system existence, the academic community has also reflected on the existing normative system, for the system itself can be embedded in the existing legal system, but can also maintain the system authority and guarantee its effectiveness. Therefore, the legislative aspects of the people's supervisor system have become the basic path and the key of the further development of the people's supervisor system.

1.1 Consensus on the Legislation of the People's Supervisor System

Upon the preparation of the relevant legislative theory of the people's supervisor system, scholars mainly analyzed the legitimacy, significance, necessity, feasible strategy and adjustment of the legislation, then, some common views formed.

First, about the value legitimacy of the legislation of the people's supervisor system (hereinafter referred to as "the legislation of the system"). To the question, the theoretical community generally believes that the legislation of the system is in line with the general development pattern of the rule of law, and belongs to an inevitable part of the development. A more representative viewpoint is the transition from the jurisprudential basis and value claims of the people's supervisor system to the value legitimacy of the legislation of the system, which emphasizes that the legislation of the system conforms to the principles of the ontology, the axiology and the methodology of modern legislation, at the same time, it further shows that the

Q. Qin, *Legislative Research on the People's Supervisor System*,
https://doi.org/10.1007/978-981-95-7972-3_3

legislation of the system can set up the procedure of the prosecutorial power obeying the governance rules at the system level, which embodies the rational humanistic concern for the criminal prosecuted and takes into account the standard of right.[1] In this regard, some scholars have also responded that the legislative purposes of the system includes both direct and fundamental purposes, the former focuses the balance of prosecutorial power by the rule of law, while the latter cares the safeguarding of human rights.[2] In short, it generally recognized that the legislative legitimacy of the system lies in safeguarding of fundamental rights through the normative legal system, and that it is the embodiment of the democratization of the legislative process and the scientific modernization of the legislative objectives in the legislation of the system.

Second, about the necessity of the legislation of the system. The theoretical community has studied this issue more fully, then, they has basically reached the consensus, which is established in the actual situation of the system, it shows that there was a clear lags in the operational effectiveness, form of existence and nature of the people's supervisor system, and that the legislative process should be accelerated. Specifically, it is generally recognized that, although the people's supervisor system is adequately regulated by legal principles, these provisions are still too abstract and provide neither sufficient legal support for this system nor practicality, therefore, laws are needed to clarify the specific content and operational procedures of the people's supervisor system and to link the people's supervisor system with the norms of the relevant systems.[3] Some scholars have further pointed out that the current people's supervisor system can only be understood as a reform of the internal working system of the procuratorial organs, but that, from the development trend, this system will inevitably have to be taken outside the system, that the current law does not presuppose such an organization as people's supervisor or authorize procuratorates to set up such an organization, and that it is devoid of any legal basis as a kind of external supervisory organization, and that the people's supervisor system, with its qualities as a litigation system, is in contradiction to the principle of law reservation stated in the *Legislation Law of the People's Republic of China*.[4] Simultaneously, the existing people's supervisor system is put on various normative documents formulated by

---

[1] See Gao Zhenyu & Lü Guofu, *Theoretical Basis and Legislative Issues of the People's Supervisor System*, at http://nx.people.com.cn/GB/channel65/152/226/200508/10/33782.html, last visited on June 5, 2009.

[2] See Dai Xiongying & Pan Hongru, *Some Reflections on the Legislation of the People's Supervisor System*, at http://www.cnjccn.com/html/2007829422.html, last visited on June 5, 2009.

[3] See Xia Zhenglin, *On the Necessity and Feasibility of the People's Supervisor System*, Journal of Lianyungang Technical College, 2005;

Niu Baocheng, *The People's Supervisor System Needs to Be Incorporated into Legislative Planning*, People's Procuratorial Semimonthly, 2004;

Wang Lei, *On the Legalization of the People's Supervisor System*, People's Procuratorial Semimonthly, 2006;

Luo Changxi & Zhou Jian'gao, *Legislative Thoughts on the People's Supervisor System*, People's Procuratorial Semimonthly, 2005, and other major journal articles.

[4] See Li Weidong, *Accelerating the Legislation on the People's Supervisor System is Imperative*, Legal System and Society, 2008; Zhou Yongnian ed., *Introduction to the People's Supervisor System*, China Procuratorial Press, 2008, p. 345.

the Supreme People's Procuratorate and the local procuratorates and local people's congresses from various regions. Since the people's supervisor system involves a large number of issues relating to the rights and obligations of the supervision participants, the absence of legal adjustments not only runs counter to the basic concept of the rule of law,[5] but also jeopardizes the neutrality of the system.[6]

Third, about the feasibility analysis of the legislation of the system. On the basis of consensus on the necessity and urgency of the legislation of the system, the theoretical community has also explored the feasibility of legislation of the system, and they believe that the legislation of the people's supervisor has basis of norms, practice and rule of law. The first basis means that this system has a normative basis, in the sense that the system has a constitutional and legal foundation, is in keeping with *Constitution of the People's Republic of China* which states that citizens of the People's Republic of China have the right to criticize and make suggestions regarding any State organ or functionary, and is also consistent with the provisions of the *Criminal Procedure Law of the People's Republic of China* and *Organic Law of the People's Procuratorates of the People's Republic of China*, which provide that procuratorial organs shall accept the supervision of the public[7]; The second basis implies that the people's supervisor system, through the prior pilot work, has led to the gradual standardization and improvement of the supervision procedures, and further summarized and promoted many of experiences,[8] which has accumulated lessons for the legislation of the system[9]; Finally, it is generally recognized that the legislation of the system shows strong practical significance and complies with the direction and content of the socialist judicial reform, and has the base of the rule of law for the generation of the system.

Fourth, about the legal positioning of the people's supervisor system. In the legislative research on the system, it has become a consensus that the legal positioning of the people's supervisor system should be the primary issue of the legislation. On this basis, most scholars are of the view that, the legislation of the system shall characterize the nature of the system as a democratic, non-judicial supervision of rights, and that the voting opinion of the people's supervisor is only an important opinion to which the procuratorial organs must refer when making decisions and lacks the

---

[5] See Xu Weilin, *Rational Reflections on the Legalization of the People's Supervisor System*, Hubei Social Sciences, 2009; Zhou Yongnian ed., *Introduction to the People's Supervisor System*, China Procuratorial Press, 2008, p. 346.

[6] See Chai Chunyuan, *Promoting the Legislation to Highlight the Vitality of the People's Supervisor System*, People's Procuratorial Semimonthly, 2006.

[7] See Ma Zengmin & Wang Xuechen, *On the Legislative Feasibility of the People's Supervisor System*, The Chinese Procurators, 2004; Xia Zhenglin, *On the Necessity and Feasibility of the People's Supervisor System*, Journal of Lianyungang Technical College, 2005; Zhao Ruifang & Lei Shanshan, *Discussion on the Legislation on the People's Supervisor System*, Today Hubei (Theory Edition), 2007, and other articles.

[8] For example, the legislative model of the people's assessor could be drawn upon.

[9] See Qiu Xueqiang, *On the Necessity and Feasibility of the People's Supervisor System*, at http://www.legalinfo.gov.cn/misc/200801/08/content_777102.html, last visited on June 5, 2009; Zhou Yongnian ed., *Introduction to the People's Supervisor System*, China Procuratorial Press, 2008, p. 352.

inevitable consequences of the procedural law, and they believe that such positioning is in keeping with the principles of the basic law of criminal procedure.[10] At the same time, the mechanism that the system produces its effect should be taken into account in the legislation. It is established as an "outside the system" supervision mechanism, thus achieving homogeneity with the nature of supervision.

Fifth, about the content of the legislation of the system. Although there is still much controversy in the theoretical community over the planning and strategy of legislation of the system, it has been possible to reach a relatively unanimous view as to the main content of the legislation of the system. First, the design principle the system should be incorporated into the legislation, i.e., the legislative process of the people's supervisor system should embody the basic qualities of the system and establish the basic principles of the system, which further guides the direction of the entire legislative process[11]; At the same time, the theoretical community, in conjunction with the basic connotations of the people's supervisor system and the effects it seeks to achieve, has summarized the entire system as a mechanism for setting up personnel and institutions for the operation of the system, a mechanism for the supervision methods and procedures, and a mechanism for the supervision effectiveness and safeguards, which should be taken into account in the legislation. For example, some scholars have suggested that a scientific legal form should be constructed in the legislation in terms of the selection system, the selection procedure, the supervision method and the guarantee for the duty performance.[12]

Sixth, about the significance of the legislation of the system. The general view is that the legalization of the people's supervisor system can promote the implementation of the system, and safeguard the rights of the main participants in the people's supervisor system well through the establishment of specific safeguard mechanisms, so that the content of the criminal procedure included in the system can be clarified.[13] On this basis, the legislation can be adopted to promote the realization of fairness and justice in society as a whole and to provide effective judicial guarantees for the promotion of social harmony.[14]

---

[10] See Wen Shengtang, *Theoretical Basis and Legislative Analysis of the People's Supervisor System*, People's Procuratorial Semimonthly, 2005; Zuo Weimin & Wu Weijun, *People's Supervisors: Deepening and Developing the Concept and System*, People's Procuratorial Semimonthly, 2005. There are also a small number of scholars who believe that the supervision of the people's supervisors belongs to the supervision of rights, which is basically from the point of view of the real, but only these arguments cannot explain the existence of the system of certain specific problems, such as how to guarantee the effectiveness of supervision, see Li Jianmin, *Discussion on the Effectiveness of Supervision Opinions of People's Supervisor*, People's Procuratorial Semimonthly, 2005.

[11] There is still controversy as to how the specific principles of the people's supervisor system should be established in the legislation. However, this does not prevent the establishment of principles from being important in legislation.

[12] See Xu Weilin, *Rational Reflections on the Legalization of the People's Supervisor System*, Hubei Social Sciences, 2009.

[13] See Wang Lei, *On the Legalization of the People's Supervisor System*, People's Procuratorial Semimonthly, 2006.

[14] See Jia Chunmei, *On the Necessity of Legislating the People's Supervisor System*, at http://fy.jcrb.com/fyfz/rmjdy/lilunyantao/200812/22.html, last visited on June 5, 2009.

1.2 Lacks of Legislative Research on the People's Supervisor System

Although a number of consensus views have been reached in the legislative research on the people's supervisor system, these views are either based on the traditional thinking mode of "a problem and a countermeasure", which is only formed on the effectiveness of the system operation, or on an idealized imagination of the value objectives that can be achieved by the legislation of the system, or simply on a purely legislative wish because of the superiority of the hierarchical level of "law" to that of the "general norms". Objectively speaking, these theoretical consensus fail to concern the fundamental question of the legislation, including why we should have the legislation? These inquiries are not only the objective needs for pursuing the operational effect, but also a kind of jurisprudence interpretation about why and how the system exists. The question about what kind of legislation should be established mention the determination of the legislative body and object, and the connotation and extension of the "law". The question about how to legislate involves the choosing of the legislative procedure and path.

1.2.1 The Rationality of the Legislation of the System

As mentioned earlier, it is generally recognized in the theoretical community that the reason why the people's supervisor system should be incorporated into the legislative process is because of the inadequacy of the existing normative system, both in terms of its low level and the aims of ensuring its impartiality. However, according to the deduction rules of mathematical models, this kind of empirical judgment is subject to the assumption that the existence of the people's supervisor system has its value. This definition of this value is not an universal value under the aura of the rule of law, such as the promotion of human rights guarantees and judicial justice, as the aforementioned academic community believes, but rather the existence of the people's supervisor has its own uniqueness, and the people's supervisor system must be used as an external supervision method of procuratorial power among many institutional choices and constructions, "The need for the supervision of prosecutorial power does not necessarily mean that it shall be subject to the supervision of people's supervisors, still less does it mean that the public needs to participate in the exercise of prosecutorial power. Moreover, even if judicial democracy should attract popular participation in the administration of justice, it does not follow that any specific judicial power should be subject to the scrutiny of specific individual citizens… Some powers require popular participation, while others should not.[15]" Therefore, before introducing the people's supervisor system into the legislation from a kind of working system norms, it is necessary to first explain the problem of why this kind of supervision method is needed to solve the problem of supervisors being supervised, and

[15] Yu Feng & Xie Xiaojian, *Calm Thinking of the People's Supervisor System*, Jiangxi Social Sciences, 2005.

whether it has any superiority over other supervision systems, such as whether there is any existential value of the people's supervisor system in comparison with the supervision of "judicial power, right of private prosecution, the system of lawyers, as well as that of the organs of state power, the Chinese People's Political Consultative Conference (hereinafter referred to as "CPPCC"), the Communist Party of China (hereinafter referred to as "CPC"), and the media, etc. and whether this system is just a piece of cake[16]". This belongs to a kind of theoretical preparation that must be made to establish the legislative legitimacy, a necessity argument that the system itself cannot be replaced by a mere political discourse and empirical evidence. If the independence of the people's supervisor system cannot be resolved, the legislation is undoubtedly just an empty and unrealistic fantasy.

1.2.2 The Carrier of the Legislation of the System

In the current legislative research on the people's supervisor system, the more general view is that the legislation is the best way to solve the system defects. But what laws should be legislated in the people's supervisor system? The "law" is just an abstract meaning from a jurisprudence point or a special reference? Is the purpose of the legislation to further improve the normative qualities of the people's supervisor system or is it based on other considerations? Above questions remain unclear in the legislative research on the people's supervisor system.

For one thing, the connotation and extension of "law". According to the classical interpretation that "law is a system of behavioral norms reflecting the will of the class, with the relationship of rights and obligations as the main content, confirming, protecting and developing specific social relations, social order and social goals".[17] If, according to this interpretation, the existing norms of the people's supervisor system have the characteristics of a system of behavioral norms, so what is the significance of promoting and advocating the legislation of the system? If the narrow sense is taken that the law just refers only to national laws, then there is a lack of a logical conditional deduction from the need for legislation of the system to the fact that only laws can be enacted. At the present time, there is a tendency to equate legislation with the enactment of laws when talking about the issue of legislation of the people's supervisor, which is a simplistic manifestation of the convergence of mentalities. We believe that it is necessary to address the carrier of the legislative research on the people's supervisor system, including the connotation of "law"— whether the "law" or "legal norms" shall be established? What level of legislation should be adopted? Can local legislation cover the people's supervisor system? What is the extent of such involvement? If not, what are the reasons?

---

[16] See Xu Xin, *Criticism of the People's Supervisor System*, from a speech delivered at the Seminar on the People's Supervisor System of Southwest University of Political Science and Law, Center for Judicial Studies, Nov. 29, 2005.

[17] Zhang Wenxian ed., *Jurisprudence (2nd Edition)*, Higher Education Press, 2003, p. 58.

For another, the purpose of the legislation of the system needs to be further clarified after clearing the connotation and extension of "law", whether it aims to make the norms of the people's supervisor system more operational or to harmonize with the existing legal supervision system? This will affect the basic direction of the legislation and the final establishment of the legal category.

1.2.3 The Legislation Strategy of the People's Supervisor System

Even if the assumption that the legislation of the system is subject to centralized legislation is valid, there is still a question of the choice of a legislative strategy — what kind of legal norms of morphology should be adopted. According to the hierarchical categorization of laws in the *Legislation Law of the People's Republic of China*, laws should be divided into basic laws and general laws. Moreover, among the normative documents with binding effect formulated by the Standing Committee of the National People's Congress, there are a large number of cases fail to appear in the form of laws. In the current legislative research on the people's supervisor system, a great deal has been referred how to choose the legislative model — the inclusion of corresponding content in the *Criminal Procedure Law of the People's Republic of China* or *Organic Law of the People's Procuratorates of the People's Republic of China*, or the formulation of a separate *People's Supervisor Law*. However, the choice of such a model is merely a conceptualization, which lacks the systematic justification, to be specific, what are the reasons for choosing such a model? What are its unique features? All of questions need to be further explored in depth in the legislative research.

2 Empirical Analysis of the Pilot Work and Operational Conditions of the People's Supervisor System—Effectiveness and Problems

2.1 The Pilot Work and Operational Conditions of the People's Supervisor System

The basic claim of the constitutionalism is that power shall be balanced. Such balance is not only reflected in a regulation state of legal rules, but also "deeply embedded in the modern ordering process of 'spirit-system-behavior-relationship' of the concept of the rule of law, legal beliefs, legal system, judicial activities and rules and orders. This process must face the rules regulation and rational balance between power and rights, rights and rights, rights and obligations, so as to guarantee rights, freedom, justice and order."[18] Since the trial implementation of the people's supervisor system, its supervision modes and procedures have gone through a gradual process from immaturity to gradual improvement and even to the deepening of the development, roughly through three stages—the launching of the pilot work, the comprehensive pilot work and the further development of the pilot work. These pilot works has achieved obvious social effects and provides a more effective solution to the lack of supervision of the procuratorate organs in the self-investigating cases.

2.1.1 The Launching of the Pilot Work

This stage began with the Conference on Comprehensive Pilot Work of People's Supervisor convened by the Supreme People's Procuratorate in 2003, and was marked by the promulgation of *the Provisions of the Supreme People's Procuratorate on Implementing the People's Supervisor System (For Trial Implementation).* The time span was from August 2003 to July 2004. During this period, the Supreme People's Procuratorate decided to launch the pilot work in 10 provinces, autonomous regions and municipalities, namely, Tianjin, Hebei, Inner Mongolia, Liaoning, Heilongjiang, Zhejiang, Fujian, Shandong, Hubei and Sichuan. Then, a symposium on the pilot work was convened in Beijing in January 2004, at which time it was decided to expand the pilot work to 13 provinces. In May of the same year, a symposium concerning the periodic summary of the pilot work was held in Chengdu.[19]

Soon, each pilot unit set up the office of people's supervisor in succession, and some of the pilot units, such as Shandong, Fujian, Hubei, Heilongjiang and other provinces, successively formulated the detailed implementing rules and writing rules of supervisory instrument to enhance the operability of the pilot provisions. Provincial courts in Liaoning and other provinces incorporated the supervision into their assessment systems of the law-enforcement quality, meanwhile, in Fujian and other places, the joint pilot inspection was carried out by various departments. At this stage, the people's supervisor mainly supervised the "three types of cases" as the supervisory object, and the corresponding normative documents also contain detailed provisions on the supervision methods and procedures for "three types of cases". In terms of the pilot scope, in addition to the province-wide pilot works in Fujian, Sichuan and Hubei, most provinces had implemented pilot work in some of the procuratorates, and the scope was not yet extensive enough. As for the supervision method, the supervision modes and the supervisory bodies in various places were still explored preliminarily, and the selection of people's supervisors or the configuration of offices of people's supervisor, all presented a diversified situation.

[18] Ma Changshan, *The Rule of Law Value of People's Supervisor and Its Realization*, Journal of National Prosecutors College, 2006.

[19] People's Supervisor Office of the General Office of the Supreme People's Procuratorate, *Notice of the Second Anniversary of the Trial Implementation of the People's Supervisor System of the National Procuratorial Organs*, Fangyuan Rule of Law Special Issue on People's Supervisors, 2006.

2.1.2 The Comprehensive Pilot Work

In July 2004, the CPC Central Committee (hereinafter referred to as "CPCCC") approved a special report by the Party Group of the Supreme People's Procuratorate and agreed to launch the nationwide pilot works. In August of the same year, the Supreme People's Procuratorate promulgated the *Plans for Further Expanding the Pilot Work of the People's Supervisor System*, which marks the people's supervisor system fallen into the comprehensive stage.

During this stage, the first manifestation is the further expansion of the pilot scope. The pilot work of people's supervisor system was fully implemented in procuratorates at provincial level; at the same time, the pilot was being vigorously pursued in people's procuratorates at the prefecture, city and county level or sub-procuratorates, with the specific pilot procuratorates to be decided by the procuratorates at provincial level and submitted for the record to the Supreme People's Procuratorate. By the end of 2005, all procuratorates at provincial level, 349 people's procuratorates at the prefecture and city level or sub-procuratorates, 2,407 people's procuratorates at the county level, which accounts 86% of the total number of procuratorates in China, had launched pilot works.[20] For another, in terms of the supervision scope, with the adoption of the *Implementing Rules for the Supervision by People's Supervisor of the "Five Kinds of Situations" (for Trial Implementation)* on 23 November 2005 at the forty-fifth meeting of the Tenth Procuratorial Committee of the Supreme People's Procuratorate, which further refines the supervision procedures for the "five kinds of situations", simultaneously, it provides that the supervision of the "one condition" shall also be subject to the application of these procedures, thus comprehensively regulating the supervision scopes and procedures of the people's supervisor system, which then fully tested and gradually perfected.

2.1.3 The Further Development of the Pilot Work

The opinions of the Supreme People's Procuratorate on the further development of the pilot work in 2006 marked the pilot work of people's supervisor was further developed. The Supreme People's Procuratorate, by summarizing the pilot work of the people's supervisor system carried out in 2005, put forward a proposal that in 2006 procuratorates at all levels should, while focused on the supervision of "three types of cases" and striven the case quality they supervised, strengthen the supervision of "five kinds of situations" and further deepen the pilot work of the people's supervisor. The requirements for supervision of the "five kinds of situations" have further deepened the pilot work of the supervisor system.

This stage can be said to be one of further refinement and standardization of the operation of the people's supervisor system, which finally led to further strengthening of the standardization and institutionalization of the pilot work. On the premise

---

[20] See Zhou Yongnian ed., *Introduction to the People's Supervisor System*, China Procuratorial Press, 2008, p. 13.

of further clarification of the procedures of supervisory objects and supervision methods, the harmonization of the people's supervisor system with the relevant systems was gradually emphasized. "The interface between the people's supervisor system and the approval and reporting system of duty-related crimes, the role of the people's supervisor system cannot be affected because of the application for the approval and reporting system".[21] In the meantime, the pilot work in various places has deepen the people's supervisor system actively. For example, pilot procuratorates in Jiangxi, Fujian and other provinces provided that people's supervisors should be invited to attend the discussion meetings of the "three types of cases" of procuratorial committee as far as possible, without affecting the proceedings, so as to broaden the ways and methods by which the supervisors can perform their duties. People's Procuratorate of Jiangsu Province has established a mechanism for the participation of people's supervisors in the joint reception of visits by the accusation and complaint department, which is conducive to obtaining information on "five kinds of situations" for the people's supervisor broadly, directly and truthfully, further enhancing the law-enforcement transparency and credibility of procuratorial organ, and playing a positive role in alleviating the repeated and prolonged petitions. The People's Procuratorate of Gansu Province unified the production of the *Notice Regarding the Supervision of 'Five Kinds of Situations' for People's Supervisor*, which has expanded the channels for the people's supervisor to supervise the "five kinds of situations". Nearly 10 provincial procuratorates, including those in Heilongjiang, Liaoning, Jiangsu, Shandong, Hubei, Sichuan and etc., has incorporated the pilot work into their annual target assessments. The People's Procuratorate of Henan Province has established a joint checking system of case quality, made supervision matters an important part of quality checking, and incorporated them into the target assessment.[22]

2.2 *Effectiveness Analysis of the Pilot and Operation of the People's Supervisor System*

Human beings live in a world of system, which maintain human order and implement human values. The vitality of the system lies in the fact that it is not only a rational form of rules, but also in the practical results it achieves in regulating society. Since the people's supervisor system generated, it has not only characterized the design effectiveness of the system from the beginning, but has also better reflected the value standards embedded in the judicial system itself, which highlighted the social effectiveness — the first prerequisite for the rationality of a social system.

---

[21] Jia Chunwang, *Continuing to Deepen the Pilot Work of the People's Supervisor System*, People's Procuratorial Semimonthly, 2006.

[22] People's Supervisor Department of Office of People's Supervision Work of the Supreme People's Procuratorate, *Summary of the Pilot Work of the People's Supervisor System in 2008*, Fangyuan Rule of Law Special Issue on People's Supervisors, 2009.

2.2.1 Embodiment of the Purposeful Effectiveness of the People's Supervisor System — the Process of Human Rights Protection Has Been Promoting

The protection of human rights is the basic spirit of a modern state governed by the rule of law, and is also the basic criterion for the vitality of the judicial system. In October 2005, a white paper on *Building of Political Democracy in China* issued by the General Administration of Press and Publication and the Information Office of the State Council listed the people's supervisor system alongside the systems of public trials, people's assessors, lawyers, legal aid, and people's mediators. This indicates that the people's supervisor system is an important system for safeguarding the people's democratic rights and basic human rights in China, and formally incorporated it into the system of safeguarding human rights.[23] On February 28, 2008, the people's supervisor system, as a reform of the judicial system with Chinese characteristics, was included in the white paper on *Building of Ruling by Law in China* which proclaimed the special status of the people's supervisor system as a mechanism for safeguarding human rights.

From a substantive point of view, the people's supervisor system is a legal remedial procedure specifically designed to deal with the infringements of human rights that may be caused by procuratorial power, and is characterized by normalization, relief nature and value legitimacy. In the dynamic operation process of the state power, it is a relatively common political phenomenon for rulers to emphasize unilaterally the authority and effectiveness of power. Taking the exercise of procuratorial power by the procuratorial organs as an example: since the filing, investigation, arrest and prosecution of duty-related crimes are all decisions made directly by the procuratorial organs, for the aims of improving the punishment effectiveness of the duty-related crimes and maintaining the authority of the procuratorial organs, the protection of the rights and interests of the prosecuted persons was often neglected, which finally caused the serious imbalance between the exercise of power and the relief of rights and made the investigation of duty-related crimes became a breeding ground for the abuse of power. In response, the people's supervisor system has set up a supervision method for "three types of cases" and "five kinds of situations" with the supervision of self-investigating cases from the perspective of regulating the operation ways, procedures and results of the operation of power. We take as an example "three types of cases", in which arrest, withdrawn and non-prosecution are important aspects of the work of the procuratorial organs in investigating and handling cases of duty-related crimes, and are also the aspects in which the procuratorial organs are most prone to abusing their powers, but are not subjected to any supervision in practice. By placing these three aspects under the supervision of people's supervisor, who have the attributes of civil rights, the procuratorial organs must fully listen to the opinions of people's supervisors before making decisions on the handling of cases under their direct investigation. As a matter of fact, this approach is placing the

[23] The White Book, published on October 19, 2005, is the first government statement on the construction of democratic politics since the founding of New China.

work of the procuratorate under the scrutiny of the people and embodying the basic requirements for the protection of human rights. By supervising such cases, people's supervisors effectively safeguard the legitimate rights of the parties concerned, thus realizing the organic unity of the fight against crime and the protection of human rights from a systemic standpoint, and achieving good social results.

Such as the case involving Pei X's suspected corruption handled by the People's Procuratorate of Shenyang City, Pei X appealed against the arrest and lodged a complaint because the illness, the procuratorial organ held that Pei X suffered from illnesses could not make him revoke the detention after changing the case officers to review again. Therefore, in order to handle the case smoothly and prevent the occurrence of social harm, the procuratorial organ maintained the original decision of arrest. However, the people's supervisor opposed it and raised that the evidence in this case had been fixed, his illness was a fact, the change of the coercive measures would not occur social harm. Then, the procuratorial organ adopted the supervision opinion and changed the decision of arrest into the release on bail pending trial according to law.[24] This type of case is not uncommon and has appeared in large quantities after the birth of the people's supervisor system. It can be seen that the people's supervisor system plays a role in balancing judicial power and litigation rights, realizing the organic unity of combating crime and safeguarding human rights by supervising the State's procuratorial power and protecting the human rights of the parties concerned, better resolving the contradictions and conflicts between the exercise of power and the safeguarding of rights, and compensating for the lack of a mechanism for guaranteeing the right of the citizens to appeal in self-investigating cases of procuratorial organs, and constituting a major step forward in the protection of human rights in criminal proceedings.

2.2.2 The People's Supervisor System Has Greatly Advanced Litigation Democracy

The operation of the procuratorial power is characterized by specialization, uniformity and procedure, and the various handling of cases may not necessarily fully reflect the wishes and requirements of the public, especially in terms of the awareness of the social harm of criminal acts and the intensity of the punishment required. Although there is also supervision by the National People's Congress and other supervision methods, this kind of supervision, with its macroscopic nature of the object and the diversity of the supervision methods,[25] will not be aimed at individual cases of supervision but is a kind of abstract, long-term democratic supervisory mechanism.

[24] The case originated from People's Supervisor Department of Office of People's Supervision Work of the Supreme People's Procuratorate, *The Pilot Work of People's Supervisors has Achieved Notable Results*, Fangyuan Rule of Law Special Issue on People's Supervisors, 2006.

[25] The National People's Congress supervises the exercise of procuratorial power in a variety of ways, including inspections by delegates and the submission of criticisms and suggestions, but neither its initiation nor its supervision is a specialized form of supervision, it is merely a manifestation of the functions of the National People's Congress.

Therefore, how to better integrate the social and popular characteristics of judicial power is also the focus of attention of the research of the Constitution.

Within the framework of the current people's supervisor system, people's supervisors can participate in many aspects of the self-investigating cases by reviewing the case files, listening to the reports of the personnel handling the cases and the opinions of the suspects, and commenting on and voting on the cases, and then can feed back their supervision conclusions to the procuratorial organs. As time passes, the concept of democratic supervision has really penetrated into the exercise of procuratorial power, and has perfected the long-term closure of the investigation of duty-related crimes. By the end of 2008, the people's supervisor in pilot procuratorates at all levels throughout the country had supervised a total of 26,484 of the "three types of cases" and 515 of the "five kinds of situations", and had provided feedback to people's supervisors on the investigation and the clarification of the situation in 500 cases,[26] thus initially forming a systematic system for the public to participate in the exercise of procuratorial power. It should be said that the implementation of the people's supervisor system, regardless of the positive impact of the supervision results, is an important manifestation of judicial democracy and judicial participation in the administration of justice, a brand-new reflection of socialist democracy in the field of criminal proceedings, the creation of a new way of realizing democratic supervision, and a systematic exploration and innovation that is in keeping with the rule of law and the concepts of democracy, and that is rich in the spirit of the times in which people's supervisors exercise their supervisory duties.

2.2.3 The People's Supervisor System Has Effectively Upheld Judicial Justice

From the results, the people's supervisor system has effectively prevented possible errors in the investigation and handling of duty-related crimes by the procuratorial organs, promoted the standardization of law enforcement and ensured the quality of the investigation and handling of duty-related crimes. Although the exercise of the corresponding powers of the procuratorial organs is highly specialized, the specialization should not be used as a reason for the closed exercise of procuratorial power. Without effective supervision, prosecutors are also bound to make mistakes. Hence, the positive significance of placing procuratorial power under the supervision of the people for preventing omissions in their powers is therefore self-evident. By the end of 2008, pilot procuratorates at all levels throughout the country had supervised a total of 26,484 of the "three types of cases", among that people's supervisors lodged an objection with 1,131 of the procuratorial organs' proposed decisions, and the procuratorial organs had adopted 711 of those decisions, account for 62.8% of the total. Procuratorial organs had accepted 515 cases of supervision by people's supervisors in respect of the "five kinds of situations", and had provided feedback

[26] See Luo Xin, *Continuous Promotion of the People's Supervisor System towards Legalization*, Procuratorate Daily, 2009.

to people's supervisors on the investigation, handling 500 cases.[27] The handling of these cases has been more focused on the introduction of value judgment standards on the basis of legality, has effectively prevented and promptly corrected problems that may arise in the process of arrest, dismissal of cases, and non-prosecution. At the same time, this system has pushed the exercise of procuratorial power under the direct supervision of the public, prompted further changes in the judicial style of the personnel handling cases, effectively prevented and reduced the act violating laws or disciplines in the handling of cases by procuratorial organs, and has safeguarded judicial justice. Taking the statistical data of 2005 and 2006 for example, the cases of violating laws or disciplines of cadres in the investigation departments of duty crimes of the national procuratorial organs fell by 15.4% in 2005 and by 37% in the first half of 2006.[28]

In the supervision process, the people's supervisor system has also effectively safeguarded the independent exercise of procuratorial power. The supervision duty carried out by the people's supervisor and their supervisory opinions put forward in a reasoned and substantiated manner can help the procuratorial organs to resist and eliminate outside interference and effectively safeguard the legal status. For example, before the Procuratorate of a city in Sichuan Province investigated and handled the case of a town mayor, Wang X, who had accepted a bribe, this fact that Wang X had accepted a bribe was verified by the relevant authorities and was not dealt with, but instead was transferred to an important position in the municipal authorities. The procuratorial organs filed a case to be dismissed in accordance with the recommendations of the relevant authorities, but people's supervisors involved unanimously disagreed with the case withdrawal. The procuratorial organs adopted the supervision opinion and prosecuted Wang X in accordance with the law. Finally, Wang X was sentenced to a term of imprisonment. Only taking the cases between September 2003 and April 2004 alone as an example, of the 21 cases in which people's supervisors in Sichuan Province raised objections, the proposed handling decisions in 5 cases were the result of interference by external factors. After the supervision by people's supervisors, these cases were dealt with in accordance with the law, which objectively provide the procuratorial organs with a solution to their problems and support the independent exercise of procuratorial power in accordance with the law.[29]

[27] *Ibid.*

[28] Chang Yan, *Research on People's Supervisor System*, Wuhan University Juris Doctor graduation thesis.

[29] Research Group on the Theory of the People's Supervisor System, *Research on the Theoretical Basis and Legislative Issues of the People's Supervisor System*, at http://fy.jcrb.com/shownews1.aspx?newsid=652, last visited on June 15, 2009.

2.2.4 The People's Supervisor System Has Enhanced Judicial Efficiency

Professor Posner of the school of economic analysis of law referred that the pursuit of justice must not ignore the cost of pursuing it in his *Economic Analysis of Law*, which argues for the importance of judicial efficiency.

Judicial efficiency is a constituent element of value goal system of the modern litigation law, and its basic starting point lies in the minimization of judicial inputs and the maximization of benefits. Its establishment has abandoned the traditional judicial value of justice as the only concept, embodies and reflects the plurality of modern litigation law in the orientation of value objectives, and plays an important impact and role in realizing the integration of justice, security, efficiency and other elements of the value objective system of modern litigation law. Judicial efficiency in the exercise of prosecutorial power is reflected in prosecutorial efficiency, which reflects the ratio between the effect obtained and the inputs made by the procuratorial organs in carrying out their prosecutorial activities. In the "three types of cases", for example, in cases where the procuratorial organs exercise the right to non-prosecution, after the procuratorial organs examined the facts and evidence, and believed that the conditions for prosecution had not been met, a decision not to prosecute may (or should) be made. However, since such decisions involving substantive consequences are made unilaterally by the procuratorial organs on the basis of their authority and the views of other objects was not listened in advance, the parties concerned, if they are not convinced by the non-prosecution, must file a complaint in accordance with *Rules of Criminal Procedure for People's Procuratorates* directly and have a decision made by a higher procuratorial organs, which may lead to delays in the litigation, a waste of judicial resources and a reduction in the efficiency of the litigation process. Before the procuratorial organs make the final decision of non-prosecution, people's supervisors can intervene in the review of the proposed non-prosecution and can been heard in advance, which will enhance the correctness of the application of the non-prosecution, and make the parties concerned more convinced of the transparency of this resolution, and enable it to effectively utilize the judicial resources while pursuing the judicial justice and realizing the judicial efficiency to the maximum extent possible.

A case study of the statistics of 2005 and 2006 shows that, under the people's supervisor system, the rate of withdrawing the case and non-prosecution in self-investigating cases of the procuratorial organ in 2005 fell by 0.98% and 4.4% year-on-year. In the first half of 2006, the two rate fell by 0.4% and 6.4% year-on-year.[30] To a considerable extent, it had shortened the litigation cycle and saved litigation costs.

[30] Some scholars also believe that using the rate of dismissal and non-prosecution to measure the quality of case handling is a more one-sided approach. Statistical data is from Xinhua News Agency, *The Cases of Violating Laws or Disciplines of Prosecutorial Cadres Dropped 37% Year-on-Year in the First Half of This Year*, at http://www.gov.cn/jrzg/200609/01/content_375948.htm, last visited on July 1, 2009.

2.3 *Analysis of Problems in the Experiments and Operation of the People's Supervisor System*

A new institutional system often experiences its "growing pains period" during development. The People's Supervisor System has encountered many challenges in its experiments across various regions. These challenges include not only uncertainty of the nature of the system but also conflicts in operational procedures and modes, as well as guarantee of operation effectiveness and other notable difficulties. Therefore, it is crucial to identify and find viable solutions for those problems that arise from the practical operation of the system.

2.3.1 Problems Regarding People's Supervisor

(i) Composition of Personnel

When selecting people's supervisors, many pilot procuratorates emphasize on the personal qualities of individuals, solely focusing on their knowledge and supervisory effectiveness while overlooking the fundamental values of the People's Supervisor System. As a result, a significant proportion of appointed people's supervisors hold specific social identities such as law professors, lawyers, and NPC deputies. On one hand, this undermines the legal legitimacy of the People's Supervisor System; on the other hand, as those appointed "elite" people's supervisors often hold concurrent positions, it is sometimes challenging to guarantee their participation in supervision, despite they have the status to fulfil their supervisory function. Under China's current inadequate removal system, the regularity and continuity of supervisory works are significantly compromised by such problems, affecting and constraining the supervision effectiveness. It deserves attention as it poses a serious obstacle to achieving the value goals of the People's Supervisor System.

(ii) NPC Deputies Serving as People's Supervisors

In the pilot works of people's supervisors conducted in various regions, there are many cases of appointing deputies to different levels of the people's congress to concurrently serve as people's supervisors. Such appointments are questionable and give rise to some negative impacts. Firstly, it is explicitly provided in Law of the People's Republic of China on Deputies to the National People's Congress and Local People's Congresses at All Levels that: "National Deputies to People's Congress and Local People's Congress at all levels, representing the interest and will of people, shall participate in the exercise of State power in accordance with the functions and authorities entitled by people's congresses at the corresponding level by the Constitution and laws." This stipulation clarifies that the supervision power of NPC deputies at all levels over procuratorates is a statutory power[31] entitled by

[31] Under existing law, suggestions, critics and opinions related to prosecutorial works can be raised by deputies of National Congress. Deputies can propose and organize an investigation committee targeted to specific problems, and can jointly file interpellation cases.

the Constitution and laws. NPC deputies serving as people's supervisors blurs the boundaries between the statutory duties of NPC deputies and the social supervision power created by the People's Supervisor System. In real practices, there are considerable numbers of people's supervisor conduct supervision over procuratorates with their identity of NPC deputy instead of their legal identity of "people's supervisor" in supervising individual cases. Such practices reveal drawbacks in the overlapping of both systems, causing confusion between different supervision modes such as legal supervision and social supervision, rigid supervision, and procedural supervision. Moreover, from the legal attribute of NPC deputies, it is known that they are the legal exercisers of State power, and their exercise of authority relays on State organs. Granting NPC deputies the identity of people's supervisors may allow NPC organs to intervene in judicial cases through people's supervisors, disrupting the current litigation balance. Last, one difficulty when procuratorates appointing NPC deputies as people's supervisor need to be faced is: how to set the appointing criteria? How to master the appointed objects? NPC deputies, as the constituent of representative organs, their identity was made selection through appointment by public authorities, which is conflict with the constitutional status of NPC deputies, and impairs their representative and public basis.

(iii) Origination of People's Supervisor

Tocqueville proposed an incisive argument on the public sentiment underlying the jury system in the United States in his book *De la démocratie en Amérique* that: "The list of jurors should expand or shrink in correspondence with the expansion or contraction of the list of voters",[32] emphasizing that the selection of jurors should be as open and transparent as the electoral system for congressmen. However, under the current experimental works, people's supervisors are generally recommended by the relevant authorities for final confirmation, which is subjective, closed and non-procedural.

The "subjective" refers to that people's supervisors are unilaterally recommended by recommending authorities with independent judgment on the recommended person's eligibility. As these recommending authorities are mostly State public authorities, it inevitably imbues people's supervisors with a strong character of being subjectively appointed. The "closed" means that the whole process, from the initial recommendation to the final confirmation of people's supervisor conducted by relevant authorities, is totally undisclosed to the public, which is severely contradicting with the social character of people's supervisors. And the "non-procedural" denotes the absence of standardized operating procedures during the initial screening, candidate assessment, and confirmation and appointment of people's supervisors. This arbitrary selection mode brings a weak strictness to people's supervisor system.

---

[32] TocquevillE, *Democracy in America (I)*, translated by Dong Guoliang, the Commercial Press, 1991.

2.3.2 Problems Regarding the Operation of People's Supervisor System

(i) Problems of Supervision Method

In practice, there are two methods of supervision on the "three types of cases" ex post supervision and supervision in the act. Ex post supervision is applied to cases where the disapproval of the arrest decision occurs after the decision has been made by the procuratorates. On the other hand, supervision in the act is employed for cases involving proposed withdrawal and proposed non-prosecution, where supervision takes place before the procuratorates make official decisions. The discrepancy on supervision methods gives rises to certain problems.

The first problem is related to the supervision mode established by the People's Supervisor System. When people's supervisors disagree with the opinions of relevant procuratorial departments, they can initiate discussions within the procuratorial committee. This stipulation does not have independent procedural value. In accordance with the stipulations in existing laws, for the "three types of cases", it is necessary to submitted to the procuratorial committee for study and decision, or report to the higher-level procuratorate for filing or approval, even without the People's Supervisor system.[33]

The second problem is negligence in the protection of the legitimate rights and interests of criminal suspects, which may lead to obtaining of different ways of judicial remedy for suspects of "three types of cases". For suspects whose cases are directly handled by the procuratorates during the investigation stage have a greater opportunity for remedial defense during the arrest phase compared to other

[33] Article 67 in *Criminal Procedure Law of the People's Republic of China* provides that: "The chief procurator shall make the decision on a People's Procuratorate's examination and approval of the arrest of a criminal suspect. Major cases shall be submitted to the procuratorial committee for discussion and decision."

In accordance with Article 95 of Rules of *Criminal Procedure for People's Procuratorates (2019 Revision)*, the examination of arrest filings of criminal cases investigated by the People's Procuratorate on its own initiative shall be filed to the People's Procuratorate at the next higher level.

In accordance with Article 237 of *Rules of Criminal Procedure for People's Procuratorates (2019 Revision)*, case need to be dismissed shall be reported to Prosecutor General or procuratorial committee for a decision.

In accordance with Article 286 of Rules of *Criminal Procedure for People's Procuratorates (2019 Revision)*, for cases returned for supplementary investigation, if a people's procuratorate still considers that there is insufficient evidence to meet the conditions for prosecution, it shall, after discussion and decision by the procuratorial committee, make a decision of not to prosecute.

In accordance with Article 289 of Rules of *Criminal Procedure for People's Procuratorates (2019 Revision)*, where the circumstances of the crime are so trivial as to entail no or exemption from punishment subject to the provisions of the Criminal Law, the people's procuratorate may, after discussion and decision by the procuratorial committee, make a decision not to prosecute.

In accordance with Article 292 of Rules of *Criminal Procedure for People's Procuratorates (2019 Revision)*,after the people's procuratorate makes a decision of non-prosecution for directly filed cases, the prosecution department shall file a copy of the written non-prosecution decision and the case examination report to the people's procuratorate at the next higher level.

suspects. However, in cases of proposed non-prosecution and proposed withdraw, those suspects undergo an additional scrutiny compared to other ordinary cases.[34]

(ii) Problems of Supervision Period

As the exercise of authorities by procuratorates are generally accompanied by the restriction and deprivation of freedom of relevant legal subjects, limitations on the time period of the exercise of authority aim to maximize the protection of the rights of criminal suspects under the current system of criminal procedure law. However, in the pilot works on people's supervisors, the statutory time limit for the exercise of authority by the procuratorates has led to a series of problems.

For procuratorates, with the extension of types of duty-related crimes and the increasingly covert means of crime, the deadlines for handling cases provided in the Criminal Procedure Law have become relatively tight. Under this premise, spare time must be allocated for people's supervisors to supervise the "three types of cases" and the "five kinds of situations", increasing the workload and pressure on the procuratorates within a given time frame. This may also impact the precision of case handling. On the other hand, due to the relatively short time period for people's supervisors to supervise cases, for example, the time period for the "three types of cases" is generally 7 days, and the maximum period shall not exceed 15 days. Some people's supervisors are thus unable to understand the facts and applicable laws in time and may struggle to make a correct judgment when supervising more complicated cases, impacting the effectiveness of supervision.[35] Therefore, how to define the supervision period in subsequent legislation becomes a crucial issue. It can be considered to find a more scientific legislative approach from two aspects: scientific regulation of the starting time of supervision, and the extension of the supervision period.

(iii) Problems of Supervision Effectiveness of People's Supervisor System

Firstly, there are problems with the initiation of supervision procedures. In the case of the "three types of cases", the People's Supervisor Office is notified by the case undertaking department, the people's supervisor then starts to supervise. This practice does not guarantee the intervention of people's supervisors in every case, putting them in a highly passive position. In the case of the "five kinds of situations", people's supervisors generally apply to the procuratorates to initiate supervision after discovering the case, but to which specific department do they apply? Can any people's supervisor apply directly? In practice, applications are made to the People's Supervisor Offices, to the Prosecutor General, and directly to the case-undertaking department, resulting in less effective supervision.

---

[34] Chang Yan, *Research on People's Supervisor System*, Wuhan University Juris Doctor graduation thesis.

[35] See Gao Yifei, *Exploring the Justification of the People's Supervisor System, Journal of Guizhou Minzu University (Philosophy and Social Science Edition)*, 2005; and Zuo Weimin & Wu Weijun, *People's Supervisors: Deepening and Developing of Concepts and Systems*, People's Procuratorate, 2005.

Secondly, there are problems in the specific supervision procedures. Initially, if the relevant departments of the procuratorial authorities have any objections to the selection of a people's supervisor, they are unable to apply for recusal. Moreover, in terms of the procedural steps for supervising the "three types of cases", the first step is the prosecutor introduces the case and the main evidence. Following that, officials concerned are heard to explain the reasons for the application of the law and the meaning of the law being applied, but what is the main evidence? The absence of a uniform standard regarding the scope and type of the main evidence in operations makes practical implementation challenge. At the same time, people's supervisors can also ask questions and listen to the prosecutor's interrogation of the suspect, question the witnesses, listen to the statement of the person concerned or the lawyer's opinions in the case, but there is a lack of regulations on how to listen and what procedures should be fulfilled before the hearing is conducted, which makes it difficult to operate. Moreover, in general cases, people's supervisors solely rely on information provided by procuratorial authorities to understand the case facts and application of laws, whereas in the case of major and complex cases, they only can hear interrogations and questioning when necessary, and the people's supervisors' knowledge of the facts is indirect, and they are unable to question the criminal suspects and the persons concerned directly. This potentially hinders the supervisors' ability to objectively comprehend the case.[36] Furthermore, current legal provisions require people's supervisors to enter a place of detention if they wish to witness a procurator interrogating a criminal suspect. This raises concerns about the lawful entry of people's supervisor into a place of detention.

A similar problem exists with respect to cases involving the "five kinds of situations". In general, supervision of these circumstances relies primarily on people's supervisors to self-discover and report to the procuratorates. However, due to the complexity of the cases and the absence of a platform that enables people's supervisors to have a clear understanding of the procuratorates' work, there is no clear "discovery" path, making the supervision of the "five kinds of situations" highly contingent.

Thirdly, there are problems related to the conflict between the system of people's supervisors and the current criminal procedure system and the procurator's working system. Due to its specificity of supervision object and modes, the People's Supervisor System intersects with the criminal procedure system and the procurator's work system, causing inevitable procedural conflicts in operation. For example, there is a conflict between filing dissatisfaction with an arrest decision and applying for changing coercive measures simultaneously when some criminal suspects do so. Article 40 of the People's Procuratorate Rules of Criminal Procedure provides that the procuratorate must respond to a request for release on bail within 7 days, while the current People's Supervisor System deems that dissatisfaction with an arrest decision is one situation that must be under supervision at the same time. Therefore, the conflict arises between people's supervisors conducting their supervision and

---

[36] See Long Zongzhi, *Discussion of Several Issues Concerning the People's Supervisor System*, People's Procuratorate, 2005.

the undertaking department carrying out their examination of whether to agree to release on bail pending trial.[37] It can be seen that it is particularly necessary to find harmonization between the People's Supervisor System and the existing criminal procedure system to utilize the effectiveness of the People's Supervisor System.

2.3.3 Problems of Regarding the Supervision Effectiveness of People's Supervisor System

During the initial trial phase of the people's supervisor system, there has been significant attention attached to the effectiveness of its supervision. Jia Chunwang, the then Procurator General of the Supreme People's Procuratorate, underscored that "exploring a new external supervisory mechanism with specific content and rigid supervisory procedures."[38] In the current system, the effectiveness of the people's supervisor system manifests in two key aspects: firstly, for the "three types of cases", the submission of cases to people's supervisors for supervision is a mandatory procedure. Secondly, the outcomes of the vote and opinions expressed by people's supervisors in supervision should be forwarded to the Procurator General or the procuratorial committee for examination. And when a majority of people's supervisors involved in the case supervision disagree with the decision made by the procuratorial committee, they reserve the right to request a review by the people's supervisor at a higher level.

However, on the basis of the nature and requirements of the people's supervisor system, their supervision, whether of the "three types of cases" or of the "five kinds of situations", is only a procedural effectiveness, namely, the supervisory suggestions and opinions of people's supervisors to the procuratorates, with rigidity but no decisiveness. Taking the supervision of the "five kinds of situations" as an example, in the pilot works, people's supervisors found that if the people's procuratorates investigated and handled cases of duty-related crimes with one of the "five kinds of situations", they could put forward their opinions, instead of "must" or "shall" to do so. And the procuratorates may or may not adopt the supervisory suggestions and opinions of people's supervisors. Although the majority of people's supervisors participating in the supervision evaluation procedure may request the higher-level procuratorate to review the decisions of the procuratorates when they disagree with these decisions, and the higher-level procuratorate shall provide timely feedback on the results of the review, these procedural constraints do not have the rigidity of a full sense. People's supervisors' supervision is of indirect effectiveness. Therefore, an important proposition in the practice of the People's Supervisor System is to guarantee that the legal effectiveness of supervision is ensured and legal effects

[37] The conflict between the People's Supervisor System and the system of criminal prosecution work is detailed in the section on the interface between the People's Supervisor System and the system of criminal prosecution work.

[38] See Jia Chunwang's speech during his research at the Beijing Municipal People's Procuratorate, Procuratorate Daily, December 3, 2003.

are preserved while respecting the system's legal attributes. This is crucial to avoid making the supervision work a mere formality.

During the operation and practice of People's Supervisor System, where the procuratorates shall adopt the system but not do, no corresponding mandatory measurement to constrain the procuratorates will lead to a lack of effectiveness remedy system for people's supervisor or subjects involved in relevant cases, making the procuratorates to maintain a dominant position in the People's Supervisor System.

2.3.4 Problems of Regarding the Guarantee Mechanism of People's Supervisor System

Firstly, there is a problem with guaranteeing the relevant rights of people's supervisors. In the operation of the system, understanding of people's supervisors to the facts, officials concerned, procedural processes, and intended results of supervisable cases mainly rely on the procuratorates' notification, lacking of an active supervision platform, making it difficult to effectively guarantee the right of people's supervisors to learn the truth.

Additionally, procurators occasionally provide tendentious presentations when presenting cases and evidence, as well as explaining relevant laws to people's supervisors, thereby impacting the supervision process. When people's supervisor supervises some sensitive cases prone to retaliation, ensuring the personal liberty and freedom of expression rights of supervisors becomes challenging. Furthermore, the consistent assurance of supervisory funds and suitable locations is often lacking, significantly compromising the overall effectiveness and independence of the supervision.

Moreover, there is a problem with guaranteeing the relevant rights of other subjects in supervision. Concerning criminal suspects, during the trial implementation of the People's Supervisor System, there is a lack of stipulations for suspects to defend and state their case, as well as proper legal channels to ask procuratorates for supervision by people's supervisors and to access the supervision results. Therefore, some scholars have pointed out that "informing procedures should be added to supervision processes, briefly explaining to criminal suspects the independent position and function of people's supervisors in the supervision procedures, as well as their own rights entitled in the procedures. This aims to provide necessary emotional support for suspects to fully express their opinions and reasons, which is helpful in discovering the truth of the case."[39]

2.3.5 Problems of Regarding Management Modes

The problems of management mode of people's supervisors mainly concern two aspects: the one is the appointment mode and regular management of people's

[39] Ji Weidong, *Reflections on the Practice of the People's Supervisor System*, People's Procuratorial Semimonthly, 2005.

supervisors, the other one is the setting up of organizations to manage people's supervisors.

As for appointment and regular management modes of people's supervisors, there are currently three main modes: the same-level supervision mode, in which the procuratorates themselves select people's supervisors to supervise cases of duty-related crimes of their own offices; subordinate supervision, in which higher-level procuratorates select people's supervisors to supervise the duty-related crimes of procuratorates at lower levels; and NPC supervision, in which the Standing Committee of the NPC at the same level selects people's supervisors to supervise cases of duty-related crimes of procuratorial organs. In the case of same-level supervision, it is of strong internality, leading to a weak social supervision effect as it involves individuals supervising themselves at the same level; the subordinate supervision mode can avoid various external interference in the handling of duty-related crimes by procuratorates, enhancing work efficiency. However, appointing people's supervisors from higher-level procuratorates to lower-level ones has notable drawbacks. Firstly, it still operates as an internal appointing mechanism. Secondly, there are certain technical challenges on how to address the interference of normal procedures posed by higher-level procuratorates to lower-level ones under the legal framework. Thirdly, the unified selection of people's supervisors by higher-level procuratorates may increase supervision costs and fail to ensure consistency. Compared to the above said two modes, the NPC supervision mode is surely more reasonable. But how to define the relationship between people's supervisor and NPC? Meanwhile, the importance attached by the NPC to the work of the supervisors has to a large extent constrained the effectiveness of supervision, which needs to be addressed by more researches.

At the same time, in accordance with the current laws, procuratorates are required to establish internal offices for people's supervisors. Based on the original intent of the system, the duties of the People's Supervisor Office are primarily to provide safeguard services for the smooth operation of supervision works. In practice, however, people's supervisors often place significant expectations on these offices, anticipating that cases meeting the both procedural and substantive criteria for supervision will be handed over to them. This expectation can lead to laxity among people's supervisors in fulfilling their responsibilities, potentially reverting the power to supervise and make decisions back to the procuratorates and hindering the realization of the system's original design intent.

3 Normative Analysis of Normative Texts Related to the People's Supervisor System: Experience and Problems

"The norm is the core issue in jurisprudence; all matters in jurisprudence must build upon it."[40] "What we refer to as 'normativism' primarily constitutes a research methodology relative to various empirical theories. This research approach is predominantly normative oriented, representing a study centered around normality issues. Given that norms inherently guide our actions, normativism research effectively embodies practical rationality, distinguishing itself fundamentally from descriptive and explanatory scientific inquiries."[41] From the existence and development of the People's Supervisor System, to analyze the basic nature of the current norms governing the System and summarize beneficial attempts for legislative activities, serves as an essential element and logical starting point for legitimacy argumentation. Which is to say, when we define the People's Supervisor System, we "shall start from the legal norms to consider the prerequisite for the analysis is the existence of norms. Aiming to explore the implications behind the norms via the analysis and conceptual clarification of legal norms."[42] Understanding the inherent compatibility between the People's Supervisor System and existing norms is a prerequisite for initiating its legitimacy argument. Only with this understanding can the specific institutional design have the potential to obtain and maintain legitimacy, allowing the People's Supervisor System to choose a nature positioning that is easily recognized and acknowledged at the design phrase, so as to reduce the costs and resistance of persuasion during the implementation of the System.

3.1 Sorting of Legal Norms and Normative Documents Related to the People's Supervisor System

In general, the existing institutional norms encompass normative documents issued by the Supreme People's Procuratorate and various local institutional norms.

[40] Xie Hui, *Legal Norms as the Core of the Legal System*, Study & Exploration, No. 6, 2003.

[41] Lin Laifan & Zhai Guoqiang, *Reflections on the Methodology of Social Sciences*, Zhejiang Social Sciences, 2006.

[42] Yu Zhong, *The Normative Analysis Method and Its Philosophical Basis in the View of Legal Methodology*, Xinjiang Social Science, 2004.

3.1.1 Corresponding Normative Documents Issued by Supreme People's Procuratorate

At present, the fundamental operation framework of People's Supervisor System mainly based on five documents issued by the Supreme People's Procuratorate: a. *Provisions of the Supreme People's Procuratorate on the Implementation of the People's Supervisor System (for Trial Implementation)*(Adopted at the Ninth Meeting of the Tenth Session of the Procuratorate of the Supreme People's Procuratorate in 2003 and amended at the Twenty-third Meeting of the Tenth Session of the Procuratorate of the Supreme People's Procuratorate on July 5, 2004); b. *Opinions on Several Issues Concerning the Application of the Provisions on the Implementation of the System of People's Supervisors (for Trial Implementation)* (Adopted at the twenty-third meeting of the tenth session of the Procuratorial Committee of the Supreme People's Procuratorate on July 5, 2004); c. *Plan of the Supreme People's Procuratorate on Further Expanding the Pilot Work of People's Supervisors*; d. *Opinions of the Supreme People's Procuratorate on Several Issues Concerning the Pilot Work of the People's Supervisor System (1)(2)*; e. *Rules of the Supreme People's Procuratorate on the Implementation of the Supervision over "Five Kinds of Situations" by People's Supervisors (for Trial Implementation)*.The Supreme People's Procuratorate has clearly defined the basic content and supervision methods of the People's Supervisor System through these documents, providing the most direct normative basis for the operation of the entire People's Supervisor System. This includes the appointment and generation of people's supervisors, their rights and obligations, the objects and scope of supervision, supervision procedures, and supervision effectiveness.

3.1.2 Normative Documents Formulated by Other Subjects

In the reform and pilot implementation of the People's Supervisor System, local pilot procuratorates have also formulated corresponding normative documents as a refinement and supplement to the Supreme People's Procuratorate's normative documents. In terms of content, these documents mainly cover the appointment method and quota determination of people's supervisors, the establishment and working methods of People's Supervisor Office, the specific methods and procedures for people's supervisors to initiate supervision, and the guarantee of supervision results and funding. In terms of formulating subjects, it can be subdivided into normative documents formulated by various levels of procuratorates, and normative documents formulated by standing committees of people's congresses at various levels and the meetings of directors of the standing committees. The former, such as the *Implementing Opinion of Shanghai Municipal People's Procuratorate on the People's Supervisor System(for Trial Implementation)* (adopted at the 6th meeting of the Shanghai Municipal Procuratorate Committee on September 16, 2004), and *Selection and Appointment Measures on People's Supervisors of Shanghai Procuratorate* formulated by Shanghai Municipal People's Procuratorate, and *the Implementing Measures of People's Supervisory System in Aihui District, Heihe City* formulated by Heihe Municipal People's Procuratorate; on the latter, the practice of the Standing Committee of the local people's congresses of formulating relevant normative documents varies. In some places, the Standing Committee of the NPC adopted a general normative document, such as People's Congress Standing Committee of Zaozhuang City made the *Opinions on Strengthening the Work of the People's Supervisors (for Trial Implementation)*, the Standing Committee of the People's Congress of Yinchuan City made *the Work Method of People's Supervisors of Yinchuan City*; in some places, the meeting of directors of the Standing Committee of the NPC adopted a number of specific normative documents, such as the Standing Committee of the People's Congress of Guang'an City, Sichuan Province, adopted *the Implementing Measures for Supervision Works of People's Supervisors (for Trial Implementation), the Measures for the Training and Assessment of People's Supervisors (for Trial Implementation)* and *the Measures for Confirmation of the Duties of People's Supervisors and Their Removal (for Trial Implementation)* in Guang'an City.

3.2 Empirical Analysis of Legal Norms and Normative Documents Related to the People's Supervisor System

The People's Supervisor System aims at the supervision on procuratorates and their officers in whether the work of procuratorates and their staff in directly investigating and handling duty-related criminal cases is in conformity with the Constitution and relevant criminal laws and regulations. It has established a relatively fixed membership and organizational form, making the supervisory process more systematic and procedural, and has formed a model of institutional regulation guided by the Constitution, governed by the law and regulated by normative documents. Within these norms, there are many meaningful contents, including the nature and positioning of the People's Supervisor System, the methods of generating people's supervisors, the procedures and effectiveness guarantee for the exercise of their rights. This system has played a significant role in exploring ways for citizens to participate in the exercise of public power through various channels, thereby embodying the democracy of justice. Furthermore, it provides practical guidance for the ongoing development of the People's Supervisor System and its potential elevation to the legal sphere.

3.2.1 Experience: Establishing the Supervisory Nature of People's Supervisors in Norms

"From the point of view of General Jurisprudence, there are no more than three constituent elements of a norm, namely, value, fact and logic"[43] Value judgment is the foundation of the existence of norms, and any normative system without the

[43] Sun Xiaoxia & Xia Li'an ed., *Introduction to Jurisprudence*, Higher Education Press, 2004, p. 14.

support of legitimacy will lose its life value. The Criminal Procedure Law, the Public Procurators Law, and the Organic Law of the People's Procuratorates all emphasize that the exercise of procuratorial power must rely on the people, which establishes the concept that the people's supervisor's supervision of procuratorial power is essentially a social supervision. Although the interpretation of this concept is relatively simple and abstract in addressing specific issues related to the People's Supervisor System, it answers the essence of social supervision. It can be asserted that interpreting this essence is the cornerstone for formulating and enhancing the People's Supervisor System. Therefore, the design and operation of the People's Supervisor System should align with the provisions of basic laws, defining this supervision as one rooted in citizens' rights with legitimacy comes from the legal promotion and recognition of social supervision.

In the specific operational rules of the People's Supervisor System, the nature of supervision is clarified. At the CPC central level, the People's Supervisor System is positioned as social supervision in Article 2 of *the Provisions of the Supreme People's Procuratorate on Implementing the People's Supervisor System (for Trial Implementation)*[44] and Article 2 of *the Rules of the Supreme People's Procuratorate on the Implementation of the "Five Kinds of Situations" for Supervision by People's Supervisors (for Trial Implementation)*[45] formulated by the Supreme People's Procuratorate, which has laid the keynote for the trial implementation of the People's Supervisor System by local pilot procuratorates and the development direction of the System, thus paving the way for the deep development of the current System. Similar provisions are also commonly found in the measures for the implementation of the People's Supervisor System in various regions. Taking the implementation in Hubei Province as an example, the word "social supervision" is also mentioned in Article 2 of t*he Implementing Measures for the People's Supervisor System in Hanyang District*,[46] Wuhan City and Article 2 of *the Implementing Measures for the People's Supervisor System in Xiangyang District, Xiangfan City (for Trial Implementation)*,[47] giving a clear position of the supervision nature. This provides a clear guidance of supervision procedure and even the supervision effectiveness. As Shen Jiaben, a jurist at the end of the Qing Dynasty, put forward that "the legislator understands the reasoning of the matter, and investigates the essence of the matter",[48] which is a necessary condition for the formulation of a good law, namely, it explains

[44] This Article provides that when investigating and handling duty-related criminal cases, the people's procuratorates shall implement the people's supervisor system and accept social supervision.

[45] Paragraph 3 of this Article provides that all relevant departments of the people's procuratorates shall divide their responsibilities, cooperate with each other and handle the supervision opinions put forward by the people's supervisors impartially in accordance with the law.

[46] This article provides that the district people's procuratorates shall implement the people's supervisor system and accept social supervision in investigating and handling duty-related crimes.

[47] This article provides that the investigation and handling of duty-related criminal cases by district people's procuratorates shall implement the people's supervisor system and accept social supervision.

[48] Cited from Zhou Wangsheng, *Science of Legislation*, Law Press, 2004, p. 266.

that the understanding degree of the nature of a norm is crucial to the scientific formulation of that norm itself.

3.2.2 Experience: Dealing Well with the Relationship Between "Supervision" and "Independence"

In accordance with the Constitution, "the procuratorates shall exercise its authorities independently in accordance with the law, and shall not be interfered with by any administrative organ, public organization or individual". Therefore, people's supervisors can only conduct external supervision of the procuratorates' exercise of procuratorial power within the framework of constitutionalism, and shall not interfere with the exercise of procuratorates' authorities. Without a scientific definition of the purview of people's supervisors' supervision and the supervisory modes in the legislation, potential violations of the present legal system may arise, leading to the de facto procurator.

Therefore, in the legislative construction of the People's Supervisor System, defining the standards and boundaries of people's supervisors' supervision should be done scientifically by grasping the relationship between the exercise of supervisory power and the exercise of prosecutorial power, as provided for in the Constitution and the law. That is, when there is a conflict between the constitutional right of "letting the people to be the masters of the country and enjoy the right of criticism, suggestion, appeal, accusation and prosecution in accordance with the law" and the independent exercise of procuratorial power by procuratorates, can both be exercised simultaneously? Is there any priority? If not, how do we figure out the power implied or the nature of the right?

To solve this problem, experience can be found from the relevant normative documents. Taking Shanghai as an example, *the Opinions of the Shanghai Municipal People's Procuratorate on the Implementation of the People's Supervisor System (for Trial Implementation)* provides that: "Where the procurator general agrees with the voting opinions of people's supervisors, the relevant operational departments shall implement it; where the procurator general disagrees with the voting opinions of people's supervisors, he shall submit it to the procuratorial committee for discussion; where the procuratorial committee disagrees, it shall be handled in accordance with laws.... If necessary, the procuratorial committee may invite people's supervisors who vote on the case to attend the discussion". "Where most of people's supervisors participating in a case have objections to the decision of the procuratorial committee, they may request the people's procuratorate at the next higher level to review the case. The people's procuratorate at the next higher level shall promptly review and make a decision." The handling of the people's supervisors' disagreement by the procuratorial committee is not only a response to the regulations of the Supreme People's Procuratorate, but also an expression of the independent exercise of procuratorial power. The presence of people's supervisors at the case discussion of the procuratorial committee implies their involvement in decision-making. However, this exercise of the right doesn't directly constrain procuratorial power; it is confined to forms of criticism, suggestion, appeal, accusation, and prosecution, making it an indirect right. While this suggestion right does not entirely overlook the participation right of people's supervisors, it can lead to procedural continuity, such as the review by the superior procuratorate. Objectively speaking, this legislative strategy strikes a balance between the supervisory power and procuratorial power. It acknowledges the procedural participation and effectiveness of the supervisory power of people's supervisors while ensuring the independence of procuratorial power. At the same time, this strategy echoes the Criminal Procedure Law as the basic law, and is worthy of reference in the subsequent legalization process of the People's Supervisor System.

Such similar provisions appear in *the Implementing Measures of the People's Procuratorate of Beichen District, Tianjin Municipality for Supervision over the "Five Kinds of Situations" by People's Supervisors, the Implementing Rules of the People's Procuratorate of Fujian Province for the People's Supervisor System, the Implementing Measures of Tongling City for the People's Supervisor System* and other implementing rules of many local procuratorates.

3.2.3 Experience: Regulating the Generation and Appointment Mechanism of the People's Supervisor System

In the process of exercising the supervision power over procuratorates, the confirmation of the members of people's supervisors not only relates to the standard for judging the legitimacy of system operation, but also affects the important factors of supervision effect. Therefore, what kind of person to be the people's supervisor and what kind of procedure to generate the people's supervisor is the key to the effective operation of the system.

The qualifications for people's supervisors are outlined in various normative documents related to the people's supervisor system. Taking *the Provisions of the Supreme People's Procuratorate on Implementing the People's Supervisor System (for Trial Implementation)* as an example[49]: "people's supervisors shall have the nationality of the People's Republic of China, uphold the Constitution of the People's Republic of China, be 23 years old or above, be honest and upright, adhere to principles, be in good health, have the right to vote and the right to stand for election, and have a certain level of education, policy and legal knowledge." Briefly analyzing these conditions, they can be categorized into political, age-related, and knowledge-related criteria. As far as the political condition is concerned, because "citizens hold the right of judicial mechanism means another kind of active and positive situation of citizens to political

[49] The practices of all regions basically follow the main contents of the Provisions, such as *the Implementing Measures of the People's Procuratorate of Anhui Province for People's Supervisor System (for Trial Implementation), the Detailed Implementing Rules of Hubei Province for People's Supervisor System of Procuratorial Organs (for Trial Implementation), the Implementing Measures of Hebei Province for People's Supervisor System of Procuratorial Organs* and other normative documents, all contain similar provisions.

rule",[50] the defenders of political order and the implementers of political rule must also require citizens to have certain class nature and political orientation, that is, only those citizens belonging to the collective "people" who are in the dominant position are qualified to exercise the supervisory power. Moreover, the Provisions exclude, in an enumerated manner, persons without political orientation, such as "persons who have been subject to criminal punishment or criminal investigation; persons who get dismissed from public office or get nominally expulsed". Such stipulations are crucial in the subsequent legislative process. Provisions on the knowledge and age of people's supervisors are also common in normative documents, and stipulations on knowledge are necessary and reasonable due to the professionalism of supervisory work. Whether restrictions on age and physical condition should be adopted in future legislation is still open to discussion.

From the perspective of the generation procedures of people's supervisors, relevant normative documents, such as *the Provisions of the Supreme People's Procuratorate on Implementing the People's Supervisor System (for Trial Implementation)* and *the Opinions on Several Issues Concerning the Application of the Provisions on Implementing the People's Supervisor System (for Trial Implementation)*, have made clear provisions on the generation procedures. Generally, the candidates are selected through consultation with organs, groups, enterprises and public institutions, and basic-level organizations, and then confirmed and issued certificates by the people's procuratorate. However, this practice is controversial in the embodiment of the principle of constitutional democracy, mainly focusing on the representativeness of people's supervisors. People's supervisors are recommended by organs, organizations, enterprises and public institutions, at the same time, procuratorates can choose people's supervisors in a certain range. Under the current conditions, this kind of selection is still a way of internal supervision dominated by the procuratorates, which is difficult to get rid of the criticism of "hiring someone to supervise yourself" and "supervision becomes a mere formality". For this problem, some local people's supervisors are appointed by the NPC. For example, *the Detailed Rules for the Appointment and Removal of People's Supervisors of Hanyang District, Wuhan City (for Trial Implementation)* prescribes the basic procedures for the announcement, recommendation, registration, examination, determination of candidates, publicity process and appointment of people's supervisors, which not only ensure the openness of the selection and appointment procedures, embody the public opinion basis for social supervision, but also conform to the current legal provisions. It is a useful attempt to further externalize the People's Supervisor System.

In addition, in the selection and appointment of the People's Supervisor System in some places, the system of self-recommendation is also provided, whereby qualified social citizens act as people's supervisors by self-recommendation, which further reflects the sociality of the People's Supervisor System and the universality of participants. For example, the self-recommendation system is provided in *the Measures of Chongqing Municipality for Selecting and Appointing People's Supervisors of*

[50] Li Qi, *Chinese Constitution and Political Legitimacy*, at http://www.law-lib.com/flsz/sz_view.asp?no=1360, last visited on June 20, 2009.

Procuratorial Organs and *the Implementing Measures of the Standing Committee of the Gucheng County People's Congress for the People's Supervisor System by the People's Procuratorates of Gucheng Counties (for Trial Implementation)* issued by Chongqing Municipality.

3.2.4 Experience: Providing a Complete and Clear Supervision Procedure

Among the various existing norms on the People's Supervisor System, the provisions on the procedures for the performance of authorities by people's supervisors are relatively systematic, mainly involving the procedures for the withdrawal of people's supervisors, the procedures for the initiation of supervision, the participation and appraisal procedures of supervision. The establishment of this kind of procedure is mainly in accordance with the power operation system of the procuratorial organ and the characteristics of "three type of cases" and "five circumstances", as well as the reference to the relevant provisions of the criminal procedure legal system. From its nature, the supervision procedure of the people's supervisor is primarily a technical setting, with its foundational purpose being to ensure the effective and independent exercise of the supervision right to supervise. The supervision procedure operates on the fundamental premise of its compatibility with the current criminal procedure system, and a number of representative empirical practices has summarized.

It is common to adopt the dual provisions of duty withdrawal and supervision withdrawal for withdrawal procedure of people's supervisors. In order to ensure the sociality of supervision and the impartiality of supervision results, *the Provisions on the Application of the Provisions on Issues Concerning the Implementation of the People's Supervisor System (for Trial Implementation)* (hereinafter referred to as the "Opinions") clearly provide for the duty withdrawal, excluding the active personnel of party committee, government, judicial organs, together with lawyers, people's jurors and other legal workers. Eliminating the duty qualification of the officials at relevant public authority can avoid the mutation of the supervision nature due to their status, and ensure the allocation and balance of state power within the statutory framework. For the supervision withdrawal, the measures consistent with the relevant provisions of the Criminal Procedure Law are mainly adopted,[51] such as *the Opinions of the Shanghai Municipal People's Procuratorate on Implementation of the People's Supervisor System (for Trial Implementation), the Implementing Measures of the Shandong Provincial People's Procuratorate on People's Supervisor System for Investigation of Cases Directly Accepted(for Trial Implementation)* and *the Implementing Rules of the Ningan Municipal People's Procuratorate on the Work of People's Supervisors.* Notably, the Shanghai Procuratorate specifies that

[51] Individuals who are close relatives of a party involved in the case, those with a personal interest or a close relative with an interest in the case, those who have served as witnesses, appraiser, defenders, or agents ad litem in the case, or those with any other relationship to a party in the case that could potentially hinder the proper execution of supervisory duties are to be excluded.

if the parties concerned and their statutory agents fail to withdraw, the people's procuratorate shall decide on their withdrawal.

Currently, local initiations procedures for supervision regarding the "three types of cases" are generally refer to the provisions of *the Provisions of the Supreme People's Procuratorate on Implementing the People's Supervisor System (for Trial Implementation)*, and the case handling department shall transfer the case materials to the People's Supervisor Office, and the Office shall be responsible for organizing people's supervisors to supervise the cases. As for the supervision of the "five kinds of situations", it is provided in *the Implementing Rules of the Supreme People's Procuratorate for the Supervision over "Five Kinds of Situations" by People's Supervisors (for Trial Implementation)* that people's supervisors shall put forward their supervision opinions to the Office. The Office will then report to the procurator general for approval before transferring them to the relevant departments. However, in practice, some local authorities have made other provisions on initiation procedures to prevent issues such as the failure of the case-handling department to hand over materials or the failure of people's supervisors to organize case supervision. For example, *the Opinions of the Standing Committee of the Weifang Municipal People's Congress on Strengthening the Work of the People's Supervisors (for Trial Implementation)* provides that "the supervision procedures of people's supervisors may be initiated by the municipal procuratorial organ at its work requirements, or may be initiated by the Legislative Affairs Commission of the Standing Committee of the Municipal People's Congress at the degree of social concerns and strong complaints from the public", and *the Measures for the Administration of the People's Supervisors of the Procuratorial Organs of Tangshan Municipality* also provides that "the people's congress shall conduct special case-filing supervision over the problems with universality, tendentiousness and strong complaints from the public in accordance with the law". Although the effectiveness of this initiation method still needs further exploration in practice, it broadens the initiation modes of supervision, holding significant referential value.

There are many practices that are worth learning regarding the supervision procedures. From the standpoint of various normative documents themselves, the universal practice[52] is the basic procedures for people's supervisors to analyze materials, listen to reports (presentation of evidence and application of law), question the investigator and parties concerned, review, and vote. Through vertical comparison, they can be classified into diversion procedures (different situations are handled by different

[52] Typical examples are the Provisions of the Supreme People's Procuratorate on Implementing the People's Supervisor System (for Trial Implementation), the Implementing Rules of the Supreme People's Procuratorate on Supervision over "Five Circumstances" by People's Supervisors (for Trial Implementation) and the implementing measures formulated by all provincial procuratorates.

organs and applicate for the supervision of "five kinds of situations"), specific supervision procedures,[53] supervision opinions handling procedures,[54] result feedback procedures, reconsideration and review procedures.[55] This kind of procedural set up is based on the characteristics of the People's Supervisor System and the exercise of functions and powers of the procuratorial organs. Although there are still some problems in the operation, such as unclear authority, time and ways of participation, this kind of procedure regulation can be said to in line with the development of criminal proceedings, and provide valuable insights for various legislative modes selection of people's supervisor system.

Some regions have developed unique practices to ensure the effective implementation of the supervision procedure of people's supervisor. First, discussion about the inquiry work of the people's supervisor becomes institutionalized and standardized. For example, *the Implementing Measures for the Auditing and Inquiries of the People's Supervisor System (for Trial Implementation)* formulated by Ziyang City, Sichuan Province, have made detailed provisions on the procedures for auditing and inquiries, covering the scope and duties of cases subject to auditing and inquiry, the rights of people's supervisors, and the initiation modes for auditing. Additionally, the system of people's supervisors' return visits has been established, "implementing it for major, important, and criminal cases where all suspects originate from the same work unit audited by people's supervisors."[56]

This has played a positive role in strengthening the self-regulation of procuratorial organs, enhancing law enforcement, and ensuring the legitimacy and integrity of procedures. Secondly, the supervision mode of self-investigation cases has been expanded, with supervision transitioning from post-case supervision to whole-process supervision. For instance, the Tentative Provisions on Strengthening the Supervision of Law Enforcement and Case Handling by Procuratorial Personnel formulated by the Shanxi Provincial Procuratorate implement the system of "one

---

[53] It can be divided into reply of verification procedures and review of supervision procedures. The former refers to that after the undertaking department verifies the supervision situation and puts forward the handling opinions to the procurator general for decision, the People's Supervisor Office gives feedback to the people's supervisors. Review of supervision procedures refer to the formation of collective supervision opinions through secret ballot and the principle of majority rule, categorized according to "three types of cases" and "five circumstances".

[54] If the people's supervisors agree, it shall be reported to the procurator general for approval. If the people's procuratorate disagrees, it shall be decided by the procuratorial committee.

[55] Taking the supervision on the "five types of situations" as an example, if the people's supervisor who initiates the supervision has any objection to the handling decision made according to the reply of verification procedures, he may request the people's procuratorate to review the case. If the people's supervisor requests reconsideration, the people's procuratorate shall designate another official to handle the case, and feedback the reconsideration results to the people's supervisor within 15 days. Where most of the people's supervisors have objections to the handling decisions made by the people's procuratorates in accordance with the review of supervision procedures, they may request the people's procuratorates at higher levels to review such decisions.

[56] Zhong Tu &Chen Chongnuo, *Exploration and Practice of the People's Supervisor System's Observing and Interrogations (Inquiries)*, Fangyuan Rule of Law Special Issue on People's Supervisors, 2008.

case, three cards,"[57] focusing on the filing, approval of arrest and prosecution of self-investigation cases, as well as the adoption of coercive measures and distraint by procuratorial organs. Thirdly, attention has been given to the connection between the supervision procedure and criminal procedure. For example, *the Provisions of the Supreme People's Procuratorate on the Implementation of the People's Supervisor System (for Trial Implementation)* provides that "the case supervision work shall be completed within 7 days from the receipt of the materials by the People's Supervisor Office. For major and complex cases, the case supervision period may be extended to 15 days. The people's procuratorate shall not exceed the statutory time limit for case handling due to the supervision of the people's supervisor". *The provision of the Detailed Rules of Hanyang District, Wuhan City on the Supervision of People's Supervisors (for Trial Implementation)* provides that "the voting opinions of people's supervisors shall, after being examined and approved by the procurator general, be handled in the following ways in accordance with different circumstances: a. Where the case falls within the statutory authority of the procurator general, a decision shall be made in accordance with the law and be transferred to the case handling department of the procuratorate for implementation; and b. Where it is necessary to make a decision on case withdraw, the procurator general may make a decision within its authority or submit the case to the procuratorial committee for discussion and decision". Both provisions echo the current legal system of criminal proceedings.

3.2.5 Experience: Setting up the Guarantee Mechanism for Authority Exercise of People's Supervisors

In order to promote a better performance of the supervisory duties of people's supervisors, a guarantee mechanism is generally set up in various normative documents. First, the material guarantee mechanism which brings the work of people's supervisors into financial expenditure and grants subsidies for their work. Article 34 of *the Provisions of the Supreme People's Procuratorate on Implementing the People's Supervisor System (for Trial Implementation)* provides that "subsidies that people's supervisors are entitled to due to their participation in supervision activities, and expenditures necessary for implementing the People's Supervisor System by the people's procuratorates shall be listed in the operating expenses of the people's procuratorates, declared to the financial department at the same level and included in the financial budget".

The Opinions of the Standing Committee of the People's Congress of Zaozhuang City on Strengthening the Work of People's Supervisors (for Trial Implementation) also provides that "the municipal procuratorial organ shall give subsidies to people's supervisors for the expenses of transportation, accommodation, dining and communication that they have paid for performing their duties; for people's supervisors without fixed income, the municipal procuratorial organ shall give corresponding

[57] Namely, each case has a case-handling notification card, a case-handling personnel's feedback card on their compliance with disciplines, and a case-handling return visit supervision card.

subsidies according to the actual working days with reference to the average monetary wages of local employees in the previous year". Similar provisions exist in implementation measures on people's supervisors formulated by Hubei, Shandong, Fujian, Sichuan, and other provinces. Second, the protection of people's supervisors' right to know involves the meeting system of attendance, inviting people's supervisors to attend relevant meetings to understand procuratorial work. For example, Article 35 of *the Opinions of the Shanghai Municipal People's Procuratorate on the Implementation of the People's Supervisor System (for Trial Implementation)* (hereinafter referred to as *the Implementation Opinions of Shanghai*) has such provisions. The next is the complete informing and the communication system. Through a series of normative measures, Shandong Provincial Procuratorate has broadened the channels for people's supervisors to know. For example, the system of irregular transmission of procuratorial work information and informing system of special activities are established and people's supervisors may inspect places of custody and participate in return visits to units and parties concerned are provided. Thirdly, the guarantee mechanism for the independent exercise of supervision rights by people's supervisors. Article 36 of the *Implementation Opinions of Shanghai* provides that "it is not allowed to interfere with the people's supervisors' reviewing and voting on cases, nor to divulge the information concerned". Article 30 of *the Provisions of the Supreme People's Procuratorate on Implementing the People's Supervisor System (for Trial Implementation)* also provides that if any person interferes with or retaliates against people's supervisors' performance of duties in accordance with the law, the main liable shall be subject to disciplinary or criminal liability.

3.2.6 Experience: Constructing a Scientific and Normative System for People's Supervisor System

The current normative documents governing people's supervisors exhibit a diverse array of forms marked by inconsistencies and a lack of logical rigor in the system arrangement between norms. Consequently, there is a need for a scientifically structured formal system for the People's Supervisor System in subsequent legislative design to establish clear logic and layers. Drawing inspiration from the work mentality of "one method, three detailed rules" observed in Wuhan Hanyang District, the approach involves adopting the *Implementing Measures for the Work of People's Supervisors (for Trial Implementation)* by the Standing Committee of the National People's Congress. This method, referring to the legislative structure employed in *the Decision of the Standing Committee of the National People's Congress on Improving the People's Juror System*, focuses on providing principled provisions for the People's Supervisor System. It temporarily avoids some issues that are not mature enough in theory, facilitating the deliberation and adoption by the Standing Committee of the National People's Congress. The so-called "three detailed rules" refer to the detailed procedural provisions on the supervision over the "three types of cases" and "five kinds of situations", other supervision, withdrawal and filing by people's supervisors in *the Detailed Rules for the Work of People's Supervisors*. In *the Detailed Rules for the Work of Appointment and Removal of People's Supervisors*, further specific provisions are made on the determination of the number of people's supervisors, the establishment of the working group for appointment, the steps and methods of appointment, the removal and addition of the duties of people's supervisors. In *the Detailed Rules for the Work of the Administration and Services of People's Supervisors*, detailed provisions are made on the issues such as the administrative bodies, work guarantee, training, assessment, awards and punishments of people's supervisors, and further clarify the respective duties of the Committee for Internal and Judicial Affairs of the NPC, the committee for appointment and removal of representatives, and the People's Procuratorate Supervisor Office in managing and providing services. In general, the three rules primarily emphasize operational provisions for supporting the implementation of *the Measures for the Implementation of the Work of People's Supervisors (for Trial Implementation)*. Simultaneously, these rules address certain theoretically controversial issues for the purpose of exploration and experience accumulation. The mode of unified regulation may also be adopted in legislation if considering the longer-term periodicity of such legislative strategy, but the appointment and removal of people's supervisors, methodology of supervision work, the service functions, and the effectiveness assurance of supervision shall be separately provided so as to achieve a harmonious and unified normative system for people's supervisors.

3.3 Analysis of the Existing Problems in the People's Supervisor System

The current norms of the People's Supervisor System represent a useful attempt to supervise the self-investigation cases of procuratorial organs. This system has initially established a mechanism involving appointment-supervision-guarantees, leading to notable social impacts. However, upon closer examination of the content of the System, it becomes evident that it faces challenges not only in terms of legitimacy in form but also exhibits contradictions with the concept of the rule of law and the original intention of the system design in its nature.

3.3.1 System Operation Deviates from Its Purpose: Conceptual Confusion About Norms for People's Supervisor System

The establishment of the People's Supervisor System is designed to create a new mechanism of procuratorial supervision, emphasizing "external restraint on the internal". T*he Provisions of the Supreme People's Procuratorate on the Implementation of the People's Supervisor System (for Trial Implementation)* and the rules on the People's Supervisor System in all regions generally provide that "in order to ensure that the people's procuratorates perform their duties in accordance with the law and impartially... the People's Supervisor System is implemented and the people's procuratorates shall accept social supervision". This can be seen as an advocacy for the People's Supervisor System's operational aim of promoting the fair and lawful exercise of procuratorial power by establishing an external supervision system.

However, within the norms of the Supreme People's Procuratorate and local people's supervisor systems, the operation of the system has arisen a lot of contrary to the purposes of external supervision. Taking *the Provisions of the Supreme People's Procuratorate on Implementing the People's Supervisor System (for Trial Implementation)* as an example,[58] Article 4 provides that "the people's procuratorates shall establish the People's Supervisor Office as the office of supervisors to conduct works in implementing the People's Supervisor System", Article 9 provides that "the number of people's supervisors of local people's procuratorates at all levels shall be determined by the people's procuratorates at the provincial level at their work needs", and Article 27 provides that "the funds needed for people's supervisors to carry out the supervision work shall be paid from the operational funds of the procuratorial organs at all levels". These standards encompass the working body, appointment, and guarantee mechanism of people's supervisors, directly impacting the nature of the system and the effectiveness of supervision within the People's Supervisor System. However, these contents also exhibit a significant internalization characteristic, namely, the people's supervisor system has the very strong subjective color in the operation process, closely tied to the internal organizational structure of the procuratorial organ. The realization of system goal relays on the level of attention given by the procuratorial organ. The normative mode of system goal is subject to the system operation, bringing a contradiction between the original intention of the People's Supervisor System and its practical implementation, and becoming a bottleneck in the development of the system.

3.3.2 Chaos in System: The Question of Formal Legitimacy of the People's Supervisor System

The foundational structure of supervision relies on specific normative documents issued by the Supreme People's Procuratorate in People's Supervisor System. Simultaneously, many implementing measures or detailed rules for the supervision of people's supervisors have been established based on the regulations of the Supreme People's Procuratorate to compose the people's supervisor system. However, when scrutinizing these norms through the perspective of the rule of law, several questions arise. First, whether the normative documents of the Supreme People's Procuratorate on the People's Supervisor System have formal legitimacy? How to define its nature? Second, how to respectively judge the detailed provisions made by local procuratorial organs and local people's congresses on the People's Supervisor System? Third, how to grasp the relationship between the provisions made by the Supreme People's

[58] The local people's supervisor system also tends to adopt an internalized operational mechanism. Further enumeration of specific instances is omitted.

Procuratorate and local procuratorial organs? If these issues remain unresolved, the People's Supervisor System may continue to face existing challenges, leading to uncertainty regarding its development prospects and direction.

First is about the legal nature of People's Supervisor System of the Supreme People's Procuratorate. The Supreme People's Procuratorate, as the legal supervision organ established by the Constitution, regulates the specific legal relations in the process of realizing its basic functions. Such norms exist in the form of judicial interpretations established in the Resolution of the Standing Committee of the National People's Congress on Strengthening Legal Interpretation,[59] and judicial documents serving to procuratorial work, including judicial administrative documents involving administrative matters of procuratorial organs and other judicial documents concerning internal work systems. From the perspective of the objects of adjustment and the contents involved, the People's Supervisor System should not belong to the judicial interpretation for the purpose of specific application of laws and decrees, nor to the scope of judicial administrative documents, but to the judicial documents involving the internal working system of procuratorial organs. If the normative system of the People's Supervisor System only involves the internal working modes and working process of the people's procuratorate, it can comfortably coexist within the existing legal framework. However, due to the external characteristics of people's supervisors, the system inevitably involves the selection, appointment, rights and effectiveness of people's supervisors. And these legal relations beyond the scope of internal work system of the procuratorial authorities and reach adjustment and regulations of the fundamental rights of people. Therefore, there is a problem of determining the legitimacy of adjusting legal rights by judicial documents.

Secondly, apart from the system norms formulated by the Supreme People's Procuratorate, local procuratorial organs and local people's congresses also play a role in establishing the People's Supervisor System. Although the connotation and extension of the litigation system are not explained within the current legal framework and its scope is not clear, the litigation and arbitration system must be regulated by law in accordance with the relevant provisions of *Legislation Law*. But the related contents of the People's Supervisor System do relate to the litigation system, and the formulation of normative documents on this issue by local procuratorial organs and local people's congresses is suspected of "violating the law".

Finally, in accordance with the Constitution and the Organic Law of the People's Procuratorates, "The Supreme People's Procuratorate shall direct the work of local people's procuratorates at all levels and of special people's procuratorates; people's procuratorates at higher levels shall direct the work of those at lower levels". The relationship between leadership and subordinates should be regarded as a rigid relationship, including both functional leadership and coordination of rules and regulations. In practice, there are also local procuratorial organs to break the provisions of

---

[59] Article 2 of the Resolution provides that the Supreme People's Procuratorate shall be responsible for the interpretation of all issues concerning the specific application of laws and decrees in procuratorial work.

the superior procuratorate of the People's Supervisor System. The capability and the "degree" of breaking through, both are worth discussing.

3.3.3 Value Imbalance in Appointment Conditions: Contrary to the Concept of Equal Rights

"The right to equality lies in preventing the unjust infringement upon the people by the public power of the state... This right, especially when the rights of the people are impaired by the violation of the principle of public power, may give the people grounds for denying the constitutionality of the measure".[60] In the realm of legislation, lawmakers must govern legislative activities based on the principle of "the same event — the same norm, the different event — the different norm". In other words, legislators should consider the object of differential legislation in terms of the nature of the matter with respect to the essence of different situations. And the essence of so-called affairs "is a kind of value performance which is often outside the positive law, is a kind of concrete substantial justice, is also a kind of specific concept of natural law"[61]

In the existing People's Supervisor System, the criteria for the selection and appointment of individuals to this role are typically defined as "23 years old or above, be honest and upright, have a certain level of education, policy and legal knowledge, and be in good health"[62] Local procuratorates often specify additional requirements such as "having a broad mass base, being adept at listening to and reflecting the opinions of the masses in a practical and realistic manner,"[63] and having certain social life experience or other special conditions.[64]

Is there any legal basis or legitimacy for stipulating the age limit of "23 years old" or above when restricting the appointment of people's supervisors from physiological conditions and knowledge structure conditions? What are the reasons for excluding persons with full capacity for civil conduct at the age of 18? Does the designer of the system have an objective or subjective judgment? What is the basis of judgment? These questions create a series of questions about the basis of specified age. What is the concept of "having a broad mass base and certain social experience"? Is it a standard for people's supervisors? Is it operable? Is it a declaratory clause or a substantive judgment clause that does not follow the law of legislation?

---

[60] Chen Xinmin, *Foundations of German Public Law (II)*, Shandong People's Publishing House, 2001, p. 672.

[61] *Ibid.*

[62] The Provisions of the Supreme People's Procuratorate on *Implementing the People's Supervisor System (for Trial Implementation)* and the implementing measures for people's supervisors of all provincial procuratorates have such provisions.

[63] See the Implementing Rules of the People's Supervisor System of the Fujian Provincial People's Procuratorate.

[64] For example, Chongqing, while stipulating that citizens may recommend themselves for the post of people's supervisor, excludes qualified candidates who are studying graduate school, for lack of social experience in practice.

The requirement of "physical health" of people's supervisors brings more doubt on the value and rationality of People's Supervisor System. In the formulation of the norms, the parties concerned with the same conditions must be treated equally when the uncertain legal concept is applied to the consideration of public welfare. "Physical health" is the standard for the appointment of the People's Supervisor System. Regardless of the uncertainty of the meaning of "physical health", there is a problem that cannot be judged at all in practice. From the point of view of the concept of equality in legislation alone, "physical health" should not be the criterion of the "essence of the matter" for the differential legislation. The value rationality of the People's Supervisor System lies in the citizen's right to supervise State power, which is inherent to the citizen's legal nature. Any other social factor should not serve as a criterion for differentiating citizens' right to supervise, as this would contradict the constitutional principle of equal treatment. Therefore, giving careful consideration to how to align the design of the People's Supervisor System with the idea of the rule of law is a crucial focus.

3.3.4 Whether Supervision Power Can Be "Transferred": Doubt on the Substantive Legitimacy of Norms of the People's Supervisor System

The People's Procuratorate serves as the organ of legal supervision in accordance with the Constitution, which brings a difficult problem in the development of constitutionalism that who supervises the supervisors. The current standard of the people's supervisor system seems to have made a new interpretation of this, but if we judge this standard system calmly. Whether this kind of normative system conforms to the general law of constitutionalism operation and the basic principle of power operation established by the current legal system?

The logical starting point of the People's Supervisor System is to put the procuratorial power under social supervision and endow the people's supervisor with a supervision power, which is in line with the general concept of the rule of law in which power is subject to restrictions in terms of the goal of the system. But the modern power system is based on the citizens with sovereign consciousness, and it begins to link the power within the State and social system, thus emerging a proposition that the power of the modern State doesn't originate solely from the State itself but from the citizens in social life, with citizens enable State power to be generated or carried out in a variety of ways, including elections, delegation, direct participation, and supervision. Therefore, considering the social attribute of the origination of power, can the prosecutorial organ self-establish a system to place prosecutorial power under social supervision and endow it with a rigid binding force?

Furthermore, the procuratorial organ, acting as the exerciser of State procuratorial power, derives its legitimacy from the constitution and laws embodying popular will. However, this legitimacy becomes meaningless if it loses its public foundation. And in terms of the derivation process of power, it is irreversible and can only be granted, but not arbitrarily change the proceedings of the statutory procedures by people's supervisors to exercise procuratorial power. Even though "people's supervisors only have the right to suggest on review, but the right to review is an important part of the right to make decisions, and the review of cases by people's supervisors is actually exercising the authority that should have been specially exercised by procuratorial organs".[65] Therefore, the current People's Supervisor System faces challenges of a lack of corresponding legitimacy within the existing legal system.

[65] Yu Feng & Xie Xiaojian, *Cold Thinking of the People's Supervisor System*, Jiangxi Social Sciences, 2005.

Chapter 4
Selection of Legislative Paths and Establishment of Legislative Principles for the People's Supervisor System

1 Selection of Legislative Paths for the People's Supervisor System

The legislation of the people's supervisor system is a crucial approach to develop it into a more institutionalized and law-based system. It involves the establishment, standardization, and guidance of the system's various rules and regulations. As an integrated systematic project, particularly under Chinese context of advancing rule of law and the fundamental requirements of practicing constitution-based governance, the legislation of the people's supervisor system must not only fully consider the inherent characteristics of the system itself as the legislative object but also take into account the structural framework of a nation's constitutional system as a whole. Additionally, it should adhere to the fundamental requirements in terms of legislative guiding thought, basic legislative principles, and basic legislative techniques.

Setting aside the grand narrative on the necessity and feasibility of legislating the people's supervisor system, our focus here is on the practical operational issues of such legislation. Specifically, within the framework of China's current constitutional system, the legislation of the people's supervisor system must not only comply with universal legislative requirements but also follow the special legislative rules dictated by the unique characteristics of the system itself, as well as the specific approaches adopted for its legislation. The process of selecting legislative paths for the people's supervisor system serves as an effective means to examine the actual state of China's current legislative practices. It also reflects China's constitutional development and the true level of its rule-of-law progress. This process represents a deepening and refinement of China's legislative practices, further advancing China's constitutional progress to elevate the standards of the country's rule-of-law development.

Q. Qin, *Legislative Research on the People's Supervisor System*,
https://doi.org/10.1007/978-981-95-7972-3_4

1.1 The Concept of the Selection of Legislative Paths for the People's Supervisor System

In the context of modern Chinese, the term "Lu Jing" (路径, path) carries at least the following layered meanings: (1) a physical road or path, used for vehicles or pedestrians—a static trace, representing the most fundamental meaning of the term; (2) the route to a destination, whether planned or already traversed—a dynamic trajectory, with both the static concept of a physical road and the dynamic concept of a route or trajectory constitute the objective meanings of "path"; (3) a method or approach to accomplishing something, representing a subjective abstraction and metaphorical extension of the term's objective meanings; and (4) a specialized terminology in particular fields, such as the textual path identifiers that reference computer files or content. Regardless of the rich semantic variations of the Chinese term, a fundamental principle in using it to convey meaning is to anchor its interpretation in the specific context. This requires that when employing "path" to express a particular idea, we must carefully consider its contextual usage.

The understanding of legislative paths is contingent upon the comprehension of the specific meanings of the terms "legislation" and "path," as well as the nuanced interpretation generated by their combination. Both in China and the West, the term "legislation" has existed since ancient times, though "there has never been a standardized definition or systematic interpretation of 'legislation' as a formal category or concept".[1] Even in contemporary discourse, the term "legislation" is used in multiple senses. From the perspective of separation of powers, legislation constitutes an activity or its outcome distinct from administration and judiciary. In the broad sense, legislation is synonymous with lawmaking, referring to "all activities whereby authorized state organs formulate normative legal documents in accordance with law".[2] In the narrow sense, legislation pertains specifically to the meaning of national legislative power,[3] defined as "the activity of the supreme state authority and its standing body in enacting or modifying laws as particular normative instruments".[4] Thus, "legislation denotes both the process of creating or modifying laws and the legal norms as the product of such process."[5] With the emergence, development and maturation of the science of law as a discipline, contemporary understanding has converged toward a unified definition from this academic perspective: "Legislation is an activity whereby specific entities, exercising defined authority and procedures while employing technical methods, formulate, recognize, or modify legal norms as particular social norms."[6] Therefore, within the specific context of legislative studies, "legislative path" refers to the process whereby certain legislative

---

[1] Zhou Wangsheng, *Science of Legislation*, Law Press China, 2004, p. 24.

[2] Li Long ed., *Jurisprudence*, Wuhan University Press, 1996, p. 290.

[3] *Ibid.*

[4] Zhang Wenxian ed., *Jurisprudence*, Higher Education Press, 2003, p. 234.

[5] *Ibid.*

[6] Zhou Wangsheng, *Science of Legislation*, Law Press China, 2004, p. 30.

bodies, acting within their legislative authority and in accordance with prescribed procedures while employing certain legislative techniques, engage in the formulation, recognition, or modification of legal norms. This definition of legislative paths reveals that legislation follows not only an objectively traceable dynamic trajectory, but also bears profound subjective imprints through the legislative body's deliberate choices in the legislative process—representing both a synthesis of dynamism and stability, and an integration of subjectivity and objectivity. Such understanding significantly enhances our grasp of legislative regularities and lays theoretical groundwork for selecting appropriate paths in legislating the people's supervisor system.

The legislative path for the people's supervisor system refers to the specific process whereby lawmakers, acting within their legislative authority and in accordance with prescribed procedures while employing certain legislative techniques, formulate the normative documents of the people's supervisor system. This path fundamentally embodies both the distinctive characteristics of the people's supervisor system itself and the inherent regularities of legislative processes, representing their organic integration.

The selection of legislative paths for the people's supervisor system refers to the activity wherein, within the framework of a nation's legislative system, a choice is made among different entities possessing differentiated legislative power to ultimately determine which legislative body shall enact laws for the system, and then utilize its legislative authority and procedures with specific legislative techniques to formulate normative documents for the people's supervisor system. Such path selection is severely constrained by the constitutional architecture of a nation's legislative system, which itself emerges from complex historical, cultural, and geopolitical factors. Within China's current constitutional system, multiple potential legislative paths exist for the people's supervisor system, making the selection process essentially an optimization exercise to identify the most institutionally appropriate approach. The decisive factor in China's legislative system lies in determining the proper lawmaker—specifically, which legislative body should undertake this task and through what institutional form.

Within the framework of China's constitutional system, the legislative system refers to the macro-level structural foundation of legislation, the legislative model represents its typological abstraction, while the legislative path embodies its practical implementation. These three elements—legislative system, legislative model, and legislative path—are closely interrelated. And clarifying their relationship serves as the logical premise and solid foundation for selecting the legislative path for the people's supervisor system.

1.2 Legislative Path and Legislative Model

1.2.1 The Concept of Legislative Model

A "model" refers to the standard form of something or a replicable template that serves as a reference.[7] "The legislative model refers to a country's habitual approach, fundamental mindset, and concrete sequence of actions in enacting, revising, or repealing laws, as well as the legislative institutions and rules shaped by multiple factors."[8] Conceptually, the legislative model reflects a fixed cognitive pattern; normatively, it is embodied in legislative rules; and operationally, it translates into established practices and procedural sequences. In the process of legislative activities, the legislative model always serves as a reference specimen or template. This is precisely the functional value that the legislative model holds for the legislative process of the people's supervisor system. In the course of legislating the people's supervisor system, due consideration must inevitably be given to the legislative model shaped by the country's constitutional system.

1.2.2 Distinction Between Legislative Path and Legislative Model

Legislative path and legislative model are closely related yet distinctly different. The legislative path is the dynamic reflection of the legislative model, while the legislative model is the static abstraction of the legislative path. The legislative path can be diverse, whereas the legislative model represents a fixed "template" formed through the abstraction and generalization of these diverse paths. To some extent, the legislative model guides the selection of legislative paths, serving as a benchmark for specific legislative routes and a "touchstone" for evaluating their smooth progression. Conversely, whether a legislative path proceeds smoothly and empirically tests the scientific validity and rationality of the legislative model.

The most crucial distinction between legislative paths and legislative models lies in their qualitative differences. A legislative path refers to the process whereby certain legislative bodies, acting within their legislative power and in accordance with prescribed procedures while employing certain legislative techniques, engage in the formulation, recognition, or modification of legal norms. While a legislative model refers to a country's habitual approach, fundamental mindset, and concrete sequence of actions in enacting, revising, or repealing laws, as well as the legislative institutions and rules shaped by multiple factors. The legislative path always manifests in concrete forms, while the legislative model often represents an abstract summation. The legislative model serves as the central mast, with the legislative path being the banner that waves upon it.

[7] *Modern Chinese Dictionary*, the Commercial Press, 2002, p. 84.

[8] Guan Baoying & Zhang Shufang, *Research on the Market Economy and the Transformation of Legislative Models*, Studies in Law and Business, 1997.

This fundamental qualitative difference between the legislative path and the legislative model gives rise to the following evident distinctions.

Firstly, the typological nature of legislative models versus the dynamic nature of legislative paths. Legislative models possess a typological characteristic. Although legislative models may vary across different historical periods—and even within the same era, they may differ due to the specific national conditions of each country—however, "they can nonetheless be categorized based on spatiotemporal criteria as a spatiotemporal existence."[9] Based on this understanding, legislative models can be classified according to different standards, thereby achieving a typological comprehension of the issue.[10] In contrast, the legislative path does not share this typological characteristic. Different legislative matters may adopt varying specific approaches, and even for the same legislative issue, the path may differ across different stages of the legislative process. The legislative path is neither fixed nor typological; rather, it is in a constant state of flux, exhibiting a distinctly dynamic quality. Regardless of the perspective from which it is interpreted, the dynamic nature of the legislative path invariably manifests in the course of practical implementation.

Secondly, the stability of legislative models versus the adaptability of legislative paths. Legislative models inherently possess a characteristic of stability. Precisely because of their typological nature, legislative models maintain relatively stable within a specific historical period and national context. This relative stability manifests in the clearly defined legislative bodies, demarcated jurisdictional competences, and established frameworks for legislative content—all demonstrating considerable determinacy. Such stability in legislative models imposes elevated requirements on concrete legislative approaches: when enacting legislation on specific matters, whichever legislative path is adopted must endeavor to maintain compatibility with the nation's existing legislative model. This adaptive function serves to effectively preserve, at minimum, the formal consistency, stability, and continuity of a country's rule of law framework.

Thirdly, the mutability of legislative models versus the variability of legislative approaches. The typological nature of legislative models does not negate their inherent mutability. Society exists in a constant state of development, with each historical stage exhibiting distinct characteristics. The transition between historical stages represents an external manifestation of quantitative changes culminating in qualitative transformation, and legislation, as a driving force of social development, is no exception. When society progresses from one historical stage to another, previously stable legislative models become disrupted, resulting in mutation. Taking China's post-1949 legislative practice as an example, the nation largely followed a "transformative legislation" model during its first fifty years (particularly after the 1980s)—a rational choice under specific national conditions. However, after

---

[9] Jiang Guohua, *Legislation: Ideal and Transformation*, Shandong People's Publishing House, 2007, p. 254.

[10] *Ibid.*, pp. 254–283.

In Professor Jiang's work, he categorized legislative models from both temporal and spatial dimensions. This analytical approach to understanding legislative models is worthy of reference.

entering the twenty-first century, as China's modernization became more established and civil economic forces matured alongside diversified interest groups, the adaptive efficacy of "transformative legislation" showed declining returns while its negative effects, such as institutional confusion and risks, became increasingly apparent. Consequently, China should appropriately adjust its legislative model in response to changing national conditions by gradually phasing out "transformative legislation" in favor of "autonomous legislation".[11] Thus, the mutation of legislative models follows specific causal mechanisms rather than reflecting arbitrary decisions by particular social classes. As Jiang Guohua notes, "The genuine impetus for legislative model transformation lies in the development of socio-political, economic, and cultural conditions."[12] The mutability of legislative models represents qualitative and fundamental change, whereas variability in legislative approaches reflects ongoing quantitative adjustments in implementation, demonstrating continuous refinement of operational practices without compromising the fundamental framework of established legislative models or disrupting a nation's stable legal architecture.

The legislative path selection for the people's supervisor system is inherently linked to the legislative model determined by a country's constitutional system. The significance of distinguishing between legislative paths and legislative models lies in clarifying that, when selecting a legislative path for the people's supervisor system, we must to some extent rely on our understanding of the legislative model and its role as a "template" for legislative activities—serving as a reference or source of inspiration. Such reference or experience learning can better guide and facilitate a more scientific and rational selection of the legislative path for the people's supervisor system.

1.3 Legislative Path and Legislative System

1.3.1 The Meaning of Legislative System

The term "system" generally refers to an organizational system and a normative institution or framework. A legislative system generally refers to the institution or framework governing the division of national legislative powers and the establishment of legislative bodies.[13] Although scholars may differ in their precise definitions

[11] See Qin Qianhong, *The Evolution of China's Legislative Model from a Constitutional Perspective: From "Transformative Legislation" to "Autonomous Legislation"*, China Legal Science, 2005.

Professor Qin's analysis of the historical context and rationale for "transformative legislation", along with the inevitable transition to "autonomous legislation", precisely illustrates the mutable characteristic of legislative models.

[12] Jiang Guohua, *Legislation: Ideal and Transformation*, Shandong People's Publishing House, 2007, p. 248.

[13] See Liu Shengping, *On the Legislative System in the Primary Stage of Socialism in China*, Tribune of Political Science and Law, 1989.

of a legislative system, there is broad consensus that its core function lies in institutionalizing the division of legislative authority—that is, determining which state organs and relevant officials hold the power to enact, revise, and abolish various legal instruments as well as to recognize various legal norms within a nation.[14] Thus, a legislative system constitutes the institutional framework that defines legislative bodies, allocates legislative powers, establishes legislative procedures, and addresses other fundamental aspects of lawmaking. At the macro level, it shapes a nation's overarching legal architecture, providing both the skeletal structure and foundational support for its legal order. To a significant degree, the legislative system forms the bedrock of a country's legal regime and represents one of its most critical components. During same given historical period, the formation of a nation's legislative system is influenced by multiple factors, including: (1) a nation's state system, which determines the nature of its legislative system; (2) a nation's political system and the form of state structure, which determine the specific form of its legislative system. Every nation's legislative system develops within the constraints of its state structure, making it impossible for its division of legislative authority to transcend the limitations imposed by its political system or the form of state structure.[15] Broadly speaking, contemporary global legislative systems generally fall into three categories: unitary, composite, and checks-and-balance models.[16] However, China's existing legislative system falls into none of these classifications. Instead, it bears distinct Chinese characteristics. As Professor Zhou Wangsheng explains, "China's current legislative system operates under unified central leadership with appropriate decentralization, featuring multi-tier coexistence and hybrid integration of legislative types."[17]

This understanding is fully substantiated by the provisions of *the Legislation Law of the People's Republic of China* (hereinafter referred to as the "*Legislation Law*"), adopted on March 15, 2000, at the Third Session of the Ninth National People's Congress. According to the *Legislation Law*, in China, the entities vested with legislative power include not only the National People's Congress and its Standing Committee but also the State Council, its constituent departments, authorized local people's congresses and their standing committees, as well as authorized local people's governments. From the perspective of the entities vested with legislative authority, aside from the organs of state power, there are also administrative bodies; apart from central lawmakers, there are relevant local state organs within certain scopes. Moreover, the hierarchy, legal effect, and nomenclature of normative documents formulated by different legislative entities vary. The National People's Congress and its Standing Committee have the authority to formulate laws, the State Council to formulate administrative regulations, the departments of the State Council

---

[14] See Zhu Liyu, *A Study on the Models of Legislative Systems*, Journal of Renmin University of China, 2000.

[15] *Ibid.*

[16] See Zhou Wangsheng, *On the Current Legislative System in China*, Journal of Peking University (Philosophy and Social Sciences), 1989.

[17] *Ibid.*

and relevant local people's governments to issue rules, and the relevant local people's congresses and their standing committees to formulate local regulations. Additionally, China's legislative system reflects special legislative authority for areas of ethnic autonomy, where the people's congresses of these areas have the power to enact autonomous regulations and separate regulations. In summary, China's legislative framework encompasses both a horizontal division of legislative authority among state institutions and a vertical distribution of legislative powers between central and local authorities.[18]

1.3.2 The Regulation of the Legislative System on Legislative Paths

Legislative paths are evidently distinct from the legislative system. The legislative system, from a macro perspective, defines legislative bodies, their authority, procedures, and other elements, whereas legislative paths pertain to how legislative bodies are determined or which legislative body is established for specific legislative matters, as well as the specific forms of legislation. The legislative system is unique to a country at the current stage, while legislative paths vary for different legislative matters and may even differ across various stages of the same legislative matter. The legislative system constitutes the macro legal framework under a country's constitutional structure, providing the foundational skeleton and operational space for legislative activities. Any legislative activity detached from this operational space is like water without a source or a tree without roots. Thus, the legislative system constrains the choice of legislative paths, meaning that the selection of legislative paths must reflect legislative activities conducted within the confines of the current legislative system. The regulation of legislative paths by the legislative system precisely illustrates the dependence of legislative paths on the legislative system. Examining the legislative system established by China's *Legislation Law* as an example, the system, which allocates legislative authority, is deeply imprinted with the realities of China's national conditions, including current political, economic, cultural, and other factors. Among these, the influence of a country's political system and form of state structure is particularly significant. These influencing factors of the legislative system also profoundly shape the selection of legislative paths for specific legislative matters.

Regarding the legislative path to the people's supervisor system, the legislative system established under China's *Constitution* and the *Legislation Law* forms the

---

[18] In his research, Professor Zhu Liyu points out that there are four distinct theories regarding the horizontal division of legislative authority: first, the model of legislative organs priori; second, the model of administrative organs priori; third, a model of tripartite parity and mutual checks; and fourth, the model of legislative organs supremacy. Similarly, there are four models for the vertical division of legislative authority: first, the model of complete centralization; second, the model of complete decentralization; third, the decentralization-centralization model; and fourth, the centralization-decentralization model. Professor Zhu Liyu also provides an analysis of both horizontal and vertical divisions.

For details, see Zhu Liyu, *A Study on the Models of Legislative Systems*, Journal of Renmin University of China, 2000.

foundational basis for its path selection. The legislative path to the people's supervisor system must operate within the current legislative system of China and must not attempt to "start from scratch" to create a so-called "castle in the air." The establishment of any system must be rooted in the soil that sustains it to ensure long-term viability and enduring vitality. Only by aligning the legislative path of the people's supervisor system with China's legislative system can it achieve rationality and legitimacy, thereby maintaining long-term sustainability and continuous dynamism.

1.4 Legislative Path Selection for the People's Supervisor System

1.4.1 The Constraint on Legislative Path Selection for the People's Supervisor System—China's Current Legislative Framework System

The legislative path selection for the people's supervisor system is not arbitrary; rather, it must be appropriately determined within China's existing legislative system, guided by the country's legislative model. This ensures that the people's supervisor system can maximize its unique functions in the process of legalization. An interpretation of the *Legislation Law* reveals the following content of its specific provisions governing the legislative framework:

Article 7 provides that "the National People's Congress and its Standing Committee exercise the legislative power of the state." It further clarifies that The National People's Congress shall formulate and revise basic laws governing criminal offenses, civil matters, state institutions, and other matters. The Standing Committee of the National People's Congress shall formulate and revise laws other than the ones to be formulated by the National People's Congress, and when the National People's Congress is not in session, shall supplement and revise the laws formulated by the National People's Congress, on the premise that the supplementation and revision are not in contradiction to the basic principles of such laws.

Article 8 specifies nine categories of matters that shall only be governed by laws, and includes a catch-all provision—"other matters on which laws must be formulated by the National People's Congress or its Standing Committee"—thereby reserving legislative authority over all remaining matters. From the provisions of Article 8, the nine explicitly listed categories of exclusive national legislative matters are overt and can be directly discerned, whereas the scope of legislative matters reserved under the catch-all clause is latent—their precise boundaries can only be determined under specific conditions. Viewed solely through the lens of overt matters, the scope of national legislative power appears limited. However, when considering latent matters, this scope becomes virtually unlimited: the NPC and its Standing Committee may exercise national legislative power over any matter they deem to fall under "other matters on which laws must be formulated by the National People's Congress or its Standing Committee." Thus, while the reach of national legislative power may seem narrow on the face of it, it is in fact exceptionally broad.

Articles 9, 10, and 11 have made provisions on enabling legislation, which at minimum clarify the following:

First, the authorization body and the delegated body. Article 9 provides: "In the absence of a law on any of the matters specified in Article 8 of this Law, the National People's Congress or its Standing Committee has the power to make a decision to authorize the State Council to formulate, in light of actual needs, an administrative regulation first on part of the matter, except for those matters concerning crimes and criminal punishments, the compulsory measures and penalties involving the deprivation of citizens of their political rights or the restriction of their personal freedom, and the judicial system." Thus, the authorization body for enabling legislation is exclusively the National People's Congress and its Standing Committee, while the delegated body can only be the State Council—not any other entity, such as the constituent departments of the State Council, local governments, or local legislative organs.

Second, the preconditions and scope of authorization. Article 9 clearly provides the precondition for authorization: only under the circumstance that the NPC and its Standing Committee in the absence of a law on their legislative authority have the power to make a decision to "authorize the State Council to formulate, in light of actual needs," an administrative regulation first on part of the matter. Given that the scope of national legislative power under Article 8 of the *Legislation Law* is exceptionally broad, all matters within this scope could theoretically be delegated to the State Council for prior regulatory formulation—provided the precondition of "in the absence of a law" is met. Thus, the potential range of matters subject to enabling legislation is also extremely extensive. However, this broad scope is subject to specific exceptions provided in Article 9: "...except for those matters concerning crimes and criminal punishments, the compulsory measures and penalties involving the deprivation of citizens of their political rights or the restriction of their personal freedom, and the judicial system." For these exceptions, even if no law has been enacted by the NPC or its Standing Committee, the State Council is prohibited from formulating administrative regulations—even with the authorization by the NPC or its Standing Committee.[19]

Third, the method and content of authorization. Article 10(1) provides: "an authorization decision shall specify matters such as the purpose and scope." Therefore, the method of authorization is exercised by the NPC or its Standing Committee in the form of a "decision", the content of which must define the purpose of authorization and the scope of matters.

[19] In fact, the NPC and its Standing Committee would never authorize the State Council to regulate these excluded matters, such as those pertaining to crimes and penalties, the deprivation of political rights or personal freedom, or judicial systems, given the explicit prohibitions of the *Legislation Law*. To do so would violate their functions and powers and expose them to legal risks under the *Legislation Law*.

Fourth, restrictions and termination of authorization. There are two restrictions on authorization: For the authorization body, when making an authorization, it must specify the purpose and scope in the form of an "authorization decision". For the delegated body: Article 10(2) and (3) require that the State Council shall exercise the authorized power strictly in compliance with the authorization purpose and scope and may not redelegate the authorized power to any other organ. Additionally, Article 11 clarifies the conditions for termination of authorization: "Where an administrative regulation on a matter formulated under authorization has been tested in practice and when the conditions are ripe for making a law on the matter, the National People's Congress or its Standing Committee shall make a law thereon in a timely manner. The authorization with regard to the matter in question shall be terminated upon the formulation of the law."

Articles 7 to 11 of the *Legislation Law* primarily delineate the scope of national legislative power, specifically the legislative authority of central organ of state power.[20] The *Legislation Law* also provides: the scope of authority for the State Council to enact administrative regulations[21]; the scope of authority of the people's congresses and their standing committees of the provinces, autonomous regions, municipalities and other large cities to enact local regulations[22]; the scope of authority of people's congresses in areas of ethnic autonomy to enact autonomous regulations and separate regulations[23]; the scope of authority for constituent departments of the State Council and authorities directly under the State Council with administrative

[20] Authorizing legislation involves the division of central legislative authority, reflecting the coordination of legislative authority between central organs of state power and central administrative bodies. See Articles 11 and 56(3) of the *Legislation Law*.

[21] See Article 56 of the *Legislation Law*. The power to formulate administrative regulations is exclusively vested in the State Council, grounded not only in constitutional provisions but also directly in the *Legislation Law*.

[22] See Article 64 of the *Legislation Law*. In accordance with the administrative division system established by the *Constitution* of the People's Republic of China and other relevant laws, the local people's congresses and their standing committees have the power to formulate local regulations are limited to two categories: first, the people's congresses and their standing committees at all provincial-level (including provinces, autonomous regions, and municipalities); second, the people's congresses and their standing committees of "other larger cities" (as specified in the *Constitution* and the *Legislation Law*, the scope of other larger cities specifically includes the cities where the people's governments of provinces or autonomous regions are located, the cities where special economic zones are located, and "other larger cities" approved by the State Council).

[23] See Article 66 of the *Legislation Law*. In accordance with the *Constitution* and relevant laws, the people's congresses of ethnic autonomous areas specifically refer to the people's congresses at three levels: autonomous regions, autonomous prefectures, and autonomous counties. The people's congresses at all three levels of autonomous areas have the power to formulate autonomous regulations and separate regulations. However, it is important to note the distinction in legislative authority: while both the people's congresses of autonomous regions and their standing committees have the authority to formulate local regulations, the exclusive power to formulate autonomous regulations and separate regulations lies solely with the people's congresses of autonomous regions. The standing committees of these congresses do not have the authority to enact autonomous or separate regulations.

functions to make rules[24]; as well as the scope of authority for the people's governments of provinces, autonomous regions, municipalities and other large cities to make rules.[25] Beyond these general legislative authorities, the *Legislation Law* also provides the scope of legislative authority of the special legislatures.[26]

It can be confirmed that the division of general legislative authority under China's *Legislation Law* technically clarifies its three components[27]:

Firstly, it clarifies the competent legislative bodies. Legislative bodies refer to organs (institutions) with the power to enact, recognize, revise, supplement, interpret, and repeal laws (in the broad sense). These include the National People's Congress and its Standing Committee, the State Council, the people's congresses of provinces and other large cities and their standing committees, the people's congresses in areas of ethnic autonomy, the constituent departments of the State Council and the authorities directly under the State Council with administrative functions, as well as the provincial governments and governments of large cities. These encompass both organs of power and administrative organs, and include both central and local organs.[28] If China's legislative system is defined by its legislative bodies, it will be both a system of central-local power division and a system of legislative-executive power separation.

Secondly, it clarifies the forms of legislative authority. The forms of legislative authority refer to the manner in which legislative bodies exercise their legislative powers and the resulting manifestations of such exercise. Differences in the manifestations give rise to a legal system structured in a hierarchical order.[29] In a broad sense, the Constitution is also a form of legislative authority. Under the provisions of the *Legislation Law*, the forms of legislative authority further include basic laws, laws other than basic laws, administrative regulations, local regulations, autonomous

---

[24] See Articles 71 and 72 of the *Legislation Law*. According to prevailing theories, the rules formulated by a constituent department of the State Council and a division with administrative functions directly under the State Council are referred to as departmental rules.

[25] See Article 73 of the *Legislation Law*. According to prevailing theories, the rules formulated by a people's government of provinces, autonomous regions, municipalities, and other large cities are referred to as local government rules. The entities authorized to formulate rules correspond to and are consistent at the administrative level with the entities authorized to formulate local regulations, namely the people's governments at the provincial level and of "other large cities".

[26] These include the authority of the Central Military Commission to enact military regulations and of its General Departments, military branches, and military area commands to enact military rules. See Article 93 of the *Legislation Law*.

[27] Dr. Li Lin, researcher at the Institute of Law, Chinese Academy of Social Sciences, argues that "Technically speaking, the division of legislative authority under China's Constitution and laws mainly consists of three components: legislative bodies, forms of legislative authority, and content of legislative authority."

See Li Lin,*On the Theory and Practice of Division of Legislative Authorities*, Chinese Journal of Law, 1998.

[28] *Ibid.*

[29] *Ibid.*

Here, the legal system does not refer to a system of different legal branches formed by classifying all existing legal norms of a country according to certain criteria consisting with different laws, but rather to the system of legal norms.

regulations, separate regulations, departmental rules, and local government rules. Among these forms of legislative authority, the Constitution holds the highest legal force, followed by laws enacted by the National People's Congress and its Standing Committee, while administrative regulations take precedence over local regulations, autonomous regulations, separate regulations, and rules. As legislative forms, normative documents such as laws and administrative regulations are constrained by the content of legislation—that is, the scope of legislative authority—and serve as their external manifestations. At the same time, however, they also delineate the boundaries within which different legislative authorities may exercise their legislative authority.

Thirdly, it clarifies the content of legislative authority. The essential requirements for the division of legislative authority should primarily include the determination of the attribution of legislative matters, i.e., legislative content.[30] Articles 7–11, 56, 64, 66, 71, 72 and 73 of China's *Legislation Law* respectively provides the legislative authority of the National People's Congress and its Standing Committee in enacting laws; the State Council in formulating administrative regulations; the provincial people's congresses and their standing committees as well as the people's congresses and their standing committees of large cities in making local regulations; people's congresses in areas of ethnic autonomy in formulating autonomous regulations and separate regulations; constituent departments of the State Council and authorities directly under the State Council with administrative functions in formulating departmental rules; provincial governments and governments of large cities in formulating local government rules.

1.4.2 The Denial of Local Legislation as a Legislative Path of the People's Supervisor System

An analysis of China's legislative system based on the provisions of the *Legislation Law* provides us with clear guidance for selecting the legislative path for the people's supervisor system. The *Legislation Law* delineates the legislative authority of different legislative bodies, offering specific path options for the legislation of this system. Generally, the possible legislative paths for the people's supervisor system are as follows:

First, the enactment by the National People's Congress or its Standing Committee in the form of law. This means adopting a legislative selection where the NPC or its Standing Committee, in accordance with its legislative power and procedures, enacts a law to establish the people's supervisor system.

Second, the enactment by the State Council in the form of administrative regulations. This approach entails the central people's government, i.e., the State Council formulates administrative regulations on the people's supervisor system in accordance with its legislative power and corresponding legislative processes.

Third, the enactment by the relevant local people's congresses and their standing committees in the form of local regulations. The relevant local people's

[30] *Ibid.*

congresses and their standing committees include those at provincial level (provinces, autonomous regions, and municipalities) and those in large cities (specifically, the cities where provincial people's governments are located, cities where special economic zones are established, and large cities approved by the State Council[31]). This legislative selection for the people's supervisor system is the path of formulating local regulations by relevant local people's congresses and their standing committees, which means that the provincial governments and the people's congresses of large cities and their standing committees enact local regulations in accordance with their respective legislative authority and procedures.

Fourth, the enactment by the people's congresses in areas of ethnic autonomy in the form of autonomous regulations or separate regulations. This path selection refers to the people's congresses of autonomous regions, autonomous prefectures, and autonomous counties formulating autonomous regulations and separate regulations on the people's supervisor system based on the political, economic, and cultural characteristics of their respective ethnic regions.

Fifth, the enactment by the constituent departments of the State Council and authorities directly under the State Council with administrative functions in the form of departmental rules. This means selecting a legislative path where the following entities formulate departmental rules for the people's supervisor system in accordance with their respective legislative power and procedures: ministries and commissions under the State Council, the People's Bank of China, the National Audit Office, and authorities directly under the State Council with administrative functions.

Sixth, the enactment by relevant local people's governments in the form of local government rules. These local governments correspond to their respective local people's congresses, covering provincial governments and the governments of large cities. This path selection of formulating local regulations for people's supervisor system by provincial governments or governments of large cities refers to that they formulate local government rules in accordance with their legislative authorities and corresponding procedures.

The selection of a legislative path for the people's supervisor system means determining the specific method to legislate for this system. Among these possible legislative paths, the first, second and fifth belong to central legislation, while the third, fourth and sixth belong to local legislation.[32] The primary consideration in selecting

[31] Excluding the four municipalities, i.e., Beijing, Shanghai, Tianjin, and Chongqing, as well as Taiwan Province, and the Hong Kong and Macao Special Administrative Regions, China has 27 provincial capital cities. The cities designated as locations of special economic zones are Shenzhen, Xiamen, Zhuhai, and Shantou, totaling four. In addition, the State Council has, over four separate occasions, approved a total of 18 "large cities." As such, up to now, there are exactly 49 "large cities" that are granted the power to formulate local regulations.

[32] The division between central and local legislation presupposes vertical decentralization of legislative power, with the criterion being whether the legislative authority resides in central or local state organs. In China's central legislation hierarchy, the entities vested with legislative authority are limited to the National People's Congress and its Standing Committee, the State Council, the constituent departments of the State Council and divisions with administrative functions directly under the State Council. In local legislation, the entities vested with legislative authority are limited to provincial people's congresses and their standing committees, provincial governments, people's

a legislative path for the people's supervisor system is making a choice between central and local legislation.

Local legislation and central legislation form a pair of corresponding categories. The so-called local legislation refers to the activities whereby specific local authorities, in accordance with certain authorities and procedures, employ certain techniques to enact, recognize, revise, supplement, or repeal normative documents whose legal force does not exceed the boundaries of their respective administrative regions.[33] Whereas the so-called central legislation refers to the activities whereby central authorities, in accordance with statutory authorities and procedures, enact, revise, or repeal certain normative documents that possess universally applicable legal force.

Local legislation possesses comparative advantages over central legislation. Its primary advantage lies in the autonomy to legislate on local affairs, where local legislative bodies, without contravening central legislation, can fully exercise their initiative and independence to legislate according to the political, economic, and cultural development needs of their respective regions.[34] Another advantage of local legislation is its targeted approach to local legislative matters. Different regions must formulate legally binding normative documents tailored to the actual needs and specific circumstances of their administrative jurisdictions. Given China's complex regional diversity, where actual conditions vary significantly across areas and the problems to be addressed differ considerably, local legislation must specifically target the practical issues arising from social relations within each administrative region.[35] Furthermore, local legislation offers the advantage of timeliness in addressing local affairs. For certain special or emergent local issues requiring prompt handling and adjustment, the timeliness of local legislation becomes particularly crucial. In some special circumstances where the state urgently needs legal norms to regulate certain social relations but national legislation cannot be promptly enacted due to immature conditions, the timeliness of local legislation proves particularly vital.[36]

Nevertheless, even so, it remains inappropriate to adopt local legislation for the people's supervisor system, for the following reasons:

Firstly, the characteristics of local legislation determine that the people's supervisor system should not be legislated through local means. The most distinctive characteristic of local legislation lies in its regional nature, which is reflected not only in the fact that its legislative bodies are local authorities, but also in that its scope of legislative authority is confined to local affairs within their respective regions, and is further manifested in that the legal effect of its normative documents is limited to specific areas. This characteristic of local legislation distinctly differs from that of

congresses of other large cities and their standing committees, and the people's governments of other large cities. Although the legislation by people's congresses i of ethnic autonomy areas holds special features, it is generally classified as local legislation.

[33] See Zhou Wangsheng, *Several Theoretical Issues on Local Legislation*, Administrative Law Review, 1994.

[34] See Xu Junlun, *Characteristics of Local Legislation*, Science of Law, 1996.

[35] *Ibid.*

[36] *Ibid.*

central legislation, as central legislation—whether in terms of the status of its legislative bodies, the nature of legislative matters involved, or most importantly the territorial applicability of its legal effect—operates uniformly across the entire sovereign territory.[37] Another attribute derived from this characteristic of local legislation is its subordinate legal status. This subordination refers specifically to the hierarchical nature of legal effect, meaning that normative documents produced through local legislation generally carry lower legal force than those enacted through central legislation. Taking China as an example, the legal effect of local regulations is inferior to that of national laws, and the effect of local government rules is inferior to that of administrative regulations.

Secondly, the inherent local characteristics of local legislation also determine its greater complexity, making it inconvenient to adopt local legislative approaches for the people's supervisor system. For one thing, China's local administrative units exist at different levels and in numerous quantities. Variations in developmental stages among different-tiered and different-region local units inevitably lead to substantial divergences in the content of local legislation across regions. For another thing, in accordance with relevant provisions in China's *Constitution* and *Legislation Law*, the enactment of local regulations, autonomous regulations, separate regulations, or local government rules must at minimum address their relationship with superior laws such as the Constitution, laws, and administrative regulations. Moreover, these three types of local legislation themselves involve intricate interconnections. For instance, within the same administrative region, there exists the question of the relationship between local regulations enacted by provincial people's congresses and their standing committees and those enacted by large cities in that region; the relationship between local government rules formulated by governments at provincial level and those by large cities; and the relationship between local regulations and local government rules.

Lastly, considering the overall implementation of the people's supervisor system, this system is unsuitable for local legislation.

The first reason is that the people's supervisor system was initiated through the *Provisions on the Implementation of the People's Supervisor System in Cases Directly Accepted for Investigation of People's Procuratorates (for Trial Implementation)*, adopted and issued by the Supreme People's Procuratorate on September 2, 2003. The trial implementation of this system represents a significant task in advancing procuratorial reform within the judicial system reform, in line with the spirit of the 17th CPC National Congress.[38] Therefore, the decision to implement the people's supervisor system was made by the Supreme People's Procuratorate, and its trial implementation has been conducted within the people's procuratorate system at all

[37] In China, due to historical particularities, not all central legislative normative documents take effect within the autonomous regions, even though Hong Kong, Macao and Taiwan are local units under national sovereignty.

[38] See Zhou Yongnian ed., *Introduction to the People's Supervisor System*, China Procuratorial Press, 2008, p. 12.

levels across China. From the perspective of its implementing body, the people's supervisor system is unequivocally a judicial system.

The second reason is that, under the division of legislative authority specified in China's *Legislation Law*, the legislative authority over judicial systems explicitly belongs to the National People's Congress and its Standing Committee, constituting a matter of national legislative power and a typical instance of statutory reservation. This means that legislation concerning judicial systems can only be enacted by the NPC and its Standing Committee, and no other legislative body—including all entities empowered with local legislative authority—shall exercise legislative power over judicial systems.

The last reason is that, apart from the aforementioned disadvantages compared to central legislation, local legislation itself still faces numerous problems. Cai Dingjian summarized these problems in his article "*The Development, Achievements and Problems of Local People's Congress Legislation*"[39]: First, it remains unclear which regulations local people's congresses can autonomously enact and which they cannot. Second, local people's congresses exhibit certain formalism, often mechanically copying the content of national laws while their local legislation lacks specificity, standardization and practicability. Third, there is insufficient macro-level coordination and supervision of local legislation. The mutual coordination and consistency of local legislation constitute a crucial link in maintaining legal unity. Due to the limitations of local legislation and considerations of local interests, local protectionism exists to some extent in legislation. Although the *Legislation Law* pays considerable attention to legislative authority, it would be more accurate to say that rather than redesigning the distribution of legislative authority, it merely acknowledges the status quo, transitioning from tacit approval to formal recognition of the current legislations and authority distribution.[40]

Based on the above considerations, adopting local legislation for the people's supervisor system proves impractical within China's current legislative framework. Among the possible legislative paths—local regulations, autonomous regulations, and separate regulations and local government rules—all three paths must be decisively rejected when selecting the legislative paths for the people's supervisor system.

1.4.3 The Elimination of Administrative Legislation from the Legislative Paths for the People's Supervisor System

Having dismissed local legislation as an option for the people's supervisor system, does this completely resolve the issue? Within the central legislation hierarchy, are

[39] See Cai Dingjian. *The Development, Achievements and Problems of Local People's Congress Legislation*, National People's Congress of China, 1994.

[40] See Zhang Zhongqiu & Zhang Mingxin, *Observations and Reflections on the Division of Legislative Authority and the Operation of Legislative Power in China*, Tribune of Political Science and Law, 2000.

all three approaches—laws, administrative regulations, and departmental rules—viable? Among these three potential legislative paths for the people's supervisor system, enacting laws constitutes what is generally regarded as legislation in the narrow sense. Since its legislative body is a central state authority, we may also term this "power legislation." In contrast, the enactment of administrative regulations and departmental rules originates from administrative organs, which we accordingly classify as "administrative legislation."[41]

First, the legislative path for the people's supervisor system must be conducted at the central level based on the following fundamental considerations:

(i) The matters involved in the people's supervisor system are not confined to local affairs but are of national significance. Examining the system from a constitutional practice perspective, it has undergone nearly six years from its inception to its trial implementation, evolving from initial establishment to gradual refinement, and from pilot programs to broader application. Throughout this process, the Supreme People's Procuratorate has consistently been the leading authority, while the implementing bodies have been people's procuratorates at all levels nationwide. Given the unique nature of China's judicial system, the procuratorial system falls within the scope of the judicial framework. From the perspective of general power theory in constitutional states, judicial power maintains a relatively independent status—unlike administrative power, which is hierarchical, or legislative power, which varies by region. Legislation concerning judicial systems falls within the purview of central state organs and constitutes a national rather than local matter.

(ii) Legislation on the people's supervisor system by central-level state organs aligns with relevant legislative theory and practice. In legislative theory, the division of legislative authority assigns local legislation primarily to local affairs, while central legislation addresses national matters. In practice, China's *Legislation Law* provides that the scope of legislative authority of the National People's Congress and its Standing Committee encompasses issues such as national sovereignty, the division of authority among state organs, fundamental civil and criminal systems, and judicial systems. While some enumerated legislative matters may, under specific conditions, be delegated to the State Council for regulation through administrative rules. However, some matters absolutely preclude the State Council from exercising such authority to formulate administrative regulation under any circumstances, as these constitute matters are exclusively reserved for statutory legislation. This means that such matters can only be regulated by laws enacted by the National People's Congress or its Standing Committee.

[41] Legislation by power organs and administrative legislation are, to a certain extent, a pair of corresponding categories. The criterion for this classification of legislation lies in whether the subject enjoying legislative authority is a power organ or an administrative organ. Within China's legislative system, legislation by power organs has multiple levels, and administrative legislation is also multi-level, with both having legislation at the central level and at the local level.

Furthermore, we contend that there are clear justifications for choosing statutory law as the legislative path for the people's supervisor system.

Articles 7 to 11 of the *Legislation Law* define the scope of matters for which the National People's Congress and its Standing Committee may exercise legislative authority. Article 56 specifies the scope of matters for which the State Council may enact administrative regulations. Articles 71 and 72 clarify the scope of matters for which ministries of State Council may formulate departmental rules. Based on these provisions, which delineate the legislative scope of the three central legislative bodies, departmental rules may only address matters pertaining to the implementation of laws or those pertaining to administrative regulations, decisions, or orders of the State Council. While administrative regulations may govern the following matters: (1) matters requiring the formulation of administrative regulations to implement legal provisions—this constitutes the State Council's executive legislation; and (2) matters falling within the administrative authority of the State Council as provided in Article 89 of the *Constitution*[42]—this constitutes the State Council's functional legislation. Beyond these two categories, the State Council may also enact administrative regulations on legal matters in advance with the authorization of the NPC or its Standing Committee. The matters subject to legal regulation are defined through both enumerated provisions and general provisions, demonstrating the broad scope of legislative authority vested in the National People's Congress and its Standing Committee, as well as the significance of the matters under their jurisdiction. All the lawmaking acts by the National People's Congress and its Standing Committee constitute functional legislation.

Therefore, with respect to departmental rules, the constituent departments of the State Council lack the authority to legislate on the people's supervisor system—an innovative mechanism within the judicial framework—as to date this system has neither been established through laws enacted by the National People's Congress or its Standing Committee, nor regulated through administrative statutes by the State Council. Consequently, the constituent departments of the State Council have no legal basis for formulating departmental rules regarding this matter.

As for administrative regulations, the State Council may, in theory, engage in three types of legislative action: executive legislation based on existing laws enacted by the NPC; functional legislation under the authority granted by Article 89 of the *Constitution*; or pioneering legislation with the authorization of the NPC or its Standing Committee. In terms of executive legislation, it is impossible because the NPC and its Standing Committee have not yet actually enacted any laws on this system, leaving the State Council without a legal foundation for such regulation. In terms of functional legislation, it is excluded because Article 89 of the *Constitution* does not grant the State Council any authority over judicial systems.[43] From the perspective of

[42] Article 89 of the current *Constitution* of China provides that the State Council, as the executive organ of the highest organ of state power, namely, the National People's Congress, shall exercise extensive administrative authorities in various areas including politics, economy, culture, foreign affairs, and national defense.

[43] According to classical natural law theory, to prevent the corruption of power, legislative, executive, and judicial powers should be separated and exercised by distinct institutions. China's *Constitution*,

constitutional separation of powers, this constitutional design aligns perfectly with the doctrine of power separation. Consequently, the State Council cannot resort to its functional legislative power to regulate the people's supervisor system. In terms of pioneering legislation, while the NPC and its Standing Committee may, under certain conditions, authorize the State Council to enact in advance administrative regulations on matters that normally fall under legislative authority, judicial systems are explicitly excluded from such delegable matters. This restriction further reflects the principle of power separation. Thus, the State Council neither can nor will receive authorization to enact administrative regulations on the people's supervisor system.

1.4.4 Adoption of National Legislation for the People's Supervisor System

The people's supervisor system, as a judicial mechanism, constitutes part of the exclusive legislative authority of the state under China's *Legislation Law*. Exclusive legislative authority refers to matters that can only be regulated by law in a multi-level legislative system, with all other normative documents excluded. This ensures the people's ultimate decision-making power over critical national issues while safeguarding both the uniformity of the legal system and citizens' rights.[44] In Chinese legal scholarship, the exclusive legislative authority defined in Articles 8 and 9 of the *Legislation Law* is termed legal reservation. Legal reservation represents a fundamental principle in legislative theory, originally proposed by 19th-century German administrative law scholar Otto Mayer. Through subsequent development, it has evolved into a comprehensive framework including total versus partial reservation, constitutional versus administrative legal reservation, and absolute versus relative reservation. Matters prohibiting delegated legislation are classified as absolute reservation, while those permitting authorization constitute relative reservation.[45] Article 9 of the *Legislation Law* explicitly provides "matters concerning crimes and criminal punishments, the compulsory measures and penalties involving the deprivation of citizens of their political rights or the restriction of their personal freedom, and the judicial system" as subjects of absolute reservation. As an innovative judicial reform aiming at improving prosecutorial oversight, the people's supervisor system falls within this category. Therefore, legislative authority over this system must be exercised exclusively by the NPC or its Standing Committee through statutory law.

In accordance with relevant provisions in Article 62 and Article 67 of China's *Constitution*, along with Article 7 of the *Legislation Law*, there remain substantive distinctions between the legislative matters falling within the competence of the National People's Congress and those under its Standing Committee. Specifically:

---

in its design of Article 89, evidently incorporates this theoretical principle. For discussions on the separation of powers, see the works of Locke, Montesquieu, and others.

[44] See Ying Songnian, *The Provisions of the Legislation Law on the Principle of Legal Reservation*, Administrative Law Review, 2000.

[45] *Ibid.*

The NPC holds authority to enact and amend basic laws governing criminal justice, civil matters, state institutions, and other fundamental legal domains. While the NPC Standing Committee is empowered to formulate and revise non-basic laws, excluding those reserved for the NPC. Besides, when the NPC is not in session, the NPC Standing Committee may enact partial supplements and amendments to the NPC-passed laws, provided such modifications do not contravene the fundamental principles established in the original legislation. Therefore, the issue arises here as to whether the people's supervisor system should be governed by a basic law enacted by the National People's Congress, or by a non-basic law enacted by the NPC Standing Committee.

In accordance with the relevant provisions of the *Constitution* and the *Legislation Law*, and in light of existing theoretical views on the legislative path of the people's supervisor system, the specific legislative paths by the NPC or its Standing Committee may include the following:

First, the NPC may enact a basic law, that is, the NPC formulates a basic law specifically to regulate the people's supervisor system.

Second, a non-basic law may be enacted by the NPC Standing Committee, that is, when the NPC is not in session, the NPC Standing Committee may formulate a law—falling outside the category of basic laws enacted by the NPC—to regulate the people's supervisor system. Under this legislative path of enacting a non-basic law by the NPC Standing Committee, several possible legislative forms exist:

(i) The NPC Standing Committee may enact a standalone *People's Supervisors Law*.
(ii) The NPC Standing Committee may amend laws that are closely related to the people's supervisor system, such as the *Criminal Procedure Law* and the *Organic Law of the People's Procuratorates*.
(iii) The NPC Standing Committee may adopt a decision—similar to the *Decision of the Standing Committee of the National People's Congress on Improving the People's Assessors System*—in the form of a decision of the standing committee of the national people's congress on improving the people's supervisor system.

The following sections will focus on analyzing these five possibilities in detail, in order to ultimately determine the optimal legislative path for the current people's supervisor system.

First, the enactment of a basic law. Article 62(3) of the *Constitution* states that the power of "enacting and amending criminal, civil, state institutional and other basic laws" is exclusively vested in the National People's Congress. The *Legislation Law*, in Article 7(2), similarly recognizes NPC's exclusive legislative power. By interpreting these provisions of the *Constitution* and the *Legislation Law*, we can at least identify two points: (1) the *Constitution* and the *Legislation Law* classify legal norms into two categories: basic laws and non-basic laws, with the exclusive right to enact basic laws belonging to the NPC; and (2) basic laws at least include criminal law, civil law, and laws concerning state organs. As for the scope of other basic laws, neither the *Constitution* nor the *Legislation Law* specify them explicitly, but the author believes that, based on the provisions of Articles 8 and 9 of the *Legislation Law*, such matters should at least include issues related to national sovereignty, the system of regional ethnic autonomy, the system of special administrative regions, the system of primary-level self-governing organization,[46] the deprivation of citizens' political rights, and compulsory measures and penalties restricting personal freedom.[47] Within the scope of matters clearly defined as falling under the NPC's authority to enact basic laws, the people's supervisor system is not included. From the perspective of the nature of the people's supervisor system, it is an important measure in the judicial system reform aimed at improving the procuratorial system in China. Therefore, the people's supervisor system is part of the judicial system, not part of the fundamental criminal system. According to the principle of the rule of law, strict adherence to legal requirements is a basic demand of the rule of law; thus, there is no need for the National People's Congress to exercise legislative power over the people's supervisor system.

Next, the enactment of non-basic laws. In comparison to basic laws, the legislative power over non-basic laws is exclusively vested in the NPC Standing Committee, as clearly stated in Article 67(2) of the *Constitution* and Article 7(3) of the *Legislation Law*. Interpreting the relevant provisions in the *Constitution* and the *Legislation Law*, the following points are worthy of our attention: (1) In accordance with the content of Articles 8 and 9 of the *Legislation Law*, the matters that are exclusively within the legislative power of the NPC to enact basic laws include criminal law, civil law, laws regarding state organs, the system of regional ethnic autonomy, the system of special administrative regions, the system of primary-level self-governing organization, the deprivation of citizens' political rights, and the compulsory measures and penalties restricting personal freedom. Other matters fall under the scope of non-basic laws, which are to be enacted by the NPC Standing Committee. These matters include the expropriation of non-state-owned property, the basic economic system, and the basic systems of finance, taxation, customs, finance, and foreign trade, as well as the system of litigation and arbitration. (2) Regarding the relationship between the National People's Congress and its Standing Committee, the NPC Standing Committee is an integral part of the NPC, serving as its permanent organ. Both share the same

---

[46] From the perspective of legislative practice, normative documents regulating the primary-level self-governing organizations (a residents' committee or a villagers' committee), such as the *Organic Law of the Residents' Committee of the People's Republic of China* and the *Organic Law of the Villagers' Committee of the People's Republic of China*, are the products of the NPC Standing Committee's exercising of its legislative power. Similarly, the normative document on the system of regional ethnic autonomy, i.e., the *Law of the People's Republic of China on Regional Ethnic Autonomy* and the normative documents on the system of special administrative regions, i.e., the *Basic Law of the Hong Kong Special Administrative Region of the People's Republic of China* and the *Basic Law of the Macao Special Administrative Region of the People's Republic of China*, are the products of the NPC's exercising of its legislative power. This unequal treatment of these matters deserves further consideration.

[47] In the constitutional system constructed by modern state constitutions, the effective protection of citizens' rights is dominant compared to the correct exercise of state power, and the restriction of state power by citizens' rights is the fundamental spirit of constitutional relations.

See Zhou Yezhong ed., *Constitution*, Higher Education Press & Peking University Press, 2004, pp. 38, 149.

attributes in terms of power, but they differ in status. While both are legislative bodies, the *Constitution* confers different powers for them in Articles 62 and 67. Taking the power to enact laws and the power to enact non-basic laws as examples, the NPC has the power to enact basic laws, while the NPC Standing Committee has the power to enact non-basic laws. However, this distinction is not absolute. In terms of the NPC's status, it holds the highest position among the state organs, being the central organ of state power. From a general principle, the NPC has jurisdiction over matters within the scope of authority of its permanent body, the NPC Standing Committee. However, it couldn't be reversed. In other words, the NPC has the power to enact laws other than basic laws, but the NPC Standing Committee does not have the power to enact the basic laws that are reserved to the NPC. Therefore, the legislative power of the NPC Standing Committee over non-basic laws is relative, not absolute, while the NPC's power to enact basic laws is absolute. In terms of legislative practice, the NPC will only exercise the powers vested in the NPC Standing Committee when it deems necessary. This means that, in relation to the people's supervisor system, although the NPC, in theoretical terms, can legislate on this matter and create normative documents in the form of basic law, taking into account practical considerations and the exploration of normative documents such as the *Constitution* and the *Legislation Law*, it is more in line with the two entities' division of work distribution and functioning for the NPC Standing Committee to legislate on the system of people's supervisors. Therefore, it is both appropriate and necessary for the NPC Standing Committee to legislate on the people's supervisor system.

Furthermore, regarding the specific legislative form by which the NPC Standing Committee enacts the people's supervisor system, there exists a divergence as to whether to formulate a specialized *People's Supervisor Law*, amend relevant laws such as the *Criminal Procedure Law* and the *Organic Law of the People's Procuratorates*, or enact the *Decision of the Standing Committee of the National People's Congress on Improving the People's Supervisor System*.

First, the enactment of a specialized the *People's Supervisor Law*. Solely from the perspective of legislative efficacy, the formulation of a specialized *People's Supervisor Law* represents the most idealized legislative approach. However, considering the practical aspects of the entire pilot implementation of the people's supervisor system, the normative basis for the pilot is documents formulated by the Supreme People's Procuratorate, and the scope of the pilot is confined to the organizational framework of the People's Procuratorates. Moreover, in light of the current overall environment surrounding this system, the enactment of the *People's Supervisor Law* imposes higher procedural and substantive requirements. Consequently, the timing for the NPC Standing Committee to specifically enact a "people's supervisor law" is not yet ripe, and it would also entail greater legislative costs, which would be inconsistent with the efficiency value demanded by the people's supervisor system. Moreover, as the people's supervisor system constitutes a judicial institution, it falls under the exclusive domain of statutory regulation, making it impossible for the NPC Standing Committee to authorize the State Council to enact administrative regulations in advance. Thus, although it represents the most idealized legislative approach, the enactment of a specialized *People's Supervisor Law* is presently unfeasible under current practical circumstances.

Second, there have been numerous proposals within both academic and practical legal communities regarding the revision of the relevant provisions of the *Criminal Procedure Law* or the *Organic Law of the People's Procuratorates*.[48] These proposals argue that the opportunity of revision of the *Criminal Procedure Law* and the *Organic Law of the People's Procuratorates* shall be caught, which means based on the current feasibility studies regarding the legalization of the people's supervisor system, and by drawing upon relevant foreign practices and the legislative experience of the people's assessor system, efforts should be made to include in the elements that have already received consensus and meet the conditions for adoption.[49] For instance, He Subin, deputy to the 10th National People's Congress, proposed revising the *Criminal Procedure Law* and the *Organic Law of the People's Procuratorates* to include corresponding provisions[50]; Jin Jun, deputy to the 10th National People's Congress, proposed adding relevant provisions to both the *Criminal Procedure Law* and the *Organic Law of the People's Procuratorates* and fully integrating the people's supervisor system into the framework of the two laws[51]; similarly, Chen Wenqing proposed revising the *Organic Law of the People's Procuratorates* to include relevant provisions and fully integrate the people's supervisor system with it.[52]

Third, other alternatives have also been suggested. Aside from the above-mentioned proposals, one view advocates a three-step approach to legislating the people's supervisor system: conducting in-depth research; introducing provisions in the *Organic Law of the People's Procuratorates* and the *Criminal Procedure Law*; and enacting a *People's Supervisors Law* to provide a comprehensive and systematic legal framework.[53] Another view suggests establishing general principles in the *Organic Law of the People's Procuratorates* and making corresponding revisions to the *Criminal Procedure Law*, while deferring the decision on whether to enact a separate law for further deliberation.[54] Some proposals even go further, suggesting an revision to the *Constitution* to expressly provide that "the people's procuratorates

---

[48] In a broad formal sense, legislative activity includes not only the enactment of normative documents by the legislative body, but also the revision of existing normative documents and the repeal or abolition of those that have become invalid. When the approach of enacting a dedicated *People's Supervisor Law* proves unfeasible, turning instead to revise the *Criminal Procedure Law* or the *Organic Law of the People's Procuratorates* is considered by many to be a reasonable alternative.

[49] See Luo Changxi & Zhou Jian'gao, *Legislative Reflections on the People's Supervisor System*, People's Procuratorial Semimonthly, 2005.

[50] See Zhou Yongnian ed., *Introduction to the People's Supervisor System*, China Procuratorial Press, 2008, p. 355.

[51] See Yang Jianshun, *Deputies Call for the Incorporation of the People's Supervisor System into Law*, Legal Daily, 2004.

[52] See Zhou Yongnian ed., *Introduction to the People's Supervisor System*, China Procuratorial Press, 2008, p. 357.

[53] See Ke Hanmin, *The Legislation of the People's Supervisor System Can Proceed in Three Stages*, Procuratorate Daily, November 7, 2005, at 3.

[54] See Zhou Shimin, *Nature and Function of the People's Supervisor System*, Journal of National Prosecutors College, 2004.

shall implement the people's supervisor system" and that "serving as a people's supervisor at the procuratorate in accordance with the law is a fundamental right of every citizen, and people's supervisors shall actively fulfill their statutory duties in supervisory activities". After such a constitutional revision, the relevant provisions should then be promptly introduced into the *Criminal Procedure Law* and the *Organic Law of the People's Procuratorates.* Once conditions are ripe, the Supreme People's Procuratorate should submit a legislative proposal to the national legislature to formulate a people's supervisor law with an appropriate level of legal authority and systemic coherence.[55] Evidently, among these alternative approaches, revising the *Constitution* specifically to regulate the people's supervisor system appears to be impractical.

In the *Introduction to the People's Supervisor System* edited by Zhou Yongnian, the various legislative proposals mentioned above are systematically reviewed and evaluated, with their commonalities and divergences clearly identified.[56] The commonalities are reflected in two aspects: first, most proposals do not require revisions to the *Constitution*; second, the people's supervisor system should add corresponding provisions to the *Criminal Procedure Law* and the *Organic Law of the People's Procuratorates.* The divergences, however, lie in three respects: (1) whether it is necessary to enact a specialized or separate people's supervisor law; (2) whether the people's supervisor system should be fully integrated with the *Criminal Procedure Law* and the *Organic Law of the People's Procuratorates*; and (3) differing views on the specific content relating to the people's supervisor system that should be added to these two laws.

It is our view that these proposals of legislative path and their evaluations stem from accumulated practical experience with the operation of the people's supervisor system and hopeful expectations for its legalization. Nonetheless, the choice of legislative path for the people's supervisor system must be made based on a comprehensive consideration of China's legislative system as determined by its constitutional system, as well as the legislative models summarized from legislative practice.

1.4.5 The Choice of Legislative Path for the People's Supervisor System

The legislative paths proposed for the institutionalization of the people's supervisor system contain both reasonable elements and certain drawbacks that are untimely. As a product of judicial system reform, the people's supervisor system has a number of successful precedents from which it can draw. China's judicial system encompasses both the adjudication and procuratorial systems. The people's assessor system is closely linked to the adjudication system, while the people's supervisor system is closely linked to the procuratorial system. From the perspective of institutional

[55] See Li Zemin, Jiang Hongying & Chen Xiaodong,*Studies on the People's Supervisor System*, Administration and Law, 2004.

[56] See Zhou Yongnian ed., *Introduction to the People's Supervisor System*, China Procuratorial Press, 2008, p. 362.

correlation within the judicial system, the two systems share significant similarities. Therefore, we believe that the legislative model used for the people's assessor system may serve as a useful reference for the legislation of the people's supervisor system. Specifically, the NPC Standing Committee may adopt a decision on the people's supervisor system by drawing on the model of the *Decision on Improving the People's Assessor System.*

The people's assessor system with Chinese characteristics has undergone a lengthy evolution, growing from nonexistence to existence, from simplicity to sophistication, and from fragmented regulations to specialized legislation over the course of nearly eighty years. As a fine tradition of people's justice, the system originated during the period of democratic revolution, developed during the socialist revolutionary period, and matured during the era of reform, opening up, and modernization.[57] The legislative process for the people's assessor system in the history of the People's Republic of China has also followed a tortuous path. In 1998, the Supreme People's Court began to explore the improvement of the system through dedicated legislation. In September 2000, it submitted the first draft *Decision on the People's Assessor System* to the NPC Standing Committee for deliberation, but the proposal was shelved due to irreconcilable differences of opinion. In February 2004, the Supreme People's Court once again submitted another draft *Decision on Improving the People's Assessor System* for to the NPC Standing Committee for deliberation. In April 2004, the Eighth Session of the Tenth NPC Standing Committee conducted a deliberation of the revised draft. On August 28, 2004, after six years of discussion, drafting, review, and revision, the *Decision on Improving the People's Assessor System* was finally adopted by the Eleventh Session of the NPC Standing Committee.[58]

Although the people's supervisor system represents an institutional innovation and does not enjoy the historical tradition and legal foundation that underpin the legitimacy of the people's assessor system,[59] the two systems nonetheless share numerous similarities, mainly in the following three aspects: (1) They share the same political significance. Both systems are direct manifestations of the political rights of the people to run the country and their constitutional right to participate in the administration of state affairs under the socialist system. By allowing ordinary citizens without legal professional backgrounds to participate in the judicial process, both systems enhance the substantive reliance of the socialist judicial system on the people and embody the essential nature of judicial democracy, thereby enhancing the public's identification with the judiciary. (2) They involve the same type of

---

[57] See Wang Doudou & Qiu Donghui, *A Detailed Review of the Nearly Eighty-Year Journey of the People's Assessor System*, Legal Daily, September 6, 2007, at 8.

[58] See Si Ying, *Firmly Advancing the People's Assessor System—A Legislative Review of the Decision on Improving the People's Assessor System*, National People's Congress of China, 2005.

[59] The people's assessor system, like the people's supervisor system, finds only general rather than explicit and direct constitutional basis. While Section 7 of the *Constitution* provides people's courts and related judicial systems, it contains no specific regulations concerning the people's assessor system.

See Zhou Yongnian ed., *Introduction to the People's Supervisor System*, China Procuratorial Press, 2008, p. 363.

participants. Both people's assessors and people's supervisors are ordinary citizens drawn from all walks of life, representing a wide cross-section of the population and enjoying broad public support. Their participation introduces public perspectives, ethics, and values into the judicial process, complementing the professional thinking of judges and prosecutors. This interaction enables judicial organs to better reflect the principle of justice for the people and the pursuit of social fairness and justice, achieving a unified effect in both legal and social dimensions and promoting societal harmony. (3) They serve the same function. Both systems promote judicial fairness. The implementation of the people's assessor system and the trial operation of the people's supervisor system both place the judiciary directly under public oversight, thereby enhancing the transparency and openness of judicial activities, increasing public trust, and reinforcing the authority of judicial organs.[60] Beyond these three similarities, the people's supervisor system and the people's assessor system also share at least three additional commonalities: they operate within an isomorphic institutional framework, their oversight bodies are constituted by the people, and they employ homogeneous oversight forms.[61]

The similarities and commonalities between the people's assessor system and the people's supervisor system provide ample justification for legislating the people's supervisor system by drawing on the legislative framework of the people's assessor system. The legalization process of the people's assessor system serves as a demonstrative model for legislative paths. Following this precedent, it is unnecessary to add incorporate provisions to the *Constitution* on the people's supervisor system. Instead, fundamental principles can be added to the *Criminal Procedure Law* and the *Organic Law of the People's Procuratorates*. The NPC Standing Committee can then promulgate *the Decision on the Implementation of the People's Supervisor System*, while the Supreme People's Procuratorate, in conjunction with the Ministry of Justice, formulates detailed implementation rules thereof. Moreover, the Ministry of Justice will be responsible for establishing specific regulations concerning the selection, appointment, assessment, award, and dismissal of people's supervisors, and will collaborate with the Ministry of Finance to develop provisions for financial safeguards.[62] Regarding the choice of legislative approach, this proposal represents the most appropriate path under current circumstances. The NPC Standing Committee has institutionalized the practice of issuing decisions to regulate matters that require legal framework but are not yet mature enough or do not meet the conditions for separate legislation or legal interpretation. Compared to formal statutory enactment, this approach offers greater flexibility and encounters less resistance and lower costs, as it does not strictly adhere to the formal requirements of legal norms. Given that the legitimacy of the people's supervisor system remains more contentious than

[60] See Zhong Liming, *A Comparative Study and Reflection on the People's Supervisor System and the People's Assessor System*, at http://www.law-lib.com/lw/lw_view.asp?no=7781, last visited on June 15, 2006.

[61] See Zhou Yongnian ed., *Introduction to the People's Supervisor System*, China Procuratorial Press, 2008, p. 362.

[62] *Ibid.*, p. 365.

that of the people's assessor system, and its operational maturity is still insufficient, adopting a decision-based approach is the most feasible option. Separate legislation can be pursued once the system matures and perfects. At present, the most viable and optimal path involves revisions and legislation at the central level, followed by the formulation of specific judicial interpretations or implementation rules.[63]

2 Establishment of Legislative Principles for the People's Supervisor System

Within China's current constitutional framework, the legislative system presents multiple possible paths for enacting legislation on the people's supervisor system, from which the optimal approach should be selected. The establishment of legislative principles for this system is similarly constrained by the legislative framework determined under the nation's constitutional system. The legislative process for the people's supervisor system amounts to a systematic project, so do the selection of its legislative path and the establishment of the legislative principles. The establishment of legislative principles for the people's supervisor system is interrelated with the choice of legislative path, while also maintaining close ties with the legislative guiding thought of the state. Moreover, given the distinctive characteristics of the people's supervisor system itself, its legislative principles embody both the universal features common to all legislative principles and the unique attributes specific to this particular system.

2.1 The Relationship Between the Selection of Legislative Path and the Establishment of Legislative Principles for the People's Supervisor System

2.1.1 The Distinction Between the Selection of Legislative Path and the Establishment of Legislative Principles

As two distinct aspects of the legalization process for the people's supervisor system, the establishment of legislative principles and the selection of legislative path constitute separate legislative issues with multiple differentiating features. In terms of their essential nature, the selection of legislative path predominantly operates at the practical level, representing the concrete implementation of legislative activities. While theoretical debates undoubtedly persist regarding the legalization path for this system, the choice of legislative path remains fundamentally more practice-oriented

[63] See Qin Qianhong & Huan Ji'e, *Reflections on the Development and Improvement of the People's Supervisor System: A Comparative Perspective on the People's Assessor System and the People's Supervisor System*, Journal of Hubei Minzu University (Philosophy and Social Sciences), 2009.

than the establishment of principles. It specifically addresses the operational methodology for legislating the people's supervisor system, with all theoretical discussions ultimately serving to identify effective paths for scientifically sound and reasonable legislation. Conversely, the establishment of legislative principles belongs primarily to the theoretical domain in its essential character. Legislative principles inherently constitute theoretical propositions and postulations. However, when these theoretical propositions are adopted in the legislative practice of the people's supervisor system and expressly incorporated into normative legal instruments, they acquire significant practical operability, thereby transforming into applicable rules. Nevertheless, it remains an indisputable fact that legislative principles, as generalized and abstract rules, retain their fundamentally theoretical nature.

2.1.2 The Connection Between the Selection of Legislative Path and the Establishment of Legislative Principles

(i) The Selection of Legislative Path Determines the Establishment of Legislative Principles

The selection of legislative path for the people's supervisor system represents a practical matter concerning the specific operational approach to legislation within China's current constitutional framework and legislative system. Determining the appropriate legislative path requires clarification of relevant systemic issues, including: the subject of legislative authority, the scope of legislative authority, specific legislative procedures, and the validity of legislation. It also necessitates distinguishing between legislative paths and legislative models. In the specific legislative process, the subject of legislative authority must not only adhere to fundamental legislative principles but also establish special principles tailored to the unique characteristics of the specific legislative matter. These special principles precisely reflect the distinctive features of each particular legislative subject. Given the unique nature of the people's supervisor system, its legislation must observe both general legislative principles and corresponding special principles. The legislation of the people's supervisor system constitutes an entirely new legislative practice, whose governing principles must be intrinsically linked to and constrained by the distinctive characteristics of the system itself.

(ii) The Establishment of Legislative Principles for the People's Supervisor System Guides the Selection of Its Legislative Path

Legislative principles possess abstract and general characteristics that endow them with universal applicability. Fundamental legislative principles are binding upon all legislative matters, and the legislation of the people's supervisor system is no exception. The distinctive principles governing the legislation of this system derive from its unique characteristics and special nature, and must be strictly observed throughout the legislative process. The implementation of specific legislative activities for this system is exactly the application of these legislative principles, a product of its guidance. Specifically, the relevant provisions of the *Constitution* and the *Legislation Law* establish fundamental legislative principles. The legislation of the people's supervisor system must be conducted within the framework of China's current constitutional and legislative system, strictly complying with these fundamental requirements. Moreover, the legislative principles of this system—particularly its distinctive principles reflecting unique institutional characteristics—when embodied in the resulting normative documents, serve as effective guidance for legislative practice.

2.2 *Overview of Establishing Legislative Principles for the People's Supervisor System*

2.2.1 The Concept of Legislative Principles for the People's Supervisor System

(i) The Concept of Legislative Principles

Legislative principles constitute the aggregate of norms and rules observed by legislative practitioners throughout the legislative process. Legislative activities encompass multiple dimensions, including research and feasibility studies of legislative projects, specific procedural steps, distribution of responsibilities among legislative authorities, and delineation of legislative authority. Legislative principles emerge from the abstraction and generalization of common features across different legislative activities, forming rules universally observed by legislative authorities. These principles serve as essential standards guiding legislative entities in their activities, representing the inherent spirit and character of the legislative process itself.[64]

(ii) The Concept of Legislative Principles for the People's Supervisor System

The legislative principles for the people's supervisor system constitute the system of rules to be observed by the subjects of the legislative authority during the legislative process concerning this system. The specific legislative activities for this system generally include preparatory work such as legislative research and feasibility studies, proposal of legislative bills, deliberation and discussion of bills, as well as adoption and promulgation of legislation. Throughout these legislative activities, the legislative authorities for this system must strictly adhere to the legislative principles that embody the inherent spirit and character of legislation.

[64] See Zhou Wangsheng, *On the Legalization and Institutionalization of Legislative Principles in China*, Legal Forum, 2003.

2.2.2 Characteristics of Legislative Principles for the People's Supervisor System

First, the reflection of the regularity of legislation. Legislative regularities represent the overall requirements for legislative activities—universal demands that permeate all levels of the legislative process. For instance, the determination of the subject of the legislative authorities must consider specific national contexts and historical periods. Legislative principles precisely embody such legislative regularities. These regularities are objective and independent of human will. In the process of the legislation of the people's supervisor system, the subjects of the legislative authority must follow both fundamental principles reflecting general legislative regularities and specific principles embodying the particular regularities of this system's legislation. Under constraints of the *Constitution* and in compliance with the *Legislation Law* and other requirements, they must conduct scientific legislation that fulfills the demands of people's democracy.

Second, the normative requirements for the subjects of the legislative authority. Generally, when conducting legislative activities, the subjects of the legislative authority must research legislative projects, clarify their guiding thoughts, establish fundamental principles, and adopt specific operational procedures and legislative steps. The exercise of legislative function and power by the subjects of the legislative authority is subject to two prerequisite requirements: First, their legislative authority must be constitutionally and legally authorized. During the legislative process, they must strictly observe constitutional and legal provisions that define the boundaries of their legislative power. Second, the subjects of the legislative authority must fully respect the scientific regularities of legislation. The inherent regularities of legislative activities require that legislative bodies follow corresponding normative requirements to ensure the enduring validity of the normative documents they produce. Legislative principles constitute the concentrated reflection of these scientific regularities. In the process of the legislation of the people's supervisor system, the subjects of the legislation should thoroughly consider these normative requirements and strictly implement them to achieve an ideal state of legislation.[65]

Third, the generalization and abstraction of legislative activities. As embodiments of both normative requirements for the subjects of the legislative authority and legislative regularities, legislative principles must generalize and abstract the entire process of all legislative activities. As generalized and abstract rules, they constrain and guide the subjects of the legislative authority to legislate more effectively in accordance with legislative regularities. For the people's supervisor system, these principles constrain

[65] Jiang Guohua posits that legislation embodies both the normative life patterns and paradigms which legislators seek to guide, as well as collective expectations for public order and good customs in social life. It constitutes an ideal conduit for realizing people's noble convictions, aspirations, and value expectations.

See Jiang Guohua, *Legislation: Ideal and Transformation*, Shandong People's Publishing House, 2007, p. 319.

the subjects of the legislative authority by requiring them to strictly observe legislative authorities, follow legislative regularities, adhere to due legislative procedures, and employ appropriate legislative techniques to conduct scientific legislation.

2.2.3 Legislative Guiding Principles of the People's Supervisor System

(i) Establishment of the Legislative Guiding Thought of the People's Supervisor System

Legislative guiding thought refers to the source of understanding for the rules followed and norms established in legislative practice. Legislative thought is diverse in nature; it may be a general understanding of legislation, a systematic theoretical proposition, or, under certain conditions, even the perspective of a national leader during a specific historical period. However, only those legislative ideas that have been elevated to the will of the ruling class may serve as legislative guiding thought.

At different historical periods, the content of legislative guiding thought varies accordingly.

In the West, legislative thought during the era of ancient Greece, particularly that of Aristotle, exerted a profound and enduring influence on the legislative theories of the Western world. In the modern era, classical natural law theorists have significantly impacted contemporary legislative practices both in the West and in other parts of the world.

In the historical context of the People's Republic of China, the legislative ideas of successive national leaders—such as Mao Zedong, Dong Biwu, Deng Xiaoping, and Peng Zhen—have exerted important influence on both legislative theory and practice. The academic community has systematically studied and organized these leaders' legislative thoughts.[66] Upon sorting and summarizing these studies, it is clear that China's legislative guiding principles are reflected in the following aspects:

First, legislative work must be based on the practical conditions of China. Legislation must not only provide a basis for reforms and development across various sectors in China but also serve as an effective safeguard to ensure the realization of the fundamental principles of socialist rule of law, namely: ensuring that laws are put in place, observed, and strictly enforced and that anyone who violates the law is held to account. This requires that legislative work must proceed from actual conditions. Legislation must not be detached from the realities of China; instead, it must be grounded in the specific characteristics of China's political, economic, and cultural contexts rather than the subjective assumptions of legislators. In accordance with the requirements of scientific legislation, each stage of the legislative process—from preliminary research, initiation of legislative procedures, to the substantive

---

[66] Based on current theoretical achievements, representative works are: Sun Hongqi, *On Mao Zedong's Legislative Thought*, Theory Construction, 1993; Wu Jiayou, *An Analysis of Dong Biwu's Legislative Thought*, People's Court Daily, 2004; Yu Zhenggun & Cheng Jisheng, *On Deng Xiaoping's Legislative Thought*, Jiangxi Social Sciences, 1998; Zeng Changqiu & Peng Shuai, *On Peng Zhen's Legislative Thought*, Journal of Lingling University, 2002; and others.

operation of legislative activities—must be based on in-depth investigation and rigorous scientific evaluation. Only in this way can legislative outcomes possess lasting vitality.

Second, legislative work must follow the principle of combining leadership with public participation. In terms of its nature, legislation is the exercise of legislative authority by state organs empowered under the legal system of the country. Within the national legislative structure, the organs of legislation, as state organs, have jurisdiction over specific areas of national or local affairs, which reflects their leadership status. However, from the perspective of legislative outcomes, legislation is an activity that provides public goods and serves the public interest of society. Therefore, it cannot be separated from the participation of the general populace. Public participation in legislation is an embodiment of legislative democracy. In democratic countries, the will of the people is expressed through legislation. As an act of state political power, legislation must adhere to democratic principles. The legislative process is one of concentrating the will of the people and reflecting their interests, and the ultimate goal of legislation is to safeguard and realize the rights of the people.[67] As a socialist state under the people's democratic dictatorship, all power of the state belongs to the people. From the perspective of the nature of the state, the guiding thought that legislative work must follow the path of combining leadership with mass participation is a necessary requirement.

Third, legislative work must be conducted in strict accordance with the *Constitution* as the supreme norm. China's *Constitution* is the result of the exercise of sovereign power by the state. It defines the powers and functions of state organs, among which legislative power is one of the specific functions exercised by the legislature. Legislative work, therefore, constitutes a part of the constitutional authority of the state and is a manifestation of the people's exercise of sovereign power. The *Constitution* serves as the highest criterion for legislative activity. The normative content of the Constitution explicitly affirms this principle: "This Constitution affirms, in legal form, the achievements of the struggles of the Chinese people of all ethnic groups and provides the fundamental system and task of the state. It is the fundamental law of the state and has supreme legal force. The people of all ethnic groups, all state organs and armed forces, all political parties and social organizations, and all enterprises and public institutions in the country must treat the Constitution as the fundamental standard of conduct; they have a duty to uphold the sanctity of the Constitution and ensure its compliance."[68] Accordingly, the *Constitution*, as the supreme guiding norm for legislative work, embodies and guarantees the duty of legislative bodies to safeguard the dignity of the *Constitution* and fulfill their responsibilities in ensuring its implementation.

In summary, the guiding principles of China's legislative work may be encapsulated as follows: to take the *Constitution* as the supreme norm, to be based on the

[67] See Jiang Guohua & Yi Saijian, *On the Legislative Democracy*, Journal of South-Central Minzu University (Humanities and Social Sciences), 2007.

[68] See the 13th paragraph of the Preamble to the *Constitution of the People's Republic of China*.

actual national conditions, to integrate theory with practice, and to uphold the principles of carrying out lawmaking in a well-conceived and democratic way. In light of the particular characteristics of the legislation on the people's supervisor system, the application of these guiding principles entails special requirements. Specifically, the establishment of legislative principles, the selection of legislative approach, and the legal institutionalization of matters such as the appointment, rights, and obligations of people's supervisors must all take the *Constitution* as the supreme criterion, comply with its basic principles. Besides, it must also consider our national conditions, and strive to promote socialist democracy to the greatest extent. It is essential to mobilize all positive elements in the pursuit of scientific legislation, in order to better supervise the lawful and effective performance of duties by the procuratorial organs and to facilitate the gradual improvement of China's procuratorial system.

(ii) The Dialectical Relationship between the Legislative Guiding Thought and the Legislative Principles of the People's Supervisor System

It is manifestly necessary to elaborate on legislative guiding thought, particularly for the purpose of clarifying the distinction between legislative principles and legislative thought, as well as establishing the connection between them.

Legislative guiding principles represent a concentrated expression of ideological conceptions concerning legislation. In terms of their form of existence, such principles have always existed within the realm of human consciousness, both historically and across jurisdictions, and thus belong to the sphere of ideas. Legislative principles are generalizations and abstractions of legislative activities. They possess a universal character, reflect the inherent regularities of legislative processes, and serve as normative requirements for legislative authorities. Legislative principles may exist as concepts in the public mind or be enshrined in normative legal instruments that constitute sources of law. Once explicitly confirmed by the Constitution or legislation, they acquire a certain degree of direct operability. In academic discourse, many discussions of legislative principles in fact remain at the level of legislative thought. Only those views that are adopted by legislators and directly incorporated into statutory provisions can be transformed into concrete and enforceable legislative principles. Views that are not adopted by legislators do not attain the status of legislative principles. The decisive factor lies in whether legislative thought is accepted and codified in normative documents by the legislative body.

This very distinction, however, confirms the intrinsic connection between legislative guiding thoughts and legislative principles—namely, that legislative thoughts, and in particular legislative guiding thoughts, constitutes the intellectual source of legislative principles. Under certain conditions, legislative guiding thoughts may directly evolve into legislative principles. The condition required is that legislators adopt specific legislative guiding principles. In the legislative process concerning the people's supervisor system, it is therefore essential to take into account current academic and practical understandings of the system. Useful and rational elements from these perspectives should be absorbed and applied in legislative practice. Such ideas may serve as the intellectual foundation for the legislation on the people's supervisor system, and in appropriate cases, may even be explicitly recognized in legislative documents as formal legislative principles. This approach would help improve and refine the legislative framework governing the people's supervisor system.

2.3 *Establishment of Legislative Principles for the People's Supervisor System*

2.3.1 Rationale for the Establishment of Legislative Principles for the People's Supervisor System

(i) General Requirements of Legislative Principles

At the macro level, the establishment of legislative principles for the people's supervisor system is fundamentally constrained and shaped by China's current national conditions. At this stage, China remains in the primary phase of socialist development. This overarching reality dictates that the country is still undergoing deepening economic reform and the continuous improvement of the socialist market economy system. Simultaneously, political reform in China is progressing toward further refinement and development. On the foundation of China's rich historical and cultural heritage, and in the context of increasing interaction with the international community, there remains substantial potential for further development in the sphere of cultural construction. These national realities constitute objective factors that must be taken into full account in all legislative matters at this stage, and they embody the general principles of legislation. General legislative principles reflect the universal laws governing legislative activity. Legislation concerning the people's supervisor system must comply with the requirements of these general principles and respect the universal rules of lawmaking. China's current national conditions in the primary stage of socialism provide the most substantial practical foundation for establishing the legislative principles of the people's supervisor system. As a theoretical expression of the universal and fundamental regularities inherent in legislation, legislative principles are of great significance to legislative practice. Specific legislative principles serve both as the theoretical basis for legislative activities and as a guide for their implementation.[69] Therefore, the general requirements of legislative principles constitute the rationale for establishing the basic legislative principles governing the people's supervisor system.

(ii) The Characteristics of the People's Supervisor System

At the micro level, the legislative principles for the people's supervisor system are constrained and influenced by the inherent characteristics of the system itself. The fact that the legislation for the people's supervisor system follows general legislative

[69] See Zhou Wangsheng, *Science of Legislation*, Law Press China, 2004, pp. 42–43.

principles does not imply that the system itself is ineffective in terms of legislation. The people's supervisor system possesses its own characteristics. Although there are various interpretations regarding the nature of the system, it is generally understood that, in terms of the classification of the nature, the people's supervisor system represents the exercise of the right of supervision granted by the constitution to citizens. Its essence is a form of supervision of rights. This characteristic underscores the unique requirements of the legislation of the system. For instance, in terms of the content of the legislation, a stronger emphasis shall be laid on protecting the rights of people's supervisors, which is also in line with the fundamental requirements of modern principles of constitutional law. The legislation for the people's supervisor system, while adhering to common legislative principles, also reflects specific principles unique to this system due to its inherent characteristics. The embodiment of the characteristic forms the rationale for establishing the specific principles of legislation for the people's supervisor system.

2.3.2 Categories of Principles of Legislation for Establishing the People's Supervisor System

The theoretical basis for establishing the principles of legislation for the people's supervisor system is rooted in both the common requirements of general legislative principles and the characteristic of the system itself. In adherence to the common requirements, the legislation for the people's supervisor system, like any other legislative subject, must follow basic principles commonly adopted. In following the unique characteristics, its legislation introduces special, specific legislative principles not found in others legislative subject.

(i) Basic Legislative Principles for the People's Supervisor System

Basic legislative principles are the guidelines that all legislative activities should adhere to and consider in their legislative processes, representing key standards in the practice of law-making and fundamental legislative philosophies in practical application. Legal scholars have different opinions on the precise content of these basic legislative principles. For example, Yang Jingyu, (ex-)Chairman of the Constitution and Law Committee of the National People's Congress, believes that the following principles should guide legislation[70]: taking Deng Xiaoping Theory and "the Theory of Three Represents" as its guide; adhering to the leadership of the Communist Party of China; upholding the principle of serving the people wholeheartedly; keeping a grip on and serving to development, the top priority for the governance. In the first general textbook on Jurisprudence edited by Sun Guohua and Shen Zongling, the following basic principles of legislation are outlined[71]: grounding in China's

[70] See Yang Jingyu, *China's Legislative System, Legal Framework and Legislative Principles*, Jilin People's Congress Work, 2003.

[71] See Sun Guohua & Shen Zongling, *Fundamental Theories of Science of Law*, Law Press China, 1982, pp. 242–250.

actual circumstances under the Guidance of Marxism, Leninism and Mao Zedong Thought; upholding a leadership with masses approach; applying principles with flexibility; ensuring stability and continuity of law; considering programmatic features of socialist law when formulating legal norms. By the late 1980s, a more widely accepted view was that Chinese legislation should include the following principles: (1) seeking truth from facts, and proceeding from reality; (2) combining practical experience with scientific foresight; (3) drawing lessons from both beneficial experiences in domestic and foreign history; (4) prioritizing the greatest benefit for the largest number of people while taking coordinated action that considers overall situations; (5) unifying legal principles with flexibility; (6) upholding a system that integrates centralism on the basis of democracy with democracy under centralized guidance, and a leadership with masses approach; (7) maintaining the continuity and stability of law while coordinating the abolition, revision, and promulgation of law.[72]

Clearly, the above-mentioned various propositions regarding the basic legislative principles remain at the conceptual level and belong to the realm of legislative thoughts. They do not constitute the normative requirements that should be followed in the practice of scientific legislation. "The primary value of basic legislative principles lies in their direct practicality",[73] but legislative thoughts at conceptual level clearly cannot realize such a value. As a result, it is necessary to "select basic legislative principles from the academic outcomes and include them in the legal systems, thereby making them be laws and systems".[74] On March 15, 2000, the third session of the Ninth National People's Congress passed the relevant provisions in the Legislation Law, which established the universal requirements that the subjects of the legislative authority in China must follow, i.e., the principles of the Constitution, rule of law, democracy, and science. The significance of these provisions lies in "the transformation of the basic legislative principles from a conceptual form to a legitimate and institutionalized form."[75] It is the transformation of the conceptual theory of legislative principles into institutional and legitimate ones that provides practical rules and requirements for legislative practice, making it easier for legislative activities to meet the expected outcomes of the legislative authorities.

a. Theoretical disputes over basic legislative principles. For one thing, in China, the basic legislative principles had always been established in conceptual forms. Even though Chinese legislation has developed considerably over the past two decades, such forms of basic legislative principles "existed only in legislative textbooks and in the practice of legislators before the *Legislation Law*, and these principles had never been confirmed by law as a legislative system that must be followed."[76] For another thing, owing to the basic legislative principles remaining in the conceptual level,

[72] See Shen Zongling ed., *Fundamental Theories of Science of Law*, Law Press China, 1988, pp. 320–330; cited from Zhou Wangsheng, *Science of Legislation*, Law Press China, 2004, p. 77.

[73] Zhou Wangsheng, *Science of Legislation*, Law Press China, 2004, p. 77; Zhou Wangsheng, *On the Legalization and Institutionalization of China's Legislative Principles*, Legal Forum, 2003.

[74] *Ibid.*, p. 78; *Ibid.*

[75] *Ibid.*; *Ibid.*

[76] *Ibid.*

rather than in the law and system, differing understandings have ultimately led to an inability to reach a consensus on the basic legislative principles both theoretically and in practice. Zhang Youyu, the late renowned legal scholar in Chinese jurisprudence, believed that the legislative principles of socialist legal systems in China include[77]: legislating from reality, in a socialist way, based on socialist democracy, not draconian and focused on education. Chen Lijie, Deputy Director of the former Department of Economic Legislation of the State Economic and Trade Commission, concluded the guiding thoughts for legislation as follows[78]: (a) Legislation must align with and reflect policies of the Party and State, serving the central work of the Party; (b) Legislation must be consistent with the decisions on reforms and adapt to the pace of reforms, serving the reform process; (c) Legislation must consider overall situation, safeguarding the fundamental interests of the State and the people, while maintaining the unity of law; (d) Legislation must be based on China's specific realities, while also drawing on beneficial foreign experiences.

Theoretical propositions are always in the conceptual forms, and different propositions reflect different conceptual forms. However, for these conceptual ideas to be transformed into practical applications, a process is required. First, a systematic study of the theoretical propositions of legislative principles must be undertaken to distinguish which belong to the realm of legislative thoughts and which correspond to principles that align with the understanding of basic legislative principles. Second, the selected legislative principles conforming to legislative rules must be identified, in order to pick out universal basic principles from specific ones related to particular matters. Finally, universal basic legislative principles should be legitimate in institutions, providing applicable rules for specific legislative practices, and realizing the practice value of the basic legislative principles.

b. The establishment of basic legislative principles in legal texts. The different understandings of the conceptual forms of basic legislative principles were eliminated after the promulgation of the *Legislation Law*. The relevant provisions of the *Legislation Law* clearly established the following basic legislative principles:

1. Principle of Constitution. Article 3 of the *Legislation Law* provides, "Laws shall be made in a way consistent with principles of the Constitution." The Thirteenth Paragraph of the Preamble of the *Constitution* provides, "The people of all ethnic groups, all state organs and armed forces, all political parties and social organizations, and all enterprises and public institutions in the country must treat the Constitution as the fundamental standard of conduct; they have a duty to uphold the sanctity of the Constitution and ensure its compliance." Article 5 of the *Constitution* specifies, "No law, administrative regulation or local regulation shall be in conflict with the Constitution." The provisions of the *Legislation Law* and the *Constitution* clearly define the constitutional principle as the fundamental principles to be followed in legislative activities. The *Constitution* provides the fundamental system and task of the State

---

77 See Zhang Youyu, *Legislative Principles of Socialist Legal System in China*, Dongyue Tribune Dongyue Lucong, 1980.

78 See Chen Lijie, *On Legislative Principles and Techniques*, China Economic & Trade Herald, 1996.

and has supreme legal force. Adhering to the basic principles of the *Constitution* is the most important principle in legislative activities.[79] Modern constitutional principles generally include the principles of popular sovereignty, fundamental human rights, checks and balances of power, and the rule of law.[80] Adhering to the basic principles of the *Constitution* means that legislative activities must be carried out in accordance with these principles.

As a universal requirement, the legislation for the people's supervisor system follows the basic principles of Constitution by ensuring that it complies with the provisions of the Constitution and does not contradict the spirit and principles embodied in the Constitution. Specifically, with respect to the content of people's supervisor system, relevant legislation should focus on two key aspects: strengthening supervision over self-investigating cases by the procuratorial organs and enhancing the effectiveness of such supervision, thereby fully reflecting the principle of popular sovereignty; and enhancing the protection of the rights of the supervisory body and criminal suspects, thereby fully reflecting the principle of fundamental human rights. The *Constitution* reflects the principle of popular sovereignty through its broad protection of citizens' rights and freedoms. The supervision by people's supervisors over the "three types of cases" and the "five kinds of situations" embodies the exercise of the supervisory power granted by the *Constitution*. Strengthening supervision over these cases and granting it certain effectiveness is an implementation of the constitutional rights of citizens and an important means of realizing popular sovereignty. As the supervisory body over the "three types of cases" and the "five kinds of situations," people's supervisors, by exercising certain rights, are more diligent to perform their supervisory duties actively. The granting of these rights is a necessary condition for the effective performance of the people's supervisors' duties. Therefore, when legislating for the people's supervisor system, appropriate rights should be granted to people's supervisors. Besides, the fact that the People's Procuratorate requires people's supervisors to supervise the "three types of cases" and the "five kinds of situations" somewhat indicates that the procuratorate has, to some extent, violated its own duties and infringed upon the rights of criminal suspects. As a result, strengthening the protection of the rights of criminal suspects can eliminate violations and dereliction of duties by the People's Procuratorate, while also encouraging it to perform its duties legally and effectively. This approach results in a "win–win" situation, safeguarding the human rights of criminal suspects while ensuring the people's procuratorates perform its duties lawfully.

[79] See Zhang Shicheng, *Basic Principles of the Legislation Law and Division of Legislative Authority*, Chinese Public Administration, 2000.

[80] See Zhou Yezhong ed., *Constitution*, Higher Education Press & Peking University Press, 2004, pp. 97–114.

2. Principle of Rule of Law.[81] Article 4 of the *Legislation Law* explicitly provides, "Laws shall be made in accordance with the statutory scope of authority and procedures, on the basis of the overall interests of the country, and for the purpose of safeguarding the uniformity and dignity of the socialist legal system." Article 5 of the *Constitution* provides, "The People's Republic of China shall practice law-based governance and build a socialist state under the rule of law," and "The state shall safeguard the unity and sanctity of the socialist legal system." These provisions in the *Legislation Law* and the *Constitution* clarify the principle of rule of law as one of the basic principles that legislation must follow. China is a unitary State, and adherence to the unity of the socialist legal system is an inherent requirement of the principle of rule of law and a fundamental demand for the soundness of China's legal system and the development of the rule of law.

The principle of rule of law, as an influential concept, was first articulated by Aristotle. His view of the rule of law encompasses two meanings: first, that established laws should gain universal compliance, and second, that the laws to which people comply should themselves be well-formulated laws.[82] This view has had a profound influence and continues to be a basic principle for legislation in many countries, even directly reflected in constitutional provisions.

As a general requirement for legislative activities, the principle of rule of law emphasizes: all legislative powers and their exercises should have a legal basis, the majority of legislative processes should operate in accordance with law, and social organizations or members participating in legislative activities should act in accordance with legal norms, exercising legitimate authority and fulfilling statutory duties.[83] Practicing law-based governance and building a socialist State under the rule of law have been the guiding principle for governing the State provided by *Constitution*. The principle of rule of law for legislation requires that the legislative system be promoted first, ensuring clear legal foundations for main aspects in legislation, such as the division of legislative authorities, the structure of legislative bodies, and the operation of legislative procedures. When it comes to the legislation of people's supervisor system, it means such legislation must be developed within the current legislative system under the system of Chinese constitutionalism. It must be formulated by the subjects of the legislative authority with such power within their respective realms of authority, following the proper legislative procedures and using appropriate legislative techniques to ensure that the people's supervisor system operates within the legal framework and gains sustainable vitality. Specifically, when the Standing Committee of the National People's Congress formulated the *Decision on*

---

[81] The principle of rule of law is generally recognized as a fundamental constitutional principle. However, this specific legislative requirement derives from the *Legislation Law*. As a general constitutional principle, rule of law, also called "the governance of law", refers to the governance theory and institutional system where the ruling class legalizes and institutionalizes State affairs according to democratic principle, strictly enforcing the law. Its core elements include: governing by law, equality before the law, and opposition to privileged legal status for any organization or individual.
Ibid., p. 110.

[82] *Ibid.*, p. 7.

[83] See Zhou Wangsheng, *Science of Legislation*, Law Press China, 2004, p. 81.

Improving the People's Supervisor System, it did so based on China's current legislative guiding thoughts, utilizing the legislative authorities and procedures granted by the *Constitution* and the *Legislation Law* to ensure scientific and reasonable legislation for the people's supervisor system. This is how the legislation for the people's supervisor system adheres to and implements the principle of rule of law.

The principle of rule of law for the legislation of the people's supervisor system requires that the legislative process must have clear legal bases for each aspect of the operational mechanism of the system, and that these rules must be strictly adhered to in practice. The rule of law is a dynamic concept that not only demands the soundness of the legal system but also calls for the strict enforcement of the system to ensure its effectiveness in practice. According to the explicit provisions of the *Legislation Law*, the principle of rule of law has two main aspects: that "legislation shall be conducted in accordance with the statutory power and procedures" reflects a general character of the principle of rule of law in the legislation of modern countries; and that "legislation should be on the basis of the overall interests of the State, and to maintain the unity and dignity of the socialist legal system" emphasizes the specific characteristics of China's principle of rule of law for legislation based on national conditions.[84]

China now adopts a one-tier, two-level, multi-layered legislative system which is established by the current *Constitution* and *Legislation Law* of China. The primary purpose of this system is to fully leverage the roles of both the central government and local governments under the unified leadership of the central government, within China's sovereign territory. However, in terms of local legislation, there exists a complex arrangement, involving provincial and large city-level legislation, as well as legislation belonging to both organ of State power and administrative organ. Often, these legislations overlap, creating a complex and "impressive" situation. While this complexity allows local legislation to adapt to specific local needs, it also leads to excessive "local characteristics," which undermines the implementation of the more fundamental principle of unified legal system, solidifies local interests, disrupts the establishment of order of a single market, increases transaction costs, wastes limited legislative resources, and restricts the supply and innovation of the institutional framework necessary for social development.[85] Therefore, in the legislation of the people's supervisor system, we should avoid the path of local legislation and instead choose the central legislative path. This choice is a profound embodiment of the principle of rule of law in the legislation for the people's supervisor system.

3. Principle of democracy. Article 5 of the *Legislation Law* explicitly provides, "During the process of lawmaking, the will of the people shall be reflected, socialist democracy promoted, and participation by the people through various channels guaranteed." This provision clearly defines the democratic principle as one of the

---

[84] See Zhou Wangsheng, *On the Legalization and Institutionalization of China's Legislative Principles*, Legal Forum, 2003.

[85] See Qin Qianhong, *Is There Continued Necessity for Larger Cities' Local Legislative Power*, at http://qinqianhong.fyfz.cn/blog/qinqianhong/index.aspx?blogid=487893, last visited on June 14, 2009.

basic legislative principles. Legislation is the direct reflection of State sovereignty, expressing the will of the people. The characteristic of legislation lies in its being the result of the interests game and the concentrated embodiment of democracy. Legislation emphasizes democracy because "only on the basis of widespread democracy can the true will and interests of the people be concentrated and expressed".[86] The democratic principle that Chinese legislation should follow includes three essential elements: first, the subjects of the legislation are broad in coverage. People are the ruler of legislation, and the legislative power is ultimately for and by the people. Besides, the subjects of the legislation should be diversified, with a reasonable division and supervision system of legislative authority between central and local governments, as well as between organ of State power and that of administration. Second, the legislative content is of popularity. It aims at safeguarding the interests of the people, confirming and protecting their rights, and not based on the will of the government or a minority. Finally, the legislative process and procedures are democratic, ensuring that the people can effectively participate in legislation and express their views during the legislative process by implementing the mass line tradition.[87]

Actually, in the *Legislation Law*, the democratic principle clearly provided involves two aspects: first, the essence of the democratic principle, i.e., the legislation should reflect the will of the people, which is a universal requirement in the legislation of all countries; second, the method of implementing the democratic principle, which is to promote socialist democracy and ensure the people's participation in legislation through various channels. This is a principle of democracy for legislation with Chinese characteristics.[88]

Following the basic democratic principles in the legislation of the people's supervisor system means that more members of the public should be able to participate directly, reflecting the will and interests of the people to the full. For one thing, in the selection and appointment of people's supervisors, the system should ensure that people's supervisors who are the subject of supervision come from all walks of life, making it possible for more citizens to participate in supervising the handling of cases by the procuratorial organs. This ensures that public opinion is fully considered by the supervisory process, rather than focusing solely on "elitism" which would fail to meet democratic requirements in the supervision of people's supervisor system. For another thing, the content of legislation for the people's supervisor system should also include more provisions limiting and restricting the powers of the People's Procuratorate, protecting the legitimate rights and interests of criminal suspects, and ensuring the effective exercise of supervisory rights by people's supervisors. In terms of legislative techniques, public participation in the drafting and discussion of the legislation of people's supervisor system should be allowed when it is possible, so

---

[86] Xiao Jinming & Yin Fengtong, *On Basic Principles of Chinese Legislation*, Literature, History, and Philosophy, 1999.

[87] See Zhou Wangsheng, *Science of Legislation*, Law Press China, 2004, p. 82.

[88] See Zhou Wangsheng, *On the Legalization and Institutionalization of China's Legislative Principles*, Legal Forum, 2003.

as to ensure the widest possible engagement of public opinion and the initiative of the public. Finally, the legislative procedure should be transparent, making legislative drafts available to the public, allowing media interviews, and holding legislative hearings on issues that affect public interests.[89] Procedural justice reflects substantive justice, and the legislation for the people's supervisor system via procedural justice should ultimately ensure the substantive justice that the protection of the rights of people's supervisors and the personal rights of criminal suspects while promoting the legitimate and effective exercise of prosecutorial powers.

4. Principle of scientific manner. Article 6 of the *Legislation Law* provides, "Legislation shall proceed from reality; and appropriately and rationally prescribe the rights and duties of citizens, legal persons, and other organizations, and the powers and responsibilities of state organs" This provision of the *Legislation Law* clearly defines the scientific principle as one of the basic legislative principles. According to Zhou Wangsheng, legislation under the principle of scientific manner forms scientific legislative thoughts, viewing legislation as a science to adjust the legislative process, and eliminating misleading, trendy or outdated concepts that hinder the legislative process; solves problems at the institutional level, establishing scientific mechanism for the division of legislative authority, the organization of legislative bodies, and legislation operation; addresses practical issues, such as methods, strategies, and other technical problems.[90] Therefore, the scientific principle in legislation primarily reflects the scientific approach to legislative concepts, systems, methods, and techniques.

Adopting the scientific principle in the legislation for the people's supervisor system means that, in the legislative process, it is essential to establish guiding thoughts of legislation so as to establish scientific legislation. Under China's current system of constitutionalism, the guiding thoughts of legislation can be concluded as emphasizing highest standards of the *Constitution*, adapting to China's practical conditions, blending theory with practice, and advocating for scientific and democratic legislation. Then, it is essential to choose the legislative path of people's supervisor system to clarify the scientific direction for the legislation. Now *Decision on Improving the People's Supervisor System* formulated by the Standing Committee of the National People's Congress shall be the best path. Next, in terms of legislative methods and techniques, the legislation for people's supervisor system should be specific. For instance, in the legislative procedure, it is proper and applicable to publish drafts to the public to allow maximum participation of the public. Besides, in the legislative process, scientific planning and demonstration of the legislation of the people's supervisor system should be fully implemented and reflect the scientific nature of the system, that is, guided by scientific legislative concepts and equipped

[89] Legislative hearing generally refers to procedural rights enabling citizens to participate in political activities, influence legislative decisions, supervise public authority (legislative power), and protect legitimate interests.

See Gao Weimin, *On Legislative Hearing Rights*, Journal of Postgraduate of Zhongnan University of Economics and Law, 2007.

[90] See Zhou Wangsheng, *Science of Legislation*, Law Press China, 2004, pp. 82–83.

with scientifically structured systems, so as to meet the expected effect. "Legislation should focus on legislative effectiveness, which is the clear pursuit of scientific legislation" and "legislative actions should follow the principle of maximizing effectiveness in economics, establish and strengthen awareness of costs and benefits in the legislation."[91] By considering all these factors, a scientifically sound and reasonable legislative process and outcome for the people's supervisor system can be achieved, which is the general requirement of the basic principle of scientific legislation.

The constitutional, rule of law, democratic, and scientific principles followed in the legislation of the people's supervisor system are interdependent and complement for each other. When adhered to in the legislative activities of the people's supervisor system, these principles can ensure that the results of the legislation remain vibrant and lasting. However, if these principles are deviated from during the legislative process, the legislation of the people's supervisor system will struggle to make progress.

(ii) Specific Principles for the Legislation for the People's Supervisor System

a. Lessons from legislation in ethnic autonomous areas. Specific principles of legislation refer to the concretization and refinement of the fundamental legislative principles. They represent the requirements followed during specific legislative activities, reflecting the unique characteristics of the legislative activities of different legislative authorities. Under China's current legislative system, local legislation and legislation in ethnic autonomous areas must both adhere to the basic principles, but each follows different specific principles. For ethnic autonomous areas, the most significant characteristic of their legislation is its ethnic focus. This ethnic characteristic determines the distinctiveness of the principles followed in the legislation of these regions. Both the *Constitution* and the *Legislation Law* clearly grant ethnic autonomous areas the right to make flexible provisions in laws and administrative regulations, based on this ethnic characteristic. However, any "flexible provisions" made by ethnic autonomous areas must meet certain requirements:

First, requirement for the unity of the legal system. The formulation of autonomous regulations and local-special regulations by ethnic autonomous areas to adapt to laws and administrative regulations should not be arbitrary. These adaptions only occur when they do not conflict with the content and guiding principle of the *Constitution.* Therefore, the standpoint of legislation for ethnic autonomous areas is to uphold the unity of socialist legal systems in China. "The principle of unity of the legal system is the supreme principle for socialist legislation in ethnic autonomous areas."[92] "Any legislation in ethnic autonomous areas that deviates from the principle of unity of legal system—that is, any such legislation that conflicts with the *Constitution* or general principles of law—cannot be considered socialist legislation for ethnic autonomous areas; it would only represent division or independence of ethnic autonomous areas in

[91] Xiao Jinming & Yin Fengtong, *On Basic Principles of Chinese Legislation*, Literature, History, and Philosophy, 1999.

[92] Wang Rending, *On Basic Principles of Ethnic Legislation*, Journal of Inner Mongolia University (Philosophy and Social Sciences), 1982.

the legal system."[93] The Preamble of the *Constitution* clearly provides: "The People's Republic of China is a unified multiethnic state founded by the Chinese people of all ethnic groups",[94] and any attempt to undermine the unity of the socialist legal system or the country's territorial integrity through legislation for ethnic autonomous areas is strictly prohibited by the government and the people of all ethnic groups.

Second, requirement for ethnic autonomy. China is a multi-ethnic, unitary State. A key reason for adopting this form of State structure is the distribution and composition of ethnic groups in China. Across the nation, the majority of ethnic minorities lives in regions interspersed with the Han majority, gradually forming a situation that different ethnic groups live among each other, while some live in concentrated communities of their own.[95] Based on these facts, ethnic autonomous areas are allowed to focus on legislation that aligns with the characteristics of their local regions and ethnic groups, by which such legislation[96] can effectively implement national laws, ensuring the practical application of flexible legislation.[97] In fact, ethnic autonomous areas' legislation that aligns with the characteristics of their local regions and ethnic groups also reflects the requirement of ethnic autonomy. Moreover, it guarantees the right to equality and lawful rights and interests of various ethnic groups, as well as equity and common interests. The people's congresses of autonomous regions, as the autonomous organs, have the power of autonomy in managing economic, social, and cultural affairs by legislation, as long as these matters fall within the scope of their autonomous powers. Legislation for ethnic autonomous areas not only ensures the autonomy of the regions but also ensures the protection of that autonomy.[98] The system of regional ethnic autonomy in China is an institutional guarantee of the protection of ethnic autonomy.

Third, requirement for ethnic development. While ensuring the unity of the socialist legal system, legislation in ethnic autonomous areas should aim to promote ethnic autonomy and, more importantly, to foster ethnic development. Due to historical reasons, ethnic minority areas are generally economically and culturally underdeveloped. Helping ethnic minorities to develop their economic and cultural sectors and improving their living conditions are key aspects of promoting ethnic equality, unity, and mutual assistance, as well as important measures of regional ethnic autonomy.[99] One of the main functions of legislation in ethnic areas is to regulate social and

---

[93] *Ibid.*

[94] See 11st Paragraph of the Preamble of the *Constitution of the People's Republic of China.*

[95] See Zhou Yezhong, *Constitution*, Higher Education Press & Peking University Press, 2004, p. 240.

[96] This terminology requires clarification. Legislative power resides solely with People's Congresses in ethnic autonomous areas in accordance with the constitutional provisions. The term "ethnic legislation" is used here for stylistic convenience.

[97] See Yan Wenyi, *On Legislative Principles and Characteristics of Ethnic Autonomous Areas*, Tribune of Social Sciences in Xinjiang, 1992.

[98] Wang Rending, *On Basic Principles of Ethnic Legislation*, Journal of Inner Mongolia University (Philosophy and Social Sciences), 1982.

[99] See Zhou Yezhong, *Constitution*, Higher Education Press & Peking University Press, 2004, p. 246.

economic affairs through legal means to promote economic growth and improve the quality of life in these areas. The *Constitution* in its 11th Preamble provides: "The State makes every effort to promote the shared prosperity of all the country's ethnic groups." Similarly, the *Law of the People's Republic of China on Regional Ethnic Autonomy* provides concrete measures in the Preface to realize this goal: "the State strive to help the ethnic autonomous areas speed up their economic and cultural development in accordance with the plans for national economic and social development." These legal provisions directly provide the constitutional and legal basis for the principle of promoting ethnic development through legislation.

The establishment of specific principles in the legislation for ethnic autonomous areas indicates two key points: first, different legislative matters have their characteristics. Second, these characteristics determine the distinctiveness of the specific legislative principles, which requires special principles be followed during the legislative process. The legislation of the people's supervisor system also follows this logic. The case of legislation for ethnic autonomous areas provides a vivid example that can serve as a reference for the specific principles in the legislation for the people's supervisor system. By analyzing this case, we can derive insights into the specific or special principles that should guide the legislation of the people's supervisor system.

b. Determining by the characteristics of the people's supervisor system. What are the inherent characteristics of the people's supervisor system? This is the logical premise for establishing the special principles for the legislation of the people's supervisor system. Our basic understanding is that, as an autonomous system innovation within China's prosecutorial system, the characteristics of the people's supervisor system are embodied in the specific provisions of the system, such as the mechanisms for selecting and appointing supervisors, powers and duties, supervision methods, and the effectiveness of the supervision. These characteristics are also reflected in its relationship with other systems, such as the people's assessors system, and the special nature it has in relation to these systems. At the core of understanding, this issue is determining the nature of the people's supervisor system—what exactly is the supervisory nature of this system?

In the current practical operation of the people's supervisor system, people have developed different views on its supervisory nature based on different perspectives. A rough summary of these views includes the following representative opinions.

Some believe that the people's supervisor system is an external supervision mechanism, rather than an internal constraint of the prosecutorial system. This view holds that the system represents supervision of power by rights rather than the supervision of organs of power. It is argued that the people's supervisor system is a form of social supervision, where the people are involved in judicial activities and directly participate in supervision of individual cases, aligning with the trend of judicial democracy. This is also seen as a form of self-improvement and development within the socialist system with Chinese characteristics.[100] Others argue that the people's

---

[100] See Zhou Yongnian, *Reflections on Legal Positioning of People's Supervisor System*, Law Science, 2006.

supervisor system is a power-checking system.[101] Another perspective is that the people's supervisor system should be considered a form of social supervision—an external supervision relative to the internal supervision of the prosecutorial system. According to the regulations and pilot practices of the people's supervisor system, it has been observed that for "three types of cases", especially those of duty-related system, the involvement of a people's supervisor is mandatory, highlighting the "rigidity" of the system.[102] Some see the people's supervisor system as a flexible supervision mechanism and a quasi-external supervision system.[103] Besides, some scholars have argued that the people's supervisor system is not and shall not be an external supervision.[104] Another some believe that the essential characteristics of the people's supervisor system are mainly reflected in the following: it is a kind of social supervision, not an internal supervision and restraint of the procuratorate; the supervision with a specific scope, not a general supervision; a rigid supervision, not a general supervision.[105]

Other different understandings on the supervisory nature of the people's supervisor system will not be listed one by one here. Despite these different viewpoints, judging from those above mentioned alone, the general consensus in the academic and practical communities is that the people's supervisor system represents social supervision, though disagreements persist on whether it is external or internal supervision, rigid or flexible, and whether it is a supervision of rights or power. All of these viewpoints have their merit, but each captures only a partial truth. While they may reflect certain aspects of the nature of the people's supervisor system's supervision, they fail to present a comprehensive view of its full nature, or they may only focus the characterization but the essence of the system. However, the ought-to-be value of these theories lies in providing paradigms for understanding the nature of the supervisory system, and in fact in accumulating experience for future definitions.

Correctly defining the nature of the people's supervisor system is crucial for establishing the specific principles for its legislation. We believe that at least the following three elements should be contained when defining the supervisory nature of

[101] See Shen Zhanqun, *People's Supervisor System as Power Restraint Mechanism*, Study Times, 2005.

Shen's argument focuses on three aspects supporting his core thesis of "power restraint." Therefore, his understanding of the nature of the people's supervisor system belongs to supervision of power.

[102] Tong Jianming, *Legal Basis and Supervisory Nature of People's Supervisor System*, Procuratorate Daily, 2005.

The system's rigidity manifests through three characteristics in supervising "three types of cases": conforming to the guiding principles of the Constitution and laws, strict procedural standards, and emphasized oversight outcomes.

[103] On characterization of the people's supervisor system, see Peng Huiling, *Nature and Social Value of the People's Supervisor System*, Journal of Hainan Normal University (Social Sciences), 2004.

[104] See Zhou Hailin, *The Nature and Improvement of the People's Supervisor System*, Journal of Fujian Police College, 2004.

[105] See Luo Changxi & Zhou Jian'gao, *Legislative Thoughts on the People's Supervisor System*, People's Procuratorial Semimonthly, 2005.

the system: it should be defined in the field of China's framework of constitutionalism, with the core focus being citizen rights and State power, and its basis found in the structural and functional differences between these two.[106] Therefore, we define the supervisory nature of the people's supervisor system as rights supervision. Under this classification of rights supervision, the characteristics of the system's supervision can be summarized in the sociality or generality of the supervisory body, the external feature of supervision, and the flexibility in the supervisory effectiveness.

Firstly, the characterization of the supervisory nature of people's supervisor system is the sociality of the supervisory body, i.e., the system is primarily a social supervision system. Social supervision refers to the oversight exercised by parties outside of State organs, including political parties, social organizations, and the masses through means and ways, over the legitimacy of various legal activities such as law enforcement, judicial processes, and compliance with laws.[107] The generality of social supervision is reflected by its supervisory body encompassing all political parties, social organizations, and the masses. In practice, whether people's supervisors come from elite circles or from the broader masses, they represent the general public and are distinct from professional prosecutors. Social supervision is characterized by its non-authoritative nature—it does not rely on State's name and authority or have binding legal consequences, but instead has the characteristics of being widespread and spontaneous.[108]

Secondly, the supervisory nature of the people's supervisor system is characterized by the externality of the scope of supervision, that is, the system is an external supervision. External supervision corresponds to internal supervision. In China, in accordance with the *Organic Law of the People's Procuratorate*, the People's Procuratorates at lower level will be governed by the higher level, which determines that in the process of investigating and handling duty-related crime cases by the People's Procuratorate, the internal supervision of the procuratorial system reflects the characteristics of its power attribute, and has a hierarchical relationship between upper and lower levels. However, under the same circumstances, the people's supervisor system as the external supervision mechanism differs from the internal supervision mechanisms of the prosecutorial system. Besides, the supervisory bodies of the people's supervisor system are masses rather than professional prosecutors. The rights or powers enjoyed by the supervisory bodies are inherently different to each other. While the People's Supervisor office may be housed within the prosecutorial agency, its role is limited to coordination, feedback, and facilitation, without imposing any direct management or restraint on people's supervisors. Hence, the people's supervisor system is an external supervision independent of the procuratorate.[109]

---

[106] See Qin Qianhong & Zhou Wei, *The Nature Positioning of the People's Supervisor System under Constitutional Framework Analysis*, Law Review, 2009.

[107] See Li Long ed., *Jurisprudence*, Wuhan University Press, 1996, p. 406.

[108] *Ibid.*

[109] See Zhou Yongnian, *Reflections on Legal Positioning of People's Supervisor System*, Law Science, 2006.

Finally, the supervisory nature of the people's supervisor system is characterized by the flexible supervisory effectiveness, i.e., the people's supervisor system is a flexible supervision, which is in contrast to rigid supervision in its effectiveness. The rigidity of people's supervisor system means that people's supervisors have the binding power over supervisory opinions of duty-related crime cases handled by the people's procuratorate; otherwise, it is called the flexibility of supervisory effectiveness. In the practice of the formation and implement of the people's supervisor system, the supervisory effectiveness depends on whether the people's procuratorate accepts the supervisory opinion, which implies that the final decision lies with the people's procuratorate, and the opinions of people's supervisors are not final. This in turn indicates the flexibility of the supervisory effectiveness of this system. In addition, the flexible nature of such supervisory effectiveness is logically connected to its social nature of the supervisory bodies and the externality of its supervisory scope.

c. Establishment of specific principles for the legislation of the people's supervisor system. Matched with the characterization determined by the supervisory nature of the people's supervisor system characterized by rights supervision, the specific principles for the legislation for the people's supervisor system are expressed as social supervision, external supervision, and flexible supervision.

Firstly, on social supervision principle in the legislation for the people's supervisor system. The social supervision principle requires that the legislation of the people's supervisor system fully guarantees broad public participation in the supervision of the "three types of cases" and "five kinds of circumstances" handled by people's procuratorate and ensures judicial democracy. To implement this principle, the selection and appointment process for people's supervisors should be inclusive, selecting suitable individuals from all social strata, rather than limiting the selection to only a certain group or specific class. From an analysis of the current pool of people's supervisors, it is evident that they often come from departments such as the People's Congress or the Chinese People's Political Consultative Conference (CPPCC). They are familiar with legal affairs, so they are often seen as the "elite" of society. However, judging from the original intention of establishing the people's supervisor system, its implementation is an important task for the procuratorial organs to implement the guiding principles of the 17th National Congress of the Communist Party of China to promote the reform of the procuratorial system in the reform of the judicial system, achieving fairness and justice in the whole society.[110] Therefore, restricting the selection and appointment of people's supervisors to just a few elite groups clearly does not achieve the goal of judicial reform, and it would not contribute to the realization of true social fairness and justice, nor would it effectively supervise the prosecutorial power. As such, the normative regulations in legislation for the selection and appointment of people's supervisors are an important criterion to be followed in the legislation of the people's supervisor system.

---

[110] See Zhou Yongnian ed., *Introduction to the People's Supervisor System*, China Procuratorate Press, 2008, p. 12.

Secondly, on external supervision principle in the legislation for the people's supervisor system. The external supervision corresponds to internal supervision. While the boundary between the two lies in the apparent differences in their respective supervisory bodies and the latent differences in the rights and powers they hold, this does not mean that, in the legislative process, the rights of people's supervisors cannot be clearly defined. In fact, the original intention of making of the people's supervisor system by the Supreme People's Procuratorate was to allow external citizen rights to restrict the internal power of the prosecutorial system. Based on this, it is crucial during the legislation of the people's supervisor system to clearly define the different rights enjoyed by the external supervisory bodies, as opposed to the rights of the prosecutorial system itself. This distinction forms another important criterion to be followed by the legislative bodies in the legislation of the people's supervisor system.

Thirdly, on flexible supervision principle in the legislation of the people's supervisor system. The rigidity and flexibility of the supervisory effectiveness of the people's supervisor system are relative in some extent. On the surface, the effectiveness of the people's supervisors' opinions depends on whether the people's procuratorate accepts them, which makes the supervision effectiveness appear flexible. However, "this does not mean that the procuratorial organ can arbitrarily decide whether or not to accept the supervisory opinions."[111] This requirement calls for the regulation of the relationship between people's supervisors and the people's procuratorate to ensure that the people's supervisor system can effectively perform its function in practice. As a specific principle to be followed, the principle of flexible supervision provides guidelines for the people's supervisor system to legislate the relationship between people's supervisors and procuratorial organs. It requires that the original intention of designing the people's supervisor system be fully considered in the content and regulations of legislative normative documents to effectively supervise the exercise of procuratorial power. This effective means of supervision also fully protect the rights of people's supervisors in a timely manner, which is also in line with the modern principle of constitutional law of limiting State power through citizen rights.

The above-mentioned principles of social supervision, external supervision and flexible supervision in the legislation of the people's supervisor system naturally align with one another. This consistency unifies the system under the overarching framework of rights supervision. As a supervisory system of rights, the people's supervisor system is developing towards greater emphasis on voluntary participation, democracy, procedural fairness, and externality from the citizenry.[112]

Together with the basic principles of the people's supervisor system, these specific principles form a cohesive and indivisible framework for the legislation of the people's supervisor system, establishing a set of rules for the legislative process.

---

[111] Qin Qianhong & Zhou Wei, *The Nature Positioning of the People's Supervisor System under Constitutional Framework Analysis*, Law Review, 2009.

[112] *Ibid.*

Chapter 5
Institutional Framework for the Legislation of the People's Supervisor System

1 Selection, Appointment and Removal Mechanism of People's Supervisors

The scientific construction of the selection, appointment and removal mechanism for people's supervisors necessitates addressing the following interrelated propositions: the determination of the competent authority responsible for their selection, appointment and removal, which is pivotal to defining the institutional nature of the people's supervisor system; the delineation of eligibility criteria for candidates, balancing the imperative of social representativeness against the need for professional expertise to ensure supervisory efficacy; the procedural design of the selection and appointment process, which must adhere to the principle of procedural fairness intrinsic to the system; and the establishment of management and removal mechanisms to impose rational constraints on supervisors, thereby safeguarding accountability and integrity as inherent requirements of the institution.

1.1 Establishment of the Selecting and Appointing Entity for People's Supervisors—The Model of Appointing People's Supervisors by the Standing Committee of the People's Congress

Under current regulations, people's supervisors are typically selected and appointed by procuratorial organs after recommendations from the Party Committee, the National People's Congress, the Chinese People's Political Consultative Conference, and related organs. While this approach serves as a stopgap measure, it cannot avoid the tendency of procuratorial organs to favor certain candidates during the selection

Q. Qin, *Legislative Research on the People's Supervisor System*,
https://doi.org/10.1007/978-981-95-7972-3_5

process. "It also risks transforming the external supervisory force of people's supervisors, a form of heterologous supervision, into homologous supervision",[1] thereby undermining the effectiveness and impact of supervision. As above mentioned, the people's supervisor system is defined as an independent external supervision mechanism distinct from procuratorial organs. To ensure its independence, people's supervisors should be appointed by an entity outside the procuratorial organs and remain independent of it. This shift from an "internal" to an "external" system is essential to create distance between the supervisors and the supervisees, thereby enhancing the authority and efficacy of supervision.

From the perspective of China's current judicial system, it is more reasonable and feasible for the standing committee of the people's congress to undertake the selection, appointment, and management of people's supervisors.

First, the selection and appointment of people's supervisors by the standing committee of the people's congress has a legitimate legal basis. In accordance with relevant laws,[2] local standing committees as permanent bodies of local people's congresses are empowered to ensure the application of the Constitution and laws within their respective jurisdictions. The establishment of the people's supervisor system embodies the exercise of social supervision power by the public, which constitutes a statutory right. In safeguarding the transformation of statutory rights into substantive rights, local people's congresses should play a pivotal role. Furthermore, in accordance with the *Organic Law of the Local People's Congresses and Local People's Governments of the People's Republic of China*, the local people's congresses have the authority to decide on matters related to political democracy and legal system development within their administrative regions. By designing institutional frameworks for the selection and appointment and management of people's supervisors within their statutory powers, local standing committees of the people's congress are exercising their functions and powers under the authority scope.

Secondly, the standing committees of the people's congresses may, through the selection and management of people's supervisors, make the supervision of procuratorial organs by the people's congresses more concrete. Given the abstract and macro-level natures of the NPC's supervision over procuratorial organs, such supervision often becomes merely procedural. By placing the selection, appointment and management authority of people's supervisors under the standing committee of the people's congress, the NPC can gain a comprehensive and direct understanding of procuratorial work. This approach achieves an organic integration of the "macro-to-specific" supervision model, while also enhancing the authoritativeness of the people's supervisor system. Consequently, it promotes greater transparency and legalization in the participation of people's supervisors in the supervision process.

Lastly, under China' current legal framework, "the people's supervisor is preferably conducted through the same power source selection and appointment model".

---

[1] Liu Qingsheng, *Research on the Reform of the System of the Selection, Appointment and Management of the People's Supervisor*, Social Sciences Hunan, 2008.

[2] See Article 44 of the *Organic Law of the Local People's Congresses and Local People's Governments of the People's Republic of China.*

This is because "adopting an independent institution appointment model would first require establishing a separate entity, which must be formed in accordance with the law, involving complex issues such as organizational structure and staffing. In contrast, the same power source appointment model aligns with China's institutional framework. China's procuratorial organs are legal supervision organs. They shall be created through the people's congresses and shall be responsible to them and subject to their supervision. If people's supervisors are appointed by the people's congresses, then both procuratorial organs and people's supervisors share the same source of power. This makes the system simpler to implement, with strong practicality and operational feasibility".[3]

However, scholars have questioned the selection and appointment of people's supervisors by the standing committee of the people's congress: "while this approach appears to combine the social supervision of people's supervisors with the supervisory power of the people's congress to enhance supervision effectiveness, it overlooks the dual constitutional role of the people's congress as both the legislative organs and supervisory organs. When the standing committee appoints people's supervisor, it may convert their oversight into an extension of state power supervision, which fundamentally contradicts the original intent of establishing a social and rights-based supervision mechanism. Furthermore, this arrangement could make people's supervisor subordinate to state power organs, effectively creating a channel for the people's congress and its standing committee to influence how procuratorial organs handle individual cases. The resulting relationship between people's supervisor and the people's congresses at all levels and their standing committees would resemble a rigid hierarchy where superior bodies control subordinate ones. Such intervention would extend congressional supervision into litigation procedures, disrupting the balance among litigation parties and undermining both the status and authority of congressional supervision."[4] In addressing these concerns, a fundamental distinction must be drawn between the congressional selection and appointment of people's supervisor and the representative exercise of supervisory power by people's supervisors. The "selection and appointment" process constitutes a procedural mechanism for qualification determination, deriving its normative value from institutional neutrality. The concept of "representation", by contrast, constitutes a de facto authorization between power-exercising entities and their source of power. Crucially, the relationship between the standing committee and people's supervisor does not constitute an affiliated one. The appointment framework by standing committees serves primarily to resolve the inherent conflict of interest in self-supervisory mechanisms within procuratorial organs. People's congress organs maintain no participatory role in case-specific supervision exercised by people's supervisor, with the relationship of the two parties is one of guidance and being guided, and there is no confusion or interference regarding supervisory power. This will not necessarily lead to people's

[3] Wang Xin, The *Preliminary Study on the People's Supervisor System*, at http://www.scdujiangyan.jcy.gov.cn/xuestantao/rmjdy.htm, last visited on July 3, 2009.

[4] Liu Qingsheng, *Research on the Reform of the System of the Selection, Appointment and Management of the People's Supervisor*, Social Sciences Hunan, 2008.

congress organs bringing supervision into judicial proceedings from outside them by controlling people's supervisors, and even less will change the nature of people's supervisors as social supervision.

1.2 Establishment of the Scope of the Selection and Appointment for People's Supervisor: Adopting "Popularization" as the Criterion

Since the inception of the system, there has been debate over whether the scope of the selection and appointment of people's supervisor should follow an "elitist", "popularized" or "moderate" approach.[5] Proponents of "popularization" argue that the supervision exercised by people's supervisor embody social supervision rather than professional supervision, aligning with the intrinsic nature of the people's supervisor system. Advocates of the "elitist" approach contend that the purpose of establishing the people's supervisor system is to enhance the supervisory capacity of procuratorial organs. Therefore, people's supervisor should possess considerable legal expertise and professional competence to facilitate effective communication with legal professionals in procuratorial organs. The "moderate" approach maintains that people's supervisor should exhibit a degree of "specialization" while retaining "public accessibility". An overemphasis on either "specialization" or "public accessibility" would be unbalanced.[6]

Should the selection and appointment of the people's supervisor be based on popularization, elitism or the moderate approach between the two? We maintain that "popularization" shall constitute the fundamental criterion for the selection and appointment of the people's supervisor. This principle entails two essential aspects: firstly, regarding the nature of the system, the selection and appointment of the people's supervisor shall not constitute the establishment of an expert supervision mechanism, nor shall it aim to form a highly specialized legal team to oversee procuratorial work; secondly, the selection and appointment process should focus solely on candidates possessing the basic characteristics of social representation, allowing for identification across state organs, social groups, enterprises, public institutions, and grassroots democratic management entities, without restriction to specific social members with particular qualifications. Consequently, during the pilot implementation of the people's supervisor system, current practices of selecting an d appointing

[5] See Zhou Shimin, *Nature and Function of the People's Supervisor System*, Journal of National Prosecutors College, 2004; Yao Qiang & Mei Yisong, *Discussion on Controversial Issues of the People's Supervisor System*, Law Science, 2005.

[6] See Dai Zhongxiang, *Exploration of the People's Supervisor System*, Exploration and Free Views, 2005; Zhang Lang, *Discussion on Theoretical and Practical Issues of the People's Supervisor System*, Justice of China, 2005; Wu Weidong, *On Establishing a Dual Selection and Appointment Model of Popularization and Specialization for People's Supervisors*, Journal of Guangdong Institute of Public Administration, 2007.

supervisors exclusively from lawyers, NPC deputies, civil servants, or other legal professionals should be discontinued.

1.2.1 Adopting "Popularization" as the Standard of the Selection and Appointment of the People's Supervisor Possesses Value Legitimacy

The construction of a system of constitutionalism is premised on the fundamental principle that state power originates from the authorization by the people. In Western societies, the modern criminal justice system ensures the value legitimacy of judicial processes precisely through the effective participation of ordinary citizens, as "the jurors' partial ignorance of the law has been regarded, to some extent, as a virtue and complement in criminal trials".[7] The popularization of the people's supervisor essentially facilitates the participation of ordinary citizens from grassroots society in the state power system, with the foundation of their supervision being characterized by civilian nature and sociality. The underlying rationale is to create a novel approach that integrates "the rational standards of ordinary people into prosecutorial law enforcement. This concept stems from an ancient assumption about human nature: the innate sense of justice and moral intuition are not monopolized by any specific social class or group".[8] Moreover, from a teleological perspective, the popularization of the people's supervisor contributes to achieving broad representation and equality among supervisory entities. Conversely, while an elitist approach to selecting people's supervisors may enhance the quality and authority of judicial outcomes, it carries inherent drawbacks: the cognitive frameworks and perspectives of legally trained elites often closely resemble those of prosecutors. This similarity may result in supervisory conclusions that mirror the views of professional prosecutors, thereby leading to partiality in oversight.

1.2.2 The Logical Paradox: The Debate between "Popularization" and "Elitism" in Selection and Appointment

The rationale behind the "elitist" approach to selecting people's supervisors lies in the assumption that complex criminal cases require a comprehensive legal knowledge framework. Consequently, proponents argue that people's supervisors must possess corresponding educational qualifications, particularly legal expertise. However, this raises a fundamental question: "What is the purpose of establishing people's supervisors? Is it truly because prosecutors lack sufficient legal proficiency, necessitating external oversight by individuals with superior legal acumen? If so, an expert advisory committee would suffice—why institute a people's supervisor system at

---

[7] *Ibid.*

[8] Liu Qingsheng, *Research on the Reform of the System of the Selection, Appointment and Management of the People's Supervisor*, Social Sciences Hunan, 2008.

all?"[9] Here, it is essential to distinguish between the value legitimacy of appointing people's supervisors and the operational effectiveness of their supervisions. The "elitism" argument is grounded in the premise that the work of the people's supervisor is specialized; without such specialization, the legal and social functions of the system may be compromised. Notwithstanding the closer examination, this argument derives from an effectiveness-based assessment rather than a legitimacy-based justification. The efficacy of a system and its inherent legitimacy are considerations at different layers—much like how an autocratic ruler might still advance social and economic development. Thus, this perspective exhibits partiality, conflating functional outcomes with institutional validity.

The popularization of selecting and appointing the people's supervisor constitutes the fundamental premise for the legitimate existence of the people's supervisor system, representing a primary-level proposition pertaining to value judgment, without which the system would forfeit its essential attribute of legitimacy. By contrast, the specialization of selecting and appointing the people's supervisor relates to supervisory functions as a secondary-level proposition concerning effectiveness evaluation, and substituting value judgment with effectiveness assessment would render the system institutionally unsustainable. Specially, "while the supervisory functions necessitate certain knowledge standards for the people's supervisor, this should not be misconstrued as demanding that they be intellectual elites or legal experts so as to avoid contravening the principle of popular nature. For candidates meeting the popular representation criteria, post-selection training can equip them with the essential legal knowledge, fundamental principles, and basic methodologies required for their duties, with such specialized legal knowledge requirements being intrinsically linked to the functional specialization of supervision, the independence of supervisory deliberations, the procedural nature of supervisory activities, and the comprehensive scope of supervisory content".[10]

Therefore, in designing the selection criteria for the people's supervisor, the system shall not require them to be legal elites with sophisticated professional competence, but should instead provide that candidate possess basic cognitive capacity and ordinary judgment of values and rationality. The qualification requirements under Article 5 of the *Provisions of the Supreme People's Procuratorate on the Implementing the People's Supervisor System (Trial)* should be amended to "basic cognitive and expressive abilities", while simultaneously establishing a training mechanism for the people's supervisor to achieve the optimal combination between institutional legitimacy and supervisory effectiveness. Specifically, the training system should incorporate both initial and annual training programs: initial training refers to professional legal instruction organized by the selecting and appointing authority for newly selected and appointed supervisors prior to their official assumption of duties; annual training constitutes periodic instruction for incumbent supervisors throughout their

[9] Zhang Huaishun & Wu Minglei, *Reflections on the Selection and Appointment of People's Supervisors*, Justice of China, 2008.

[10] Liu Qingsheng, *Research on the Reform of the System of the Selection, Appointment and Management of the People's Supervisor*, Social Sciences Hunan, 2008.

tenure. The training curriculum shall cover fundamental legal knowledge relevant to supervisory activities, supervisory procedures, work discipline, and professional ethics.

Furthermore, in light of the institutional characteristics of the people's supervisor system, specific political qualifications and capacity requirements may be established for the people's supervisor. Under the current normative framework, the people's supervisor must uphold *the Constitution of the People's Republic of China* and possess the right to vote and stand for election that align with China's political system and should be retained in subsequent legislative developments. Simultaneously, referencing the civil law standard that recognizes full civil capacity at age 18, the minimum age for the people's supervisor should be reduced from the current 23 to 18 years. This adjustment may both expand the pool of eligible candidates and eliminate the existing arbitrariness in the system, ensuring consistency with statutory provisions. The current "healthy body" requirement should be abolished as it contravenes constitutional equality principles and lacks operational feasibility. In summary, the qualifications for the people's supervisor should be provided as: (1) supporting the Constitution of the People's Republic of China; (2) possessing the right to vote and standing for election; (3) reaching the age of 18; and (4) having basic cognitive and expressive capacities. Additionally, individuals "who have received criminal punishment, are under criminal investigation, have been dismissed from public office, or are subject to disciplinary probation"[11] shall be ineligible for appointment.

1.3 Procedural Design for the Selection and Appointment of the People's Supervisor by the Standing Committee of the People's Congress

With respect to the selection and appointment procedures for the people's supervisor, central legislation should establish only fundamental principles, while allowing local standing committees of the people's congresses to formulate specific implementation measures tailored to regional conditions. The standing committee may establish a dedicated the people's supervisor's selection and appointment commission to oversee the selection, appointment, and removal of the people's supervisor. The specific appointment process shall comprise the following stages: First, the qualifications, quota, procedures, application methods, and timeline for the people's supervisor shall be publicly announced through local media outlets. Second, preliminary candidates shall be identified through a dual-channel system combining self-nomination and recommendations by relevant entities or social organizations. Following evaluation by the selection and appointment commission, the shortlisted candidates shall be submitted to the standing committee for final determination. Finally, the standing committee shall publicly disclose the proposed list of the people's supervisor for

[11] See Article 6 of *the Provisions of the Supreme People's Procuratorate on the Implementing the People's Supervisor System (Trial).*

scrutiny before formal confirmation, with the chairman of the standing committee issuing official certificates to the appointed supervisors.

1.4 Regulation and Removal Mechanisms for the People's Supervisor

1.4.1 The Establishment of the Regulatory Organs for the People's Supervisor

The "management" of the people's supervisor encompasses substantive administrative functions such as appointment and removal, disciplinary actions, and dismissal, as well as service-oriented functions, including the confirmation of supervisors for individual cases, archiving of supervisory opinions, and facilitation of supervisory activities. Substantive management constitutes an evaluation of the qualifications and competence of the people's supervisor, while service-oriented management pertains to the coordination and facilitation of their work. Given the external nature of the supervisory authority exercised by the people's supervisor, substantive evaluations must remain entirely independent of the people's procuratorates to safeguard the autonomy of their oversight functions. Future legislation on the people's supervisor may designate the standing committee of the people's congress as the authority responsible for their appointment, removal, disciplinary actions, and dismissal.

As for the existing people's supervisor offices, their roles should be strictly defined as that of a service and coordination organ. These offices shall utilize their professional expertise to guide the supervisory work of the people's supervisor, convey their opinions, facilitate communication between supervisors and procuratorial organs, and ensure compliance with supervisory resolutions by relevant procuratorial departments. Additionally, the offices may be granted the right to propose disciplinary actions or dismissal of the people's supervisor to the standing committee, though they shall hold no direct decision-making authority in such matters.

1.4.2 Conditions for the Removal of the People's Supervisor

Legislation should categorize the removal of the people's supervisor into voluntary removal and compulsory removal. Voluntary removal refers to termination under statutory conditions, primarily encompassing resignation in accordance with the law, the occurrence of circumstances rendering the individual unsuitable to serve, and the expiration of the supervisor's term. To ensure supervisory efficacy and impartiality, the term of office for the people's supervisor should not exceed two years, with no eligibility for reappointment.

Compulsory removal applies when a people's supervisor fails to fulfill statutory supervisory duties or engages in serious misconduct during supervisory activities, warranting dismissal by the competent organs. Specific conditions may include: absence from two or more supervisory activities without justification during the term of the deputy, or engagement in fraudulent practices or other unlawful conduct during supervision, resulting in adverse consequences. In such cases, the appointing organs shall terminate the supervisor's appointment. The people's supervisor office shall retain the authority to propose the removal of a supervisor to the appointing organs.

2 Rights and Obligations of the People's Supervisor and Other Supervision Participants

A legal relationship is, in essence, a relationship of rights and obligations. To a certain extent, the core issue of the people's supervisor system lies in defining the rights and obligations of the people's supervisor and other participants in the supervision process. Under the current normative framework of the people's supervisor system, the provisions governing the rights and obligations of the people's supervisor and other participants remain ambiguous and fragmented, with scope for expansion in the scope of these rights. Consequently, in subsequent legislative design, clarifying the rights and obligations of the relevant entities within the people's supervisor system will be instrumental in standardizing the system itself and enhancing its operational efficacy.

2.1 Rights and Obligations of the People's Supervisor

2.1.1 Definition of the Rights of the People's Supervisor

"Supervision constitutes a developmental process of negation and reaffirmation, with reasonable doubt serving as the subjective impetus for the exercise of supervisory authority".[12] Fundamentally, the premise of supervision by the people's supervisor lies in their skepticism toward the exercise of power by procuratorial organs, representing an additional layer of oversight over existing internal supervisory mechanisms. In essence, all rights of the people's supervisor may be characterized as a right to challenge, bearing certain attributes of public power. Logically, a valid challenge shall be grounded in reasonable standards, scientific methodologies, and mechanisms to monitor outcomes. Consequently, the people's supervisor system, rooted in the right to challenge, shall adhere to the general principles governing such challenges. Within this framework, the right to challenge may be further delineated as follows: the right to information regarding the subject of supervision, serving as the basis for

[12] Qiu Jinghui, *The Powers, Responsibilities and Safeguard Mechanisms of People's Supervisors*, at http://www.dffy.com/faxuejieti/zh/200406/20040624212829.htm, last visited on June 15, 2009.

reasonable judgment; the right to supervise self-investigating cases, ensuring scientific methodologies in oversight; the right to request review and the right to monitor outcomes, providing mechanisms for accountability; the right to personal freedom and the right to remuneration, safeguarding the external conditions necessary for effective supervision.

(i) Right to Information of the People's Supervisor

The exercise of the right to information inherently embodies attributes of civil society, representing a dynamic interplay between society and the state under constitutional governance. Conceptually framed, if the right to information serves as a mathematical medium, its two essential components must necessarily be civil rights and state power. Granting the people's supervisor the right to information concerning the rationale and procedures of procuratorial organs in exercising prosecutorial power constitutes both a fundamental prerequisite for sound value judgment and a basic safeguard for the system's operational legitimacy. When categorized substantively, this right to information manifests as the right to access case-specific information relevant to supervision, and the right to know the evidence and legal reasoning applied in cases.

The right to information regarding supervised cases shall be expressly recognized in legislation, entitling people's supervisors to access fundamental case details, including the basic facts of the case, the case-handling department, and the case-handling officer. This right shall encompass the right to question relevant prosecutor for detailed explanations and to observe the interrogation or questioning of suspects and witnesses by case-handling officer, thereby enabling comprehensive understanding of the case. Furthermore, the people's supervisor shall be granted the direct right to interrogate suspects and witnesses to ascertain relevant case information. It shall be clarified that conferring this right through legislation does not equate to recognizing independent investigative authority for the people's supervisor, but rather serves the purpose of facilitating their thorough comprehension of the case. In this context, scholars have noted that current legal provisions restrict access to detention facilities such as detention centers to authorized personnel, a qualification people's supervisors inherently lack.[13] To address this, legislation may provide that people's supervisors, when necessary,[14] may enter detention facilities accompanied by relevant procuratorial personnel to question suspects regarding case facts.

The right to information concerning the application of evidence and legal reasoning in cases shall be statutorily guaranteed, entitling people's supervisors to inquire with the case-handling department regarding the rationale for disposition decisions and the specific legal provisions applied. This right shall include the right to pose follow-up questions to the responsible officers and to demand explanations on the interpretation of the invoked legal norms. Where doubts persist, the people's supervisor may seek separate consultations with legal experts or practitioners without

---

[13] Zhou Yongnian, *Introduction to the People's Supervisor System*, China Procuratorial Press, 2008, p. 149.

[14] It shall be limited to the purpose of understanding the case facts.

obligation for immediate determination. Concurrently, the right to review all legal instruments relevant to case disposition conclusions shall be expressly conferred.

(ii) The Supervisory Right of the People's Supervisor

The supervisory right vested in people's supervisors differs fundamentally in juridical nature from statutory supervisory powers. Whereas legal supervision constitutes a form of rigid supervision that inherently belongs to the domain of public power, the supervisory right of the people's supervisor is strictly confined to the right to articulate evaluative opinions concerning case facts and legal application, thereby furnishing referential input for procuratorial organs' final determinations. In essence, such right embodies procedural supervision characteristic of civil rights rather than state power. This right specifically comprises five constituent elements: the right to initiate supervision procedures, enabling people's supervisors to lawfully commence oversight processes; independent exercise right, guaranteeing unimpeded performance of duties free from interference by any institution, groups or individual, with their qualifications revocable solely under statutory conditions, a safeguard reflecting the system's foundational purpose; commenting right, permitting substantive evaluation of both factual and juridical aspects of cases; voting right, facilitating formal resolution of divergent opinions through democratic consultation; and the right to submit supervisory opinions, requiring procuratorates to duly consider collective conclusions. The existing normative framework of the people's supervisor system has established these rights through operational protocols that demonstrate significant referential value for future legislative refinement, particularly in balancing supervisory efficacy with procedural legitimacy.

(iii) Right to Request Review and Right to Monitor Outcomes

Given the relationship between the supervisory right of the people's supervisor and the prosecutorial power of procuratorial organs, the final disposition of self-investigating cases shall remain within the exclusive purview of procuratorial organs. It shall be emphasized that without any mechanism to monitor final determinations, the people's supervisor system may risk becoming merely a superficial formality. Accordingly, legislation should provide that when the procuratorial organ's final disposition diverges from the supervisory opinions submitted by the people's supervisor, the latter shall possess the right to raise objections. However, given the procedural nature of their supervisory role, such objections shall be confined to procedural significance, specifically, the right to demand that the relevant procuratorial organ conduct reconsideration or review and render a new decision. Furthermore, the people's supervisor shall be granted the right to ongoing outcome monitoring, including the right to report or file complaints with disciplinary inspection authorities upon discovering violations of law or discipline by relevant departments in handling duty-related crime cases.

(iv) Right to Personal Liberty and Right to Remuneration

These two rights fundamentally constitute extrinsic safeguards essential for the regular exercise of supervisory right by people's supervisors. The right to personal liberty entails protection for supervisors' oversight activities and related expressions during the performance of their duties, ensuring freedom from unlawful deprivation or restriction of personal freedom and safety. The right to remuneration refers to the entitlement to receive financial compensation for participation in supervisory activities, including standard remuneration and reimbursement for lost wages, as prescribed by law.

2.1.2 Establishment of Obligations for People's Supervisors

Within the framework of legal relationships, rights and obligations are inherently interconnected. Jurisprudentially, "legal obligations, as requirements governing the conduct of social actors, are ostensibly and perceptibly defined by legal rules [...] Legal obligations constitute requirements imposed on social actors to perform or abstain from specified conduct".[15] The essence of legal obligations thus lies in these prescriptive or prohibitive requirements, which derive from value-based legal judgments and are expressly codified in normative provisions. The People's Supervisor System originates from the fundamental pursuit of judicial justice, while empirically the "acts" and "omissions" of people's supervisors shall align with existing institutional norms and conform to the criminal procedure framework. Consequently, the obligations of people's supervisors serve both the ideal of judicial justice and the imperative demands of the national institutional system. Accordingly, the obligations of people's supervisors may be categorized into the duty to uphold judicial impartiality and the duty to safeguard institutional functions and the legal order.

(i) Obligation to Uphold Judicial Impartiality

Judicial impartiality entails unbiased conduct in judicial proceedings. To fulfill this obligation, people's supervisors shall first adhere to defined value assessment standards to ensure the equitable exercise of their supervisory functions, which fundamentally serve to safeguard the proper implementation of prosecutorial power and preserve social equity and justice. Second, their deliberative conclusions shall be strictly grounded in verifiable legal bases and factual determinations, free from subjective preferences. Third, to guarantee the integrity of deliberations, people's supervisors shall observe the fundamental principle of "recusal for conflict of interest", abstaining from participation in cases where impartiality may be compromised, and refraining from unauthorized contact with case parties or their representatives. Lastly, they shall neither interfere with fellow supervisors' voting nor blindly conform to others' opinions, but rather maintain unwavering adherence to objective facts in service of judicial impartiality.

(ii) Obligation to Comply with the National Legal System

The People's Supervisor System shall adhere to mandatory national norms. Given the nature of duty-related crimes, the supervision process may involve extensive

---

[15] Yao Jianzong, *Jurisprudence: General Legal Science*, China University of Political Science and Law Press, 2006.

confidential information concerning the operational systems and procedures of state organs. Consequently, people's supervisors are obligated to strictly observe relevant national laws, safeguard state secrets, and refrain from disclosing any case-related information or details of deliberations and voting.

Additionally, people's supervisors shall rigorously comply with the prescribed regulations governing their duties, including adherence to fundamental case supervision procedures, and may not unjustifiably abstain from or evade participation in supervisory deliberations. However, since the obligations of people's supervisors are constrained by imperative national laws, the legislative framework should place greater emphasis on safeguarding their rights to enhance the system's operational efficacy.

2.2 *Rights and Obligations of Suspects and Other Litigants*

Within the criminal procedure legal framework, suspects are endowed with a systematic set of rights, including but not limited to the right to request recusal, the right to legal assistance, the right to apply for bail pending trial with restricted liberty of moving, the right to petition for lifting compulsory measures, and the right to file appeals. Under the People's Supervisor System, however, the rights of suspects should primarily revolve around enhancing the effectiveness of supervision, thereby ensuring targeted protection. To this end, legislative provisions should "emphasize respect for suspects' procedural choice and participation rights, embodying the dual principles of combating crime and safeguarding human rights".[16] Specifically, suspects should be granted the right to initiate supervision, the right to present case statements, defense right, the right to be informed of supervision outcomes, and recusal right.

Right to request supervision initiation and to file petitions or complaints. Under the current people's supervisor system framework, the initiation of supervision over the "three types of cases" typically occurs through notification by procuratorial organs to people's supervisors, placing the right to commence supervision with the procuratorate. This initiation mechanism fails to ensure comprehensive case coverage by people's supervisors, effectively granting procuratorial organs discretionary control over case selection. Consequently, legislative consideration should be given to empowering suspects with the right to request supervision over these "three types of cases".[17] Regarding cases involving the "five types of situations", which require verification of authenticity by relevant sectors, suspects who identify such circumstances should be granted the right to petition or lodge complaints with people's supervisors, thereby enabling the lawful initiation of supervision procedures by the supervisors.

---

[16] Zuo Weimin & Wu Weijun, *People's Supervisors: Deepening and Developing the Concept and System*, People's Procuratorial Semimonthly, 2005.

[17] It generally applies to cases where the suspect disagrees with the arrest decision.

Right to present case statements and defenses. The recipients of such statements and defenses should be people's supervisors rather than procuratorial organs, corresponding to the supervisors' authority to interrogate suspects regarding case facts. The content of these statements and defenses should be strictly limited to factual accounts of the case and the suspect's personal understanding of the events.

Right to be informed of supervision outcomes. This entails the suspect's right to access information concerning supervision outcomes related to their case. Specifically, "the supervisory opinions of people's supervisors and the disposition decisions of the people's procuratorate shall be read to the suspect, with written records prepared and signed by the suspect."[18]

Right to request recusal. As a fundamental requirement of judicial impartiality and a basic litigation right, this empowers suspects to seek recusal of any People's Supervisor who has an interest in the case or other circumstances potentially compromising impartiality.

The obligations imposed on suspects primarily consist of a duty of truthful disclosure, which is strictly limited to the factual circumstances of the "three types of cases" and "five types of situations" themselves, excluding other case details. Expanding the scope of this obligation may "violate the principle of procedural non-action obligations for suspects and undermine safeguards for the right to silence".[19]

Within the framework of people's supervisors' oversight activities, additional participants in the supervision process may include parties with direct interests in the case, suspects' legal representatives, victims, private prosecutors, plaintiffs in incidental civil actions, incidental civil litigation agents, defense counsel, and witnesses. Consequently, the protection of these litigants' rights constitutes an essential consideration in the design of the People's Supervisor System.

First, rights of relevant participants to lodge complaints and petitions, and right to request recusal. The concerned participants shall possess the right to file complaints and petitions with people's supervisors regarding the "five types of situations" in self-investigating cases, thereby initiating statutory supervision procedures. For instance, victims may report cases that fail to file a case that should be filed, while witnesses may report instances of evidence obtained through coercion, both of which shall be incorporated into the formal supervision process.

Second, participants with a substantive interest in the case outcome shall have the right to request recusal. For example, where victims face non-confirmation or non-enforcement of legally mandated criminal compensation decisions, or where people's supervisors have a conflict of interest or other circumstances potentially compromising impartiality, such participants may demand the supervisors' recusal.

---

[18] Zhou Yongnian, *Introduction to the People's Supervisor System*, China Procuratorial Press, 2008, p. 170.

[19] Liu Meixiang, *Analysis of Suspects' Obligations*, Journal of Southwest University of Political Science and Law, 2007.

2.3 Obligations of Relevant Departments of Procuratorial Organs

2.3.1 Obligations of Case-Handling Officer in Procuratorial Organs

The relationship between rights and power inherently manifests as a dynamic of checks and balances. Within the normative framework of the People's Supervisor System, the realization of rights by people's supervisors and other supervision participants necessarily entails constraints on prosecutorial power. To safeguard the effective exercise of such rights—including but not limited to the right to information, supervisory right, right to request case review, and right to personal liberty by people's supervisors, as well as rights of other case participants—legislation shall expressly define the corresponding obligations of case-handling officer in the procuratorial organs.

First, the obligation to notify. This primarily entails informing people's supervisors of the essential details of cases subject to supervision, including the identity of the case-handling officers, and providing relevant case materials to the supervisors. Given the operational responsibilities of case-handling officers, the legislative framework may provide that such materials shall be transmitted to the people's supervisor office for subsequent delivery to the supervisors. Additionally, officers shall notify all case participants of their respective rights, including informing suspects of their right to request supervision by people's supervisors, and advising suspects and interested parties of their right to seek recusal of supervisors. Finally, officers are obligated to disclose supervision outcomes to suspects and other case participants.

Second, the obligation to accept supervision. This entails, first, providing people's supervisors with an overview of the case structure and key evidentiary materials; second, explaining the applicable legal provisions, including the interpretation and jurisprudential basis for their application; and finally, responding to all inquiries raised by the supervisors, arranging their attendance during the interrogation of suspects and examination of witnesses, and when necessary, facilitating direct questioning of relevant case participants by the supervisors.

Third, the obligation to ensure supervisory impartiality. Prosecutorial departments shall refrain from interfering with the independent deliberation of cases by people's supervisors and shall maintain the confidentiality of deliberation outcomes. For cases subject to reconsideration or review initiated by supervisors, prosecutors shall provide full cooperation.

Furthermore, given the distinctive nature of the "five types of situations", case-handling officer shall promptly examine and verify supervision matters raised by people's supervisors, communicate the results without delay, and maintain readiness for ongoing supervision.

2.3.2 Obligations of the People's Supervisor Office

By nature, the people's supervisor office functions as a working organ dedicated to facilitating the supervision activities of people's supervisors. Consequently, its obligations are primarily coordinative and service-oriented in character.

The Office bears the obligation to impartially determine case-specific supervisors, ensuring neutrality through randomized selection procedures.

It shall assist people's supervisors by accepting supervision applications, inviting their participation in duty-related crime meetings and law enforcement inspections, and providing necessary working conditions to safeguard their rights to information, personal liberty, and remuneration while preserving their operational independence. The Office is further obligated to organize supervision activities, including timely notification of schedules and venues, as well as scientific arrangement of case deliberation sessions.

Additionally, the Office shall oversee procuratorial organs by ensuring case-handling units fully cooperate with supervision procedures, prepare complete case materials, and diligently implement supervisory conclusions. For cases involving the "five types of situations", it assumes the duty to properly channel and process relevant supervision materials.

The Office also undertakes ancillary responsibilities, including maintaining supervisor rosters, archiving case files, documenting supervision activities, coordinating with superior and subordinate offices, and executing tasks assigned by the chief procurators or procuratorial committee.

3 The Scope of the People's Supervisor Supervision

The scope of the people's supervisor supervision is definitely provided in Articles 13, 14, and 15 of *the Provisions of the Supreme People's Procuratorate on the Implementing the People's Supervisor System (Trial)*, all of which pertain to cases directly investigated by procuratorial organs. Specifically, the people's supervisor should perform the duty to cases (a) where the procuratorate plans to withdraw the case, not to prosecute, or where the criminal suspect object to a decision on arrest; (b) situations where, the procuratorate, in handling cases directly accepted by the people's procuratorate, fails to file a case when it should file, unlawfully detains suspects beyond statutory limits, conducts illegal searches, seizures or freezes of property, fails to recognize or enforce criminal compensation as required by law, or where procuratorial personnel engaged in misconduct, abuse of power, or corruption; and (c) certain circumstances where the people's supervisor may also be invited to participate in other activities of supervision to law enforcement by the procuratorate in handling duty-related crime cases, and may provide suggestions and opinions to any violations of laws or regulations. In summary, the aforementioned scope of the people's supervisor supervision can be referred to as the "three types of cases," the "five type of situations," and the "one category of circumstance."

The *Provisions* defines the people's purcuratorate self-investigating cases as the main supervisory subjects of supervision, offering significant reference value for future legislation. However, during the trial implementation of the people's supervisor system, academia has also engaged in reflection and reconstruction of the scope of supervision. Meanwhile, local regulations on the system of the people's supervisor vary in their definitions of supervisory scope, even affecting the understanding of the nature and fundamental direction of the system. Therefore, discussing the scope of supervision of the people's supervisor and clarifying the essence of these disputes are of vital importance for determining the legislative orientation of the system. This book holds that the legislative confirmation of the scope of the people's supervisor supervision should not be defined solely from a certain perspective of the system's existence, nor should it remain a utopian vision supported by abstract theoretical foundations. Instead, it should be based on the purpose of the system's existence, comprehensively considering its actual operation and relationship with the procuratorial system, so as to clarify the scope of the people's supervisor supervision. On this basis, we believe that defining the scope of the people's supervisor supervision in terms of the "three types of cases", "five types of situations," and "one circumstance" is an appropriate choice in accordance with current conditions. Of course, with the advancing of judicial democracy reform, the scope of the people's supervisor supervision remains potential for further expansion in future legislation.

3.1 Debate on the Scope of the People's Supervisor Supervision

During the pilot implementation of the people's supervisor system, there have been divergent views regarding the scope of supervision exercised by the people's supervisor, commonly categorized as the "Expansion Theory" and the "Contraction Theory."

The representative view of the expansion theory holds that the scope of supervision should be extended beyond self-investigating cases by procuratorates to encompass all criminal cases, which means that the people's supervisor be entitled to perform its duty of supervision over all stages of criminal proceedings and to all litigation participating institutions. The part of proponents of the aforesaid theory argues that: "In a holistic view, non-self-investigating cases should also be included within the scope of supervision by the people's supervisor… The procuratorial organs are following the proper course to facilitate citizens' participation in or supervision of its judicial decisions through establishing the people's supervisor system, but should not limited its scope to self-investigating cases by procuratorates. With the implementation of pilot programs and the accumulation of experience and exercise, the Supreme People's Procuratorate should actively propose legislative recommendations to the national legislature and formulate the *People's Supervisor Law* with legal authority, thereby expanding the scope of supervision to cover ordinary cases and embodying the principle of procedural justice."[20] Scholars of the theory also express their opinions, from the perspective of protecting the fundamental rights of parties, to further justify expanding the scope of supervision that "solely emphasizing the supervision of self-investigating cases by procuratorates may lead to procedural injustice, as criminal suspects and victims in different types of cases suffer unequal treatment. A suspect who is arrested in a self-investigating case by procuratorates can have the arrest decision supervised by the people's supervisor if they object, whereas suspects arrested upon approval by the procuratorate in other cases lack such a remedy. This discriminatory treatment based on the nature of the offense is unfair to suspects."[21] Other scholars note that although the full expansion of supervision to all aspects of the procuratorate's authority may take time, there still remain rooms for expansion in at least three areas: (a) Supervision over passive exercise of procuratorial powers. For example, when the procuratorate fails to supervise the police fails to file a case that should be filed or fails to object erroneous judgments or rulings by the court that should be objected; (b) Supervision over unlawful external interference. People's supervisors should supervise cases involving external power interfering with case handling and assist the procuratorate in overcoming difficulties; (c) Supervision over other improper conducts of the procuratorate. Supervision to people's procuratorates who abuse their power during case investigations should be enhanced.[22] Regardless of their specific justifications, all expansion theory arguments go beyond the existing scope limited to the "three types of cases" and the "five types of situations."

In contrast, advocates of the contraction theory propose narrowing the scope of supervision, particularly by removing "cases where criminal suspects object to arrest decisions" from the supervision scope. Their reasons include: (a) Arrest is merely a procedure in criminal litigation and a measure of enforcement, intended only to prevent subsequent crimes or escape. It does not impact the substantive outcome of the case; (b) Supervision to objections to these cases constitutes mid-procedural supervision, which may negatively affect subsequent legal processes. Since a suspect can only object after the people's procuratorate has made and executed the arrest decision, the investigation process will have already moved into the next phase; (c) The arrest involves complex conditions, such as whether a sentence of imprisonment or higher is likely and whether arrest is necessary, issues involving legal interpretation and investigative expertise that the people's supervisor may not be qualified to assess.[23]

Both the expansion and contraction theories offer reasonable perspectives, yet each has its limitations.

---

[20] Zuo Weimin & Wu Weijun, *People's Supervisors: Deepening and Developing the Concept and System*, People's Procuratorial Semimonthly, 2005.

[21] Yuan Zhi, *A Comparative Study of the People's Supervisor System and Japan's Prosecution Review Commission*, at http://review.jcrb.com/zyw/n98/ca179602.htm, last visited on May 5, 2009.

[22] Dan Wei, *A Proper Understanding of the People's Supervisor System and the Solid Promotion of Procuratorial Reform*, People's Procuratorial Semimonthly, 2004.

[23] See Cheng Dewen & Wang Hongnan, *An Analysis of the Supervisory Scope of the People's Supervisor System*, Fangyuan Rule of Law Special Issue on People's Supervisors, 2006.

Firstly, both views approach the supervision scope from a single perspective. The expansion theory is rooted in the ideal of equality of litigation rights for participants in criminal proceedings but lacks consideration for the practical foundation and systemic integration of an expanded supervisory scope. Its idealism is evident. Conversely, the contraction theory emphasizes operational difficulties but overlooks the fact that practical challenges are not the fundamental reason of denying a system. At its essence, the contraction theory raises issues about how the system should operate, rather than whether the scope of supervision should change at all. With institutional optimization, these practical difficulties could be better addressed.

Secondly, both theories fail to accurately define the nature of the people's supervisor system. Advocates of the expansion theory aim to fully protect participants' rights in criminal proceedings and envision "a comprehensive supervisory system that ensures equal access to remedies for both suspects and victims, thus promoting fairness and justice in society".[24] However, many issues have to be solved such as the definition of nature of parties' litigation rights; decision in protecting all of parties' litigation rights or in facilitating parties' litigation remedy; understanding of relationship between protection of parties' litigation rights and supervision of the society; and the boundary and effectiveness of social supervision in protecting parties' litigation rights. This view challenges the basic framework of the current criminal procedure system and raises social concerns about the legitimacy of supervisory powers. The contraction theory's proposal to remove "object to arrest decisions" from the scope of supervision conflicts with the fundamental principle of human rights protection. It severely weakens the supervisory role of the people's supervisor by excluding arrest-related issues from their supervision. Therefore, taking into account both the theoretical and practical shortcomings of the expansion and contraction theories, it is not advisable to alter the current scope of supervision at this stage.

3.2 An Analysis of the Rationale for Defining the Scope of Supervision by the People's Supervisor

In order to resolve the ongoing debate surrounding the scope of supervision exercised by the people's supervisor, it is necessary at the current stage to adopt the supervisory scope explicitly provided in Articles 13, 14, and 15 of the *Provisions of the Supreme People's Procuratorate on the Implementing the People's Supervisor System (Trial)* as a legislative reference in the future. This approach is not only necessitated by the intrinsic characteristics of the system but also follow the organic logic and evolutionary path inherent in institutional development.

[24] Xu Qianquan, *Several Issues Concerning the Supervisory Scope of the People's Supervisor*, Journal of Yunyang Teachers College, 2009.

3.2.1 Institutional Origins and Purposes: The Supervisory Scope Should Remain Unchanged

Pursuant to Article 129 of *the Constitution of the People's Republic of China*, "The People's Procuratorates of the People's Republic of China are state organs for legal supervision." Within the criminal proceedings system, this right to supervise manifests primarily in two dimensions: right to supervise over criminal investigation and right to supervise over judicial adjudication. Specifically, the people's procuratorates exercise its investigative supervision over the Public Security Organs through case-filing and arrest approval, and its judicial supervision over the people's courts through the right to protest and the right to supervise judgment. Therefore, the people's courts may exercise legal judgment over the prosecutorial authority of procuratorial organs through judicial proceedings. At the same time, the investigation of the procuratorates over duty-related crimes remains in a state of external supervision. This power without oversight bears the risk of abuse. Against this backdrop, and with a view to safeguarding human rights and enhancing the fairness of judicial processes, the Supreme People's Procuratorate decides to establish the people's supervisor system to enable external supervision of its handling of duty-related crimes. It not only embodies the essence of rule of law and value orientation of constitutionalism but also forms an institutional innovation to respond to the accountability vacuum in prosecutorial investigations.

The people's supervisor system, therefore, emerges as a mechanism to balance the unlimited exercise of the procuratorial power, with its institutional design explicitly targeting self-investigating cases. By introducing social oversight into an area previously devoid of external checks, it achieves a synthesis of external and internal supervisions, as well as of right and power supervisions mechanisms. If the system were now to expand its supervisory scope beyond self-investigating cases by the people's procuratorates, a convincing normative and practical foundation should be established. In light of pre-existing statutory supervision at the stage of some judicial proceedings, the necessity and legitimacy of introducing an additional layer of societal superversion should be critically examined.

3.2.2 Outcomes of the People's Supervisor System: Expansion Is Unnecessary

As previously articulated, the people's supervisor system constitutes a form of right supervision, which lacks binding legal force by its position. Its authority is inherently inferior to authority supervision as provided by law, and its performance is also inferior to that between state organs. Superficially, an expanded supervisory scope may appear to enhance supervision over related cases, which empowers the social supervision over the fields that statutory supervision has already supervised; however, in substance, it would represent a waste of resources giving supervisory activities a merely symbolic function, thereby undermining its effectiveness and efficiency.

3.2.3 Conflict Between Procedural and Substantive Justices in the Expansion of Supervisory Scope

In contemporary discourse on evidentiary standards in criminal proceedings, procedural justice theory, as a critical counterpoint to traditional substantive approaches, has increasingly gained traction. This theory foregrounds the legitimacy of legal procedures and emphasizes the decisive role of litigation process (including the evidentiary process) in determining facts.[25] Procedural justice has, to a certain extent, become synonymous with judicial fairness due to its establishment and development. Nevertheless, procedural justice must be grounded in substantive justice; absent such grounding, it risks degenerating into a hollow or incomplete form of justice. Proponents of expanding the supervisory scope argue that the litigation rights of criminal suspects differ substantially across case types, resulting in de facto inequality. Consequently, they advocate for the extension of the people's supervisor' jurisdiction to promote procedural equality among suspects.

However, in accordance with the *Criminal Procedure Law*, investigations of non-self-investigating cases by procuratoial organs are conducted by public security organs, and these investigations are already subject to statutory supervision by prosecutorial organs such as case-filing and investigative supervision, as well as other statutory supervision by the people's courts and higher people's procuratorates. Introducing these litigations into people's supervision would result in a dual-layered supervisory system for such cases, while investigations of duty-related crimes by the procuratorial organs would remain only under the people's supervisor supervision. Such asymmetry could engender a new procedural inequity and affect the legitimacy of judicial outcomes, creating new forms of differential treatment contrary to the aims of justice.

3.2.4 The Rule of Institutional Development: Adherence to Gradualism of Institutional Reform

"Analogous to technological innovation, institutional reform follows a path characterized by increasing remunerations and the self-reinforcing mechanism, which renders a system or institution on its way and tends to be reinforced through subsequent developments... Establishment and operation of a system or institution typically unfolds through five stages: conceptual design, pilot testing, model adjustment, normative structuring, and full-scale implementation[26]". While introducing the concept of "path dependence" from the field of economics into legal reform remains a further discussion of its standpoint, the general principle of gradualism in these two fields in institutional development remains similar. Following the intrinsic rule of institutional

---

[25] Wu Hongyao, *The Basis of the Standard of Proof in Criminal Cases: Procedural Justice or Substantive Justice*, Legal Daily, 2001.

[26] Xu Hanming, *An Economic Analysis of the Concept and Characteristics of the People's Supervisor System*, Fangyuan Rule of Law Special Issue on People's Supervisors, 2005.

development facilitates us encounter considerably less pressure and difficulties in institutional operation.

The establishment of the people's supervisor system is a direct response to the absence of effective supervision over self-investigating cases by the procuratorial organs. To now extend supervisory scope to the entirety of criminal proceedings, encompassing all case types, would entail a fundamental re-positioning of the legal supervisory system. Such an undertaking would require not only a reallocation of powers among the supervision, procuratorate and judgment of National People's Congress, but also a reconsideration of the status of the people's supervisor's supervisory power within the current legal framework. From an institutional perspective, the expansion of supervisory scope is not merely a matter of legal technique. Rather, it would necessitate legal revisions or interpretations of fundamental criminal law. The social costs of such reforms would be significant, while the potential social benefits remain to be specified. It is in accordance with the gradualism of institutional development that we keep the current supervisory scope at first and then make prudent decision to optimize the institution after its fulfillment of certain social value.

3.3 Conclusion

Upon a comprehensive analysis of both the rationale behind and the practical effects of the current supervisory scope, this study contends that retaining the existing parameters of the people's supervisor system is the most appropriate approach at present, which reflects not only the considerations in the original institutional design, but also the imperative of maintaining overall equilibrium within the supervisory framework. Nonetheless, this conclusion does not preclude the possibility of future expansion. In the long run, introducing social supervision into the judicial process and enhancing transparency of judicial activities represent inevitable trends. It is reasonable to believe that, through the rational reallocation of the authority between legal supervisions and social supervisions, the latter will yield increasingly beneficial outcomes.

4 Supervisory Procedures of the People's Supervisor

In the current legislative design, it is still inappropriate to comprehensively expand the scope of supervision exercised by the people's supervisor. The primary focus should remain on the supervision of the "three types of cases" and the "five types of situations." Although the methods of supervision over these two fields are generally similar, there are still essential differences: supervision over the "three types of cases" is essentially a judgment on judiciary outcomes, emphasizing supervision of individual cases, while supervision over the "five types of situations" evaluates the prosecutorial conduct, focusing on supervision of judiciary activities. Therefore, regulatory frameworks for the people's supervisor system should provide separate procedures for supervision of these two fields.

4.1 Procedural Design for the Three Types of Cases

From the logical progression of a people's supervisor's involvement in a case, the supervision procedure may be structured into the following stages: initiation of supervision, pre-procedures of supervision, deliberation and voting of supervision, handling of supervisory outcomes, feedback of supervisory outcomes, and review procedures.

4.1.1 Initiation of Supervision

The procedure of supervisory initiation designed in this book mainly provides that the people's supervisor are entitled to initiate supervision and the procuratorial organs are obligated to provide necessary helps for activities.

Regarding the supervisory initiation in cases where criminal suspects contest a decision of arrest, the approach of *the Provisions of the Supreme People's Procuratorate on the Implementing the People's Supervisor System (Trial)* can be adopted. In the provision this entails a conditional supervision mechanism: if a suspect contests an arrest decision, the case should first undergo a re-examination by the investigative supervision department. If the suspect accepts the decision or the original arrest decision is withdrawn following reassignment and review, the supervisory initiation needs not to be activated. This approach aims to utilize the internal error-correction mechanism of the procuratorial organ to save judicial resources.[27] However, if the procuratorial organ upholds the original arrest decision after reviewing, the suspect or their representatives, defenders, etc., must be informed of their right to request supervision by the people's supervisor. Upon such a request, the supervisory initiation may be activated.

A mechanism should be established for the people's supervisor to initiate supervision for the procuratorial organs via the people's supervisor office. To protect the right to information, before any final decision is made in a "three types of cases" matter (except those contesting arrest decisions, which are post-supervision), the procuratorial organs should regularly provide detailed case materials to the people's supervisor through specific means. The people's supervisor may have the right to make decision to initiate the supervisory procedure.[28] The people's supervisor also can initiate supervision for the "three types of cases" after having a complete understanding for

[27] In view of the common occurrence of objections by criminal suspects to arrest decisions, the conditional referral of such cases to people's supervisors serves to minimize blind supervision and substantially improve its efficiency.

[28] However, granting people's supervisors with the authority to initiate supervisory procedures raises certain technical challenges—specifically, whether the procedure should be initiated by designated

the case in response to information from suspects, close relatives, their representatives and defenders. To enhance communication between the people's supervisor and the public, necessary information for communication with the people's supervisor should be published via media to facilitate public complaints. Once the supervisory initiation is triggered, the people's supervisor office should notify the relevant departments to transfer the case materials for the supervisor.

4.1.2 Pre-procedures of Supervision

Once the supervisory initiation is triggered, a confirmation process is required to determine the people's supervisor participating in the case. Currently, supervisors are selected either by random draw or by predetermined order. The random draw method is preferred, as it better ensures the impartiality of supervision. The reasons include that if selection solely follows a predetermined order, the identity of future supervisors could be anticipated, compromising neutrality; while random draw, except to the fluctuation of selection probability, ensures the impartiality for the supervisory outcomes. Thus, the Office should confirm the supervisors through random draw from the supervisor list, selecting an odd number (typically three; five for complex or difficult cases). This selection should be determined within two days of initiation and supervisors should be notified of the date and location of supervision at least two days in advance. The authority handling the case must inform the parties and their representatives within 24 h after the selection,[29] including notice of their right to challenge against the supervisors.

The procedure of filing challenge divided in two situations: (a) Supervisors may voluntarily challenge themselves; (b) suspects or other parties of interest may also challenge with the procuratorial organs. Challenge should be made before supervision begins, by the suspect, their statutory agent, or defense counsel. As current regulations lack specific provisions on the form and timing of such requests, a consultation procedure should be established, wherein the case handler informs the parties of their right to challenge before supervision begins, and any written feedback is promptly submitted to the people's supervisor office.

As for grounds for challenge, Article 23 of the Provisions can be adopted.[30] Although some scholars suggest adding three circumstances, in accordance with the

---

supervisors or any individual supervisor. We contend that any people's supervisor should be granted the authority to proactively initiate the supervisory mechanism ex officio in order to ensure the system's effectiveness. At the same time, in cases where supervisors do not initiate such procedures, relevant departments of the procuratorial organs should transfer materials to the people's supervisor office and submit to supervision as a supplementary measure. It must be emphasized that if the procuratorial organs fail to fulfill its obligation to guarantee the supervisors' right to information, the procedural design allowing supervisors to initiate supervision would be rendered meaningless.

[29] The relevant time-related provisions are primarily based on Zhou Yongnian ed., *Introduction to the People's Supervisor System*, China Procuratorial Press, 2008, p. 210.

[30] In accordance with this provision, in any of the following situations, the people's supervisor participating in case supervision shall voluntarily recuse, and the parties to the case and their legal representatives shall have the right to demand the recuse: (a) where the people's supervisor is a party

Provisions of the Supreme People's Court on Strict Implementation of Withdrawal System by Judicial Officers promulgated by the People's Supreme Court in 2001, that (a) meet one of the parties to the case or any of their agents or defenders privately without approval; (b) accept property or other benefits from the parties to the case or from their entrusted persons; (c) accept treats from the parties to the case or the entrusted persons, or participate in various activities with their expenses paid by the parties to the case or the entrusted persons,[31] we think such adjustments is inappropriate currently. The reasons for that include: First, the people's supervisor differs from judicial officers in its legal nature. And then, they exercise a right rather than judicial power, and do not have final decision-making authority. Furthermore, existing provisions already cover "other interests that may affect impartiality," making additional grounds unnecessary.

Decisions on challenge should be made by the people's supervisor office and provided in writing to the applicant before supervision begins.

4.1.3 Deliberation and Voting of Supervision

During this stage, supervisors, in accordance with the current related provisions, should first elect a presiding supervisor to facilitate the sound operation of proceedings involving deliberation and voting.

The formal supervisory procedure makes progress through three stages in time order: hearing of opinions, deliberation, and voting.

Hearing of opinions refers to the process where the case handler presents key facts, evidence, legal application, legal interpretation, and intended resolution to the supervisors. Supervisors may question to case handler, where supervisors deem necessary may attend hearings with suspects, witnesses, or defense counsel, or directly question these parties. Some scholars advocate for an "objection-based" approach where the supervisors act as neutral evaluators between the prosecutor and the defense in terms of case facts and application of laws. The trial process is integrated into the consultation phase with people's supervisors, where the judicial body adopts a deliberative model. People's Supervisors preside over the examination of arguments between the procuratorial organs and the suspect, as well as their representatives or defense counsel, regarding the facts of the case and the application of law.[32] However, at this stage, we believe it is not yet appropriate to take overly ambitious steps in the reform process, based on that first, by nature, people's supervisors do not possess

or a close relative of a party to the case; (b) where the people's supervisor or a close relative people has an interest in the case; (c) where the people's supervisor has served as a witness, expert witness, defender or litigation representatives in the current case; or (d) where the people's supervisor has any other relations with a party to the case that could affect the impartial performance of supervisory duties.

[31] Cheng Weigang et al., *Designs on Improving the Procedures Related to the People's Supervisor System*, Law Science, 2006.

[32] See Ji Weidong, *Reflections on the Practice of the People's Supervisor System*, People's Procuratorial Semimonthly, 2005.

the legal attribute to exercise discretionary judgment. Second, the "objection-based" approach also raises questions about how it should be integrated with the statutory powers of the procuratorial organs. Therefore, in the current legislative framework, it is only feasible to provide that people's supervisors may, if deemed necessary, hear opinions from criminal suspects and their authorized representatives regarding case facts. Legislation could adopt the provision: "Where deemed necessary, people's supervisors may, with the cooperation of the procuratorial organs, enter detention facilities to question criminal suspects or interview their authorized representatives, witnesses, and other relevant persons" to gain a clearer understanding of the case facts.

Deliberation and voting must proceed independently, without outside presence. Discussion should focus on the issues including clarity of facts, proper legal application, sufficiency of evidence, and procedural legality. One supervisor may be designated to record the proceedings.

Voting is conducted by anonymous ballot. The decision is based on majority rule: whether to agree or disagree with the outcome of "three types of cases". The presider then submits the decision to the Office.

The duration of the entire supervisory procedures starts from the day the supervisor receives notification. If the facts are clear and no hearing or interviews occur, the process must conclude within 7 days in accordance with current provisions. If interviews or hearings are held, the period may be extended to 15 days with the procurator general's approval. The extension must be applied for before the original deadline.

4.1.4 Handling and Feedback of Supervision Outcome

This stage may reference Article 25 of the Provisions, which provides: the procurator general or the procuratorial committee shall, within its statutory authorities, review the supervisor's vote and related department opinions. The necessary explanation of supervisors and related departments may be adopted in procuratorial review. If the procuratorial party agrees, the relevant department must execute the supervisor's decision. If the procurator general disagrees, the case must be discussed by the procuratorial committee, which may issue a final decision. It is recommended to add that the procuratorial committee shall invite the supervisors involved in the case to attend meeting and hear their views. After a decision is made by the committee, the outcome should be promptly communicated to the supervisors, and some written documents should be notified to the people's supervisor who initiated the supervisory procedure and participated in the committing supervision by the Office.

4.1.5 Review Procedure

If a majority of the supervisors involved in the case disagree with the procuratorial committee's decision, they may apply for a review by the higher-level procuratorate via the Office. Following current provisions, the original procuratorate should submit case-related materials within 3 days since the review initiation for reviewing of the higher-level procuratorate. The higher-level procuratorate must issue a review opinion within 15 days and provide feedback to the supervisors.

4.2 Procedural Design for the "Five Types of Situations"

Unlike the typified "three types of cases," the "five types of situations" focus on supervision to procuratorial conducts in duty-related crimes. Despite common natures in deliberation and review procedures, procedural design must reflect their distinctions.

4.2.1 Supervisory Initiation Procedure

Supervision to the "five types of situations" should also be initiated by the people's supervisor, similar to the "three types of cases". An information disclosure mechanism should be established to ensure supervisors' rights to inquiry and information. Legislation should obligate the procuratorial organs to regularly inform filed and prosecuted cases with the people's supervisor, and publicize contents of the "five types of situations" and contact channels for the people's supervisor to facilitate public reporting. Additionally, where the procuratorial organs identify issues falling within the "five types of situations," it should invite supervisors to relevant meetings to expand the path of facilitating their understanding of such cases.

A notification mechanism must also be established. When duty-related crime investigations are launched, during the first interrogation, the suspect should be informed in writing that if any of the "five types of situations" occurs later in the criminal procedures, they or their closed relatives and defenders may report it to the people's supervisor. If not in custody, the suspect may report directly.

4.2.2 Implementation of the Diversion Procedure

The *Provisions of the Supreme People's Procuratorate on the Implementing the People's Supervisor's Supervision on the Five Types of Situations (Trial)" by the people's supervisor* (hereinafter to be referred as The Provisions on "Five Types of Situations") establishes a diversion procedure specifically applicable to the supervision initiated by the people's supervisor over the "five types of situations".[33] In contrast to the direct entry into the deliberation and voting procedure provided for

[33] Article 5 of The Provisions provides: The People's Supervisor Office shall be responsible for the unified receipt and forwarding of the supervisory opinion materials submitted by people's supervisors, for reviewing and proposing handling suggestions for approval by the procurator general. Where the case does not fall under the jurisdiction of the procuratorate, it shall be transferred to the competent people's procuratorate for handling in accordance with these Rules; if the case falls under

"three types of cases," this diversion procedure requires the related department of the procuratorial organs to conduct a preliminary review of the supervisory opinions submitted by the people's supervisor prior to the deliberation and voting phase. Where the facts are clear and the circumstances are minor, the department shall propose a handling opinion for the procurator general's decision, and forward the

---

the jurisdiction of the procuratorate, it shall be assigned to the relevant department in accordance with the following divisions of responsibility:

(1) Where a people's supervisor raises a supervisory opinion regarding the procuratorate's failure to file a case that should be filed, or the filing of a case that should not be filed, the case shall be handled by the department of investigation supervision.
(2) Where a people's supervisor raises a supervisory opinion regarding unlawful extended detention by relevant departments of the procuratorate during case handling, the case shall be handled by the department of detention facility inspection.
(3) Where a people's supervisor raises a supervisory opinion regarding illegal searches, seizures, or freezing of assets by relevant departments of the procuratorate during case handling, the case shall be jointly handled by the department of investigation supervision and the finance department; if the circumstances involve suspected violations of discipline or law, the case shall be handled by the discipline inspection and supervision department.
(4) Where a people's supervisor raises a supervisory opinion regarding the procuratorate's failure to confirm or implement decisions on state compensation in duty-related crime cases, the case shall be handled by the department responsible for criminal compensation.
(5) Where a people's supervisor raises a supervisory opinion regarding misconduct such as abuse of power for personal gain, accepting bribes, extorting confessions by torture, or obtaining evidence through violence by procuratorial personnel during case handling, the case shall be handled by the discipline inspection and supervision department.
(6) Where the matters reflected by the people's supervisor do not fall under the "five types of situations," the People's Supervisor Office shall, in accordance with the division of responsibilities, submit the matter for approval by the deputy procurator general in charge and then forward it to the relevant department for handling.

After receiving materials transferred by the People's Supervisor Office, the responsible department shall report the investigation results to the People's Supervisor Office within the prescribed time limit. If the case cannot be clarified within the prescribed period, an appropriate extension may be granted with the approval of the procurator general, and a written explanation of the reasons and the progress of the investigation shall be submitted to the People's Supervisor Office. The People's Supervisor Office shall track and supervise the handling process.

Article 6 provides:

People's procuratorates shall handle the supervisory opinions submitted by people's supervisors in a timely manner. Where the facts of the supervisory circumstance raised by the people's supervisor are clear and the circumstances are minor, the responsible department, upon receipt of the materials, shall promptly designate a staff member to review, investigate and verify the situation, and propose a handling opinion for decision by the procurator general. A written reply shall be transferred to the People's Supervisor Office within 10 days.

Where the supervisory circumstance raised by the people's supervisor is complex or has a significant impact, the responsible department shall, within 30 days from the date of receiving the materials, designate a staff member to review, investigate, and verify the situation, propose a preliminary handling opinion, and prepare to be supervised accordingly.

The People's Supervisor Office shall, based on laws, judicial interpretations, and relevant work provisions, and in light of specific circumstances, propose whether to initiate an evaluation procedure for the supervisory circumstance raised by the people's supervisor, subject to the decision of the chief procurator.

corresponding response to the people's supervisor office within 10 days from the date of submission. This diversion mechanism serves to distinguish between ordinary and major violations, thereby enhancing the efficiency of supervision, and constitutes an important innovation in promoting the self-regulation and internal accountability of procuratorial organs. However, it is noteworthy that the handling decisions that define the "simple cases" may not be accepted by the people's supervisor. First, the determination of whether "the facts are clear" and "the circumstances are minor" is made unilaterally by the procuratorial organs, not by the people's supervisor, and given the difference in perspectives between the two, such assessments are highly subjective. Second, where objections arise concerning the handling of such cases, people's supervisors are not permitted to initiate the deliberation and voting procedure or to the higher-level procuratorate for review, but only request the people's procuratorate to review. Accordingly, it is proposed that the design of the diversion procedure, while drawing upon the relevant provisions of the Supreme People's Procuratorate, should provide that, where the people's supervisor object to the procuratorate's handling decision, the matter shall, akin to cases deemed "complicated" or "having significant social impact," be referred to the supervision deliberation and voting procedure.

4.2.3 Supervision Deliberation and Voting Procedure

In respect of the confirmation procedure for the people's supervisor and the challenge procedure for participants in the relevant cases, reference may be made to the applicable procedures governing the "three types of cases."

As to the deliberation procedure, the selection and working methods of the presiding supervisor may likewise follow the procedures for the "three types of cases." During the hearing of opinions, the people's supervisor shall primarily hear the case-handling officer's report on the investigation and the proposed handling opinion, and shall answer the question issued by the people's supervisor. Unlike in the "three types of cases," the inquiry shall focus solely on issues pertaining to the "five types of situations," without delving into related case facts or the application of law. Where necessary, the criminal suspect or their representative may also be questioned to ascertain the existence of any "five types of situations."

Regarding the formulation of supervisory opinions, there shall be no simple outcome of "agree" or "disagree." Rather, through collective deliberation, a consolidated supervisory opinion shall be produced. Each people's supervisor participating in the deliberation shall state the reasons for their opinion and submit the document with their signature to the people's supervisor office for archival purposes.

4.2.4 Handling and Feedback of Supervision Outcomes

Upon receipt of the supervisory opinion from the people's supervisor, the procurator general shall promptly address the matter and, where necessary, submit it to the procuratorial committee for deliberation. The outcome must be communicated to the people's supervisor who initiated and participated in the supervision within 15 days. Furthermore, it is required that "when the people's procuratorate investigates, verifies, or deliberates on handling matters relating to the supervision of the 'five types of situations' by the people's supervisor, the people's supervisor of the procuratorate shall be invited to attend the relevant meetings."

4.2.5 Review Procedure

Where the majority of people's supervisors participating in the supervision disagree with the handling opinion of the procurator general or the procuratorial committee, they may, through the people's supervisor office, apply for review to people's procuratorates at higher level. It shall be further provided that within 3 days of receiving the application for review, the procuratorial organs must transfer the relevant materials to people's procuratorates at higher level for examination. The people's procuratorates at higher level shall render a decision on the review within 15 days and provide feedback to the people's supervisor.

In cases involving duty-related crimes where the people's supervisor determines that criminal compensation should be awarded but the procuratorate fails to confirm such compensation in accordance with law, and where, following supervision, the procurator general or the procuratorial committee intends to make a decision of non-confirmation, the criminal compensation department shall, in accordance with *the Provisions on Submitting Non-Confirmation Decisions in Criminal Compensation Cases Handled by People's Procuratorates to People's Procuratorates at Higher Levels for Approval*, directly submit the non-confirmation opinion, case files, and supervisory opinions to people's procuratorates at higher level for review and approval, without the need for the people's supervisor to apply separately for review.[34]

5 An Analysis of the Effectiveness Mechanism of the People's Supervisor System

When discussing the effectiveness mechanism of the people's supervisor system, we must first define what is meant by "effectiveness." Terms such as "effective," "having effect," "producing effect," "invalid," and "ineffective" are often associated with the supervisory activities of the people's supervisor. Yet, what exactly constitutes effectiveness? What constitutes invalid? What are the objects and boundaries of each? Does "effectiveness" refer to the actual outcomes or the institutional binding force? Is it a political concept or a legal concept? There are no clear standards for these definitions, leading to a lack of precise positioning in discussions on the effectiveness mechanism of the people's supervisor system. Consequently, determinations

[34] See Article 8 of *the Provisions of the Supreme People's Procuratorate on the Implementing the People's Supervisor's Supervision on the Five Types of Situations (Trial).*

regarding the effectiveness of the system are often made on different levels, lacking homogeneity.

The effectiveness of an institution and related issues of the effectiveness are basic standards for evaluating the existence of an institution. From the perspective of the authority of institutions, "effectiveness refers to the special existence of norms. To say a norm is effective means we assume its existence, or we assume it binds the behavior of those it regulates[35]". Essentially, institutional effectiveness is a form of binding force, either arising from political domination or from the social recognition of the law's "legitimacy effect." In a rule-of-law society, effectiveness typically manifests as legal effectiveness. "Legal effectiveness generally has two meanings: broadly, it refers to the binding force of law; narrowly, it refers to the scope of the law's effectiveness, namely, to whom, where, and when it applies[36]". Therefore, the discussion of the people's supervisor system's effectiveness mechanism mainly concerns whether the system has legal effectiveness, and whether it possesses the objectivity and stability of legal effectiveness. Broadly, it refers to the legal binding force of the people's supervisor system; narrowly, it focuses on the supervisory opinions of the people's supervisor have binding force for what circumstances and which subjects Thus, the effectiveness mechanism of the people's supervisor system can be understood in three aspects: whether the legislation should empower legal effectiveness; what kind of legal effectiveness it should have; and how to achieve legal effectiveness. It represents a combination of the institutional binding forces at both the macro level and the micro level. These issues must be clarified in legislative discussions about the people's supervisor system.

5.1 *Legislation Should Empower Legal Effectiveness on the People's Supervisor System*

Some scholars argue that, "In practice, the people's supervisor system functions merely as a procedure of suggestion or consultation without substantive functions or legal effectiveness. Its actual effectiveness subordinates to the decisions of the procuratorial organs. Therefore, the people's supervisor' supervision should not be granted direct legal force, as it could interfere with judicial independence and potentially lead to greater injustice".[37] Accordingly, it is advocated that legislation should define the supervisory role of the people's supervisor as right to advice, a form of flexible supervision. The reason is that granting supervisory effectiveness could cause the people's supervisor to become yet another victim of power abuse. In addition, based on the principle of separation of powers and the coordination of powers and

[35] Kelsen, *General Theory of Law and State*, translated by Shen Zongling, Encyclopedia of China Publishing House, 1996, p. 32.

[36] See Shen Zongling ed., *Fundamental Theories of Science of Law*, Law Press China, 1988, p.382.

[37] Xue Panlin, *The People's Supervisor System from a Constitutional Perspective*, The Chinese Procurators, 2008.

duties in a constitutional state, legal supervisory powers should only be exercised by corresponding state organs.

This concern does serve as a warning against the potential distortion of the people's supervisor system into a form of power supervision. "However, from the perspective of intrinsic nature of supervision, all supervisions in different natures and types are effect. Supervisions without effectiveness have no meaning at all[38]". Supervision is a concentrated reflection of checks and balances and oversight among different entities. Regardless of the nature of the supervising entity, the core of supervision lies in the binding force that the supervisor exerts over the supervised, although the manifestation of this binding force takes on a diverse range of forms. Without acknowledging the supervisory effectiveness of the people's supervisor, the system would lose its meaning. Social and media supervision can also exercise the right to criticize and make suggestions to procuratorial organs, which may also lead to improvements in the work of procuratorial organs. There would have been no need for the Supreme People's Procuratorate to introduce the people's supervisor system, and the systematic and unique nature of the people's supervisor system would not be demonstrated. Meanwhile, the supervisory effectiveness of the people's supervisor has constitutional and legal legitimacy. Therefore, granting supervisory effectiveness in legislation is undoubted. What remains to be explored is the effectiveness of such supervision, not whether it should be effect. Of course, in terms of legislative technique, it is not necessary to explicitly declare its legal effectiveness in the text; it can instead be implied through provisions stipulating the binding force of the people's supervisor' opinions on procuratorial organs.

5.2 The People's Supervisor Should Be Granted Procedural Binding Force

As previously discussed, the supervisory outcomes of the people's supervisor should have procedural rather than substantive binding force. The supervisory outcomes only acquire rigid binding force when accepted by the procuratorial organs. Therefore, in the legislative design the nature of the supervisory effectiveness shall not be focused on, instead, the focus shall be on how to embody this procedural binding force.

5.2.1 Effectiveness Mechanism Within the Current System

In accordance with current regulations of the Supreme People's Procuratorate, for the "three types of cases," supervision by the people's supervisor must be initiated in every instance. If the procurator general agrees with the supervisors' opinion, the relevant department must implement them. If the procurator general disagrees

---

[38] Li Jianming, *A Study on the Effectiveness of People's Supervisors' Opinions*, People's Procuratorial Semimonthly, 2005.

after review, the matter must be referred to the procuratorial committee for deliberation. If the committee agrees with the supervisors' opinion, the relevant department should implement; if not, an explanation must be provided to the supervisors via the people's supervisor office. If a majority of participating supervisors disagree with the committee's decision, they may request a review by people's procuratorates at higher levels, whose decision those at lower levels must implement. This effectiveness mechanism can be summarized as: procurator general's review—procuratorial committee deliberation—people's procuratorates at higher levels review. The people's supervisor primarily plays a role in facilitating review and reconsideration, while represents a leading mechanism by the procuratorial organs, in which the procurator general's review and procuratorial committee deliberation are mandatory steps upon meeting certain conditions, while the review by people's procuratorates at higher levels is a discretionary procedure that may be initiated when appropriate. For the "five types of situations," if the people's supervisor disagrees with the proposed handling decision, it must be submitted to the procurator general for decision and the general may send it to the procuratorial committee if necessary. In minor cases, supervisors can request a review with people's procuratorate which makes the decision; for other cases, they can request review of those at higher levels.

Thus, the current system establishes procedural effectiveness for self-investigating cases by procuratorial organs, involving reviews level-by-level for the "three types of cases" and reviews by people's procuratorates at same level and those at higher levels for the "five types of situations" in light of cases complexity. Although the supervisory effectiveness of people's supervisors is defined by nature as procedurally rigid, regulations of the Supreme People's Procuratorate use strong terms like "shall review," "shall seriously study," and "shall feedback," the binding force is a procedural petition right within an incomplete sense: the realization of supervisory effectiveness should be transformed into substantive effectiveness through the recognization and resolutions of procuratorial organs, and supervisors lack the right to monitor the transformation process. Thus, the key of the consideration of this mechanism is to "recognize supervisors' opinions should not be treated as ordinary citizen suggestions nor replace professional decisions and ascertainment of procuratorial organs. Therefore, it should not have statutory binding force. How to position the supervisory effectiveness of people's supervisors between the two extremes to avoid abuse while ensuring effectiveness is still not finished.[39]"

5.2.2 Construction of Effectiveness Mechanism for People's Supervisor System

To strengthen the rigidity of the procedural binding force and prevent arbitrary acceptance of supervisory outcomes by procuratorial organs, efforts could be made to improve the procedural design, coordination between people's supervisor's

[39] Chen Guiming, *Let People's Supervisors Become the Eyes of the People*, at https://theory.people.com.cn/GB/49150/49153/5465358.html, last visited on June 10, 2009.

supervision and power supervision of the procuratorial organs and others in the legislation.

(i) Supervisory Procedures Initiated by the People's Supervisor and the Reasonable Initiation Mechanism Should Be Established

Legislation should empower the people's supervisor to initiate supervisory procedures directly. For the "five types of situations," supervision should be initiated by the people's procuratorates' after the people's supervisor's discovery in accordance with the related provisions. For the "three types of cases," the people's supervisor office notifies supervisors to participate. In fact, initiation is still belong to people's procuratorates, which weakens supervisors' possibility in comprehensively intervening all cases and then renders the supervised cases are at discretion of the procuratorial organs. To handle with such issues, efforts should be made to further optimize the supervision initiation procedure. The practical adjustments include that to add provisions that allow parties involved in "three types of cases" to directly apply to the people's supervisor for supervision, thereby enabling the people's supervisor to initiate supervisory procedures on their own, addressing the inadequacy of having the procuratorial organs notify the people's supervisor to conduct supervision. Among the "three types of cases", it is provided that "those who are dissatisfied with the arrest decision, including suspects, defense counsel, and their close relatives, may apply for supervision to the people's supervisor. Complainants and victims in cases where the case is withdrawal or decided not to suit may also apply for supervision to the people's supervisor. The people's supervisor shall initiate supervisory procedures in accordance with their authority, and people's procuratorates must accept such supervision[40]". Similar provisions may be adopted for "five types of situations", allowing the people's supervisor to initiate supervisory procedures based on their authority.

(ii) Establishing People's Procuratorates at Higher Levels Intervention Mechanism to Improve the Rigidity of the Procedure

The Organic Law of the People's Procuratorates of the People's Republic of China provides that the Supreme People's Procuratorate shall guide local people's procuratorates at all levels and special people's procuratorates; the people's procuratorates at a higher level shall guide the people's procuratorates at lower levels. Therefore, in the supervision of the people's supervisor, the reasonable choice of improving the effectiveness mechanism is that supervisory opinions and leadership functions of procuratorates at higher levels should be better aligned. In cases where there is a divergence of opinions between the people's supervisor and the procuratorial committee at the same level, the provision allowing the people's supervisor to request a review by people's procuratorate at higher levels may be revised in legislative documents to read: "If the people's supervisor has different opinions to the final decision of the people's procuratorate, the result of such different opinions shall be submitted to people's procuratorates at the higher levels, which shall initiate a review procedure."

40 Cui Guiying, *A Brief Discussion on the Scope and Effectiveness of the People's Supervisor System*, at http://www.js.jcy.gov.cn/readnews.asp?%20nid=9958, last visited on June 10, 2009.

This would strengthen the mandatory nature of supervision initiated by people's procuratorates at the higher levels. At the same time, an accountability mechanism for people's procuratorates at the higher levels may be introduced. Specifically, if the procurator general fails to submit the different opinion, which "shall" be submitted, of the people's supervisor to the procuratorial committee for deliberation, or if the procuratorial committee fails to handle the matter, which "shall" be handled, in accordance with the law, people's procuratorates at the higher levels shall impose disciplinary and administrative sanctions on the responsible individuals in accordance with relevant regulations.

Moreover, consideration may be given to differentiating the manner in which people's procuratorates at the higher levels intervene based on the outcome of the people's supervisor' vote. In "three types of cases," if the people's supervisor unanimously passes a resolution that the procuratorial committee disagrees with, the procuratorial organs shall directly apply for a review by those at higher levels, i.e., the review procedure shall be initiated in accordance with the functions and powers. For other passed resolutions that are not accepted by the procuratorial committee, the review procedure shall be initiated upon request by the people's supervisor.[41]

(iii) Introducing Supervision by People's Congresses

People's Congresses at all levels serve as supervisory organs, and People's Procuratorates shall be responsible to the People's Congress at the same level. Therefore, to enhance the procedural rigidity of the people's supervisor, it is worth considering the introduction of a remedy mechanism involving the People's Procuratorate at the same level. This would help comprehensively integrate the macro-level supervision of the People's Congress with the case-specific supervision by the people's supervisor. Accordingly, relevant legal texts could incorporate a remedy mechanism of the People's Congress, which further gives the reviewing outcomes of People's Procuratorates at higher levels a guarantee to the procedural effectiveness. It shall provide that "if People's Procuratorates at higher levels disagree with the opinion of the people's supervisor and uphold the original decision of the Procuratorial Committee upon review, the people's supervisor may apply to the Standing Committee of the People's Congress at the same level to initiate the supervision mechanism of the People's Congress." Such involvement of People's Congresses not only addresses the coordination between the people's supervisor system and the system of the People's Congress supervision, but also strengthens the rigidity o the effectiveness of the people's supervisor.

---

[41] Some scholars argue that where a supervisory opinion is adopted by a two-thirds absolute majority vote of people's supervisors in the first round of voting, the procurator general should confirm it and instruct the relevant departments to implement it, without the need to submit it to the procuratorial committee for decision.

See Xie Pengcheng, On Measures to Strengthen the Effectiveness of the People's Supervisor System, at http://www.hxjcy.gov.cn/ReadNews.asp?NewID=217, last visited on June 15, 2009.

However, such confirmation of the effectiveness of the people's supervisors' vote constitutes a substantive judgment of power rather than a procedural effect, and is inconsistent with the fundamental principle provided in the Constitution and the law that the people's procuratorates shall exercise procuratorial power independently.

(iv) Establishing a "Supervisory Opinion Filing" Mechanism

Supervisory opinions of people's supervisors could be formally included in the case files. For instance, if a case concerning the "three types of cases" lacks the relevant supervisory opinions in its file, the decision would not acquire final effectiveness. This would also strengthen regulation on the procuratorial organs. At the same time, when people's courts hear cases involving duty-related crimes investigated by people's procuratorates, they also review and consider the supervisory opinions of the people's supervisor. This practice enhances the acceptability of supervisory opinions issued by the people's supervisor and improves the overall effectiveness of their supervisory function.

6 Guarantee Mechanism for the People's Supervisor System

The key of institutional design lies in the efficacy of its operation.[42] Since its inception, the people's supervisor system has played a significant role in promoting the fair exercise of procuratorial power, advancing judicial justice, and enhancing judicial efficiency. However, during its implementation, the system has encountered bottlenecks that hinder its further development towards standardization and legalization. A key reason is that existing institutional regulations predominantly contain declarative provisions regarding the supervisory rights and methods of the people's supervisor, while lacking enforceable safeguards. Consequently, the supervisory authority, intensity, and purposes of the people's supervisor remain in an ought-to-be state, lacking mechanisms to transition into practical application. Therefore, in the process of legalizing the people's supervisor system, constructing a comprehensive and scientific guarantee system to align the original institutional intent with actual operational effectiveness is both an important and challenging task.

Both *the Provisions of the Supreme People's Procuratorate on the Implementing the People's Supervisor System (Trial)* (hereinafter to be referred as "The Provisions") issued by the Supreme People's Procuratorate and the regulations formulated by various localities generally include dedicated chapters outlining the safeguards for the people's supervisor in performing their duties. Typical provisions cover the safeguards of supervisory conditions, independent supervision, personal safety, and funding.[43] However, overall, these safeguards are general and lack operability. For instance, many provisions provide that the people's supervisor may be invited to participate in "relevant activities" or "relevant meetings," and include ambiguous

---

[42] The guarantee mechanism for the effectiveness of the people's supervisor system has been addressed in the preceding section titled "Effectiveness Mechanism of the People's Supervisor System." This section focuses on the guarantee mechanisms for the rights of people's supervisors and the institutional conditions necessary to support their functioning.

[43] See Articles 29 to 34 of *the Provisions of the Supreme People's Procuratorate on the Implementing the People's Supervisor System (Trial).*

concepts such as "handling in accordance with law." There is an abundance of declarative provisions and a scarcity of punitive measures; safeguards within judicial institutions are prevalent, while safeguards from the public are rare. Therefore, it is necessary to further refine and improve the guarantee mechanisms of the current people's supervisor system in subsequent legislative activities.

6.1 Conceptualization of the Rights Protection Mechanism for the People's Supervisor

6.1.1 Guarantee Mechanism for the Right to Information

As previously noted, the people's supervisor conducts supervision over duty-related crime cases either upon notification by procuratorial organs or through their own "discovery". Based on this, the effectiveness of such supervision is significantly undermined, leading to the awkward predicament of limited access to information and the concurrent demand for accurate and well-founded supervisory opinions. Therefore, safeguarding the right to information for the people's supervisor in their supervisory activities becomes a primary concern in the guarantee mechanism. We propose constructing this mechanism by establishing a regular briefing system, a supervisory rights notification system, a communication mechanism between people's supervisors and procurators, and by strengthening and standardizing the procedures for case handlers to introduce and respond to questions during the supervision process.

A regular briefing system should be established. In practice, some localities adopt written briefs, delivering a *Working Brief* to the people's supervisor monthly. Others arrange for the people's supervisor to review relevant materials and case files related to duty-related crime investigations under the accompaniment of procuratorial staff.

Considering the abstract and principled nature of central legislation, it is inadvisable to specify the exact methods of the regular briefing system. The key is to provide the content of the regular briefings. Specifically, it should be mandated that basic information of supervised cases (including the number, types, stages, and proposed handling opinions), basic information on the handling departments and officers, evidence materials of the handling process, procedural records, and analytical materials on the conclusions be communicated. The specific methods of briefing should be flexibly determined by local people's procuratorates based on their conditions.

A supervisory rights notification mechanism should be established. The notification mechanism operates on two levels: first, informing criminal suspects of their right to request supervision by the people's supervisor; second, safeguarding that the people's supervisor is aware of whether the suspects have been informed of this right. For example, primary-level people's procuratorates in Nantong City, Jiangsu Province, arrange for the people's supervisor to observe the entire process of informing suspects of their rights in real-time or provide copies of the notification records for the people's supervisor to review at any time, which just a kind of available attempts in this course.[44] Similar to the regular briefing system, the central legislation should not provide specific notification methods but should clearly provide that "informing duty-related crime suspects of their rights is an obligatory duty of case handlers, to be fulfilled during the first interrogation, with corresponding notification documents prepared." Additionally, people's procuratorates should establish mechanisms to ensure the people's supervisor are aware of the suspects' notification status.

An observation and attendance mechanism and a communication mechanism between people's supervisors and procurators should be established. First, regarding the ambiguous provisions on the people's supervisor attending meetings, it is advisable to specify the relevant meetings. For cases where people's supervisors disagree with the procurator general's review opinions and the case is submitted to the procuratorial committee for discussion, it should be provided that the people's procuratorate must invite the people's supervisor to attend the committee's discussions. For meetings held by case-handling departments to decide on case handling, the people's supervisor can also be invited to attend and express their opinions. Second, it can be provided that in all procedures of handling duty-related crime cases by procuratorial organs, the people's supervisor may request to observe (except in cases involving state secrets). Legislation can also provide in principle that procuratorial organs should further disclose prosecutorial operations to the people's supervisor and establish a long-term communication mechanism between procuratorial organs and the people's supervisor, with specific contact methods determined by each people's procuratorate.

6.1.2 Guarantee Mechanism for Supervisory Authority

Supervisory authority refers to the authority necessary for the people's supervisor to achieve supervisory objectives. From the perspective of the supervision process, supervisory authority is based on the people's supervisor' understanding of the cases under supervision and is crucial to the supervisory outcome. A complete guarantee mechanism for supervisory authority includes both external conditions for exercising supervisory authority and regulations and sanctions against interference or obstruction of the people's supervisor in exercising their supervisory authority.

A time guarantee mechanism for supervisory authority will be established. Currently, in the supervision process of the people's supervisor, some are unable to participate in supervision due to time constraints, rendering their supervisory authority ineffective. For instance, some people's supervisors do not participate in any case supervision during their term, while others, due to their job conditions,

[44] See He Qiming et al., *Smoothing Information Channels to Ensure Effective Supervision: Procuratorial Organs in Nantong City Safeguard People's Supervisors' Right to Know Through Four Links*, Fangyuan Rule of Law Special Issue on People's Supervisors, 2006.

find it difficult to fully supervise a case. The former situation pertains to the adjustment of the dismissal mechanism, while the latter falls under the supervision guarantee mechanism. Therefore, legislation should provide that the people's supervisor' time for participating in supervision must be guaranteed, establishing a coordination mechanism between procuratorial organs and the work units of the people's supervisor. Legislatively, it is advisable to avoid specifying the exact time each supervisor must participate in supervision. Instead, it can be provided that the work units of the people's supervisor should support their supervisory work, consider supervision time as work time, and reasonably adjust and arrange the work nature and schedule of the people's supervisor.

An independent supervision mechanism should be established. First, it should continue the current provisions on independent supervision, stipulating that "people's procuratorates shall not control, induce, or circumvent the supervision of the people's supervisor, shall not interfere with the people's supervisor' evaluation and voting on cases, and shall not disclose the evaluation and voting results of the people's supervisor." Second, it should strengthen the punitive mechanism, stipulating that people who interferences with the independent evaluation work of the people's supervisor shall be subject to administrative sanctions and legal penalties, depending on the circumstances.

6.1.3 Guarantee Mechanism for Personal Rights

First, Article 31 of the *Provisions of the Supreme People's Procuratorate on the Implementing the People's Supervisor System (Trial)* shall be followed, which provides that "those who retaliate against or obstruct the people's supervisors from performing their duties shall be referred to the relevant authorities for disposition in accordance with the law; if a crime is constituted, criminal liability shall be pursued in accordance with law." Second, relevant provisions on the personal protection of deputies to the National People's Congress can be referred to, which provide that people's supervisors' statements shall not be subject to legal liability. In accordance with relevant laws, the statements and votes of National People's Congress deputies and members of its Standing Committee at meetings shall not be subject to legal liability. Due to the representative nature of people's supervisors, they may, during the supervision process, inadvertently infringe upon the personal rights of criminal suspects due to limitations in professional expertise. If the law strictly requires people's supervisors to bear corresponding civil or criminal liability, it will inevitably affect their initiative and enthusiasm in supervision activities. Therefore, legislation can consider providing that people's supervisors' statements shall not be subject to legal liability, while also limiting the exemption to relevant speech made in the course of performing supervisory duties.

6.2 Guarantee Mechanism for Material Conditions of the People's Supervisor

Currently, in pilot implementations, the activity funds for the people's supervisor are mostly included in the expenditure of people's procuratorates at all levels and coordinated with the corresponding financial departments to be included the government budget. However, this approach is a unilateral provision by procuratorial organs and lacks corresponding legal supports, often failing to gain recognition from local financial departments, making it difficult to guarantee the expenditure for the supervisory work of the people's supervisor. Therefore, legislation must clearly define the guarantee mechanism for the material conditions of the people's supervisor' supervisory work.

An office conditions guarantee mechanism will be established. The supervisory work of the people's supervisor is meticulous and complex, involving various procedures such as obtaining case information, evaluation, and voting. In practice, however, there is often no fixed place for supervision activities of the people's supervisor, with their duty commonly conducted at working places of relevant departments. To ensure the neutrality and fairness of supervisions, it should be provided that people's procuratorates at all levels shall arrange dedicated places for the people's supervisor to perform their supervisory duties, offering necessary working places and supplies.

A guarantee mechanism for supervisory expenditure should be established. Legislation should avoid the model where the working expenditures of the people's supervisor are included in the expenditure of procuratorial organs and declared by them. Instead, it should clearly provide that the working expenditure for the people's supervisor of procuratorial organs at all levels be included into the local government budget, planned and ensured by local governments, with the Standing Committee of the People's Congress, as the selecting and appointing body of the people's supervisor, responsible for supervising implementation.

A work allowance mechanism for the people's supervisor should be established. First, actual expense allowances should be included in the allowance mechanism. Pursuant to Article 33 of *the Provisions of the Supreme People's Procuratorate on the Implementing the People's Supervisor System (Trial)*, people's procuratorates shall provide appropriate allowances to the people's supervisor for expenses incurred in the course of performing their duties, including but not limited to transportation, communication, and accommodation. The standard for such allowances shall be determined with reference to the applicable standards for procuratorial personnel at the corresponding level. Second, for the people's supervisor without fixed sources of income, the people's procuratorates shall provide work allowances calculated based on the local daily average salary standard applicable to procuratorial personnel at the corresponding level.[45] Third, for the people's supervisor who has a job, people's procuratorates shall establish communication mechanism with the supervisors' units

---

[45] *The Provisions of the Supreme People's Procuratorate on the Implementing the People's Supervisor System (Trial)* adopt a compensation standard based on calculated based on the local daily average salary standard of employees. However, in light of the nature of the work performed

to mandate that the units shall not reduce directly or indirectly any salaries, bonuses, and other benefits of the supervisors due to their performance of supervisory duties.

by people's supervisors is same to the procuratarial staff, we propose that their remuneration be determined with reference to the average wage standard of the latter.

Postscript

This book is a collaborative effort by four authors: Qin Qianhong, Huan Ji'e, Zhou Wei, and Lü Hongbo. The specific division of the writing is as follows: Chapter I is authored by Qin Qianhong, Huan Ji'e, and Zhou Wei; Chapter II by Huan Ji'e; Chapter III by Qin Qianhong and Zhou Wei; Chapter IV by Lü Hongbo; and Chapter V by Zhou Wei.

This book represents the culmination of a project funded by the Hubei Provincial People's Procuratorate in 2008. The conceptual framework and outline of the manuscript are conceived by Qin Qianhong, the project leader, who also undertakes the revisions and finalized the manuscript.

The successful publication of this book is greatly attributed to the unwavering support of Mr. Xu Hanmin, Executive Deputy Procurator General of the Hubei Provincial People's Procuratorate, and Mr. Jin Xin, Procurator General of the Hanyang District People's Procuratorate. Furthermore, the inclusion of this book in Wuhan University's Academic Series on Humanities and Social Sciences is attributable to the consistent advocacy and support for humanities and social sciences research at Wuhan University by the Department of Social Sciences of Wuhan University. The authors hereby extend their sincerest thanks to all mentioned.

Qin Qianhong

2009 winter in Luojia Hill, Wuchang District

Q. Qin, *Legislative Research on the People's Supervisor System*,
https://doi.org/10.1007/978-981-95-7972-3

References

Chinese Monographs

1. Zhou Yongnian ed., *Introduction to the People's Supervisor System*, China Procuratorial Press, 2008.
2. Han Dayuan ed., *Research on the Constitutional Foundations of China's Procuratorial System*, China Procuratorial Press, 2007.
3. Wang Pengxiang, *Criminal Procedure Law of the United States*, Peking University Press.
4. Deng Zhenglai and [UK] Alexander, *State and Civil Society: A Sociological Approach*, Central Compilation & Translation Press, 2002.
5. Wang Lijun, *Dialectics of Power and Rights*, China Legal Publishing House, 2005.
6. Tong Zhiwei, *Legal Rights and Constitutional Governance*, Shandong People's Publishing House, 2001.
7. Qin Qianhong & Ye Haibo, *Research on Socialist Constitutional Governance*, Shandong People's Publishing House, 2008.
8. Xia Yong, *The Origins of the Concept of Human Rights*, China University of Political Science and Law Press, 2001.
9. Zhou Yezhong ed., *Constitution*, Higher Education Press & Peking University Press, 2001.
10. Zheng Xianjun, *Research on Fundamental Rights*, China Democracy and Legal System Publishing House, 2007.
11. Li Long, *Collected Works of Li Long*, Wuhan University Press, 2006.
12. Wang Renbo, *The Chinese Path to Constitutionalism*, Shandong People's Publishing House, 2003.
13. Chen Xingliang ed., *Criminal Law Review*, Peking University Press, 2006.
14. Xu Chongde, *On Studying and Discussing the Constitution*, Law Press China, 2000.
15. Liu Junning, *Republicanism, Democracy, and Constitutionalism: A study of Liberal Thought*, SDX Joint Publishing Company, 1998.
16. Xu Yawen, *On Procedural Justice*, Shandong People's Publishing House, 2004.
17. Jiang Guohua, *Legislation: Ideal and Transformation*, Shandong People's Publishing House, 2007.
18. Zhou Wangsheng, *Science of Legislation*, Law Press China, 2004.
19. Sun Xiaoxia & Xia Li'an ed., *Introduction to Jurisprudence*, Higher Education Press, 2004.
20. Chen Xinmin, *Foundations of German Public Law (II)*, Shandong People's Publishing House, 2001.
21. Sun Guohua & Shen Zongling, *Fundamental Theories of Science of Law*, Law Press China, 1982.
22. Li Long ed., *Jurisprudence*, Wuhan University Press, 1996.

Q. Qin, *Legislative Research on the People's Supervisor System*,
https://doi.org/10.1007/978-981-95-7972-3

23. Yao Jianzong, *Jurisprudence: General Legal Science*, China University of Political Science and Law Press, 2006.
24. Zhang Wenxian ed., *Jurisprudence*, Higher Education Press, 2003.
25. Su Li, *Paths Lead to Cities: Rule of Law in Transitional China*, Law Press China, 2004.
26. Song Bing ed., *Procedure, Justice, and Modernization: Lectures by Foreign Jurists in China*, China University of Political Science and Law Press, 1998.
27. Cai Yanmin et al., *Analysis of Due Process*, China University of Political Science and Law Press, 2000.
28. Ma Guixiang, *Theory of Criminal Procedural Justice*, China Procuratorial Press, 2002.
29. Rao Ai ed., *Comparative Judicial Systems*, Southwest Jiaotong University Press, 2003.
30. Li You et al., *Toward Rational Justice: A Comparative Study of Foreign Criminal Justice Systems*, China University of Political Science and Law Press, 2001.
31. Chen Guangzhong et al. ed., *A Comparative Study on Non-Prosecution Systems between China and Germany*, China Procuratorial Press, 2001.
32. He Qinhua et al., *A History of Legal Development in Japan*, Shanghai People's Publishing House, 1999.
33. Han Qiang, *Procedural Democracy*, Masses Publishing House, 2002.
34. Zhong Hairang, *Theory of Legal Supervision*, Law Press China, 1993.
35. Tang Wei & Sun Jiping, *Essays on Legal Supervision*, Peking University Press, 2001.
36. Cai Dingjian, *State Supervision Systems*, China Legal Publishing House, 1991.
37. Wang Guanghui et al., *The Path to Constitutionalism: Theory and Practice of Constitutional Supervision*, Law Press China, 2002.
38. Fan Jinxue, *Political Theory of Rights: A Liberal-Democratic Interpretation*, Shandong People's Publishing House, 2003.
39. Chen Yunsheng, *New Trends in Democratic Constitutionalism: Theory and Practice of Constitutional Supervision*, People's Publishing House, 1988.
40. Central Committee of the Chinese Communist Party ed., *Lenin on Procuratorial and Supervisory Work*, Xinhua Bookstore, 1949.
41. Song Yinghui et al. eds., *Research on Pre-Trial Criminal Procedures*, China University of Political Science and Law Press, 2001.
42. Zuo Weimin, *Between Rights Discourse and Power Techniques: New Reflections on China's Justice*, Law Press China, 2002.
43. Sun Changyong, *Investigative Procedures and Human Rights: A Comparative Study*, China Fangzheng Press, 2000.
44. General Office of the Supreme People's Procuratorate ed., *Collective Reports of the Supreme People's Procuratorate*, China Procuratorial Press, 1999.

Chinese Translations

1. [Japan] Hiroya Matsuo, *Criminal Procedure Law of Japan I*, translated by Ding Xiangshun, China Renmin University Press, 2005.
2. [Japan] Hiroya Matsuo, *Criminal Procedure Law of Japan II*, translated by Zhang Ling, China Renmin University Press, 2005.
3. [US] Ellen Hochstedler Steury & Nancy Frank, *Criminal Court Process*, translated by Chen Weidong & Xu Meijun, China University of Political Science and Law Press, 2002.
4. [UK] Martin Loughlin, *Public Law and Political Theory*, translated by Zheng Ge, The Commercial Press, 2002.
5. [US] McIlwain C. H., *Constitutionalism: Ancient and Modern*, translated by Zhai Xiaobo, Guizhou People's Publishing House, 2004.
6. [US] Stephen L.Elkin et al, ed., *New Constitutionalism: Designing Political Systems for a Good Society*, translated by Zhou Yeqian, SDX Joint Publishing Company, 1997.

7. [Austria] Kelsen, *General Theory of Law and State*, translated by Shen Zongling, Encyclopedia of China Publishing House, 1996.
8. [Germany] Schmitt, *Constitutional Theory*, translated by Liu Feng, Shanghai People's Publishing House, 2005.
9. [UK] David Hume, *A Treatise of Human Nature,* translated by Guan Wenyun, The Commercial Press, 1980.
10. [US] Robert Dahl et al., *Constitutionalism and Democracy*, translated by Tong Dezhi, Jiangsu People's Publishing House, 2008.
11. [US] Joseph Schumpeter, *Capitalism, Socialism and Democracy*, translated by Wu Liangjian, The Commercial Press, 1999.
12. [US] James H. Elster et al., *Constitutionalism and Democracy: Studies on Rationality and Social Change*, translated by Pan Qin et al., SDX Joint Publishing Company, 1997.
13. [Japan] Tanase Takao, *Dispute Resolution and the Judicial System*, translated by Wang Yaxin, China University of Political Science and Law Press, 2004.
14. [France] Tocqueville, *Democracy in America (I),* translated by Dong Guoliang, The Commercial Press, 1988.
15. [France] Gustave Le Bon, *The Crowd: A Study of the Popular Mind*, translated by Feng Keli, Central Compilation & Translation Press, 2005.
16. [US] John V. Orth, *Due Process of Law: A Brief History*, translated by Yang Mingcheng & Chen Shuangling, The Commercial Press, 2006.
17. [US] Joseph Weiler, *The Worlds of European Constitutionalism*, translated by Cheng Weidong et al., China Social Sciences Press, 2004.
18. [UK] Hobbes, *Leviathan*, translated by Li Sifu et al., The Commercial Press, 1996.
19. [US] Rawls, *A Theory of Justice*, translated by He Huaihong et al., China Social Sciences Press, 1988.
20. [US] Michael D. Bayles, *Principles of Law: A Normative Analysis*, translated by Zhang Wenxian et al., Encyclopedia of China Publishing House, 1996.
21. [US] Douglass C. North., *Structure and Change in Economic History*, translated by Chen Yu et al., Shanghai Joint Publishing, Shanghai People's Publishing House, 1994.
22. [France] Tocqueville, *Democracy in America (I)*, translated by Dong Guoliang, The Commercial Press, 1991.
23. [UK] Alfred Denning, *Due Process of Law*, translated by Li Keqiang et al., Masses Publishing House, 1984.
24. [US] James E. Stoner, *Public Policy Making: Processes and Principles*, translated by Zhu Ziwen, Chongqing Publishing & Media Co., Ltd., 2001.
25. [US] Thomas W. Merrill ed., *Political Theory of the Constitution*, translated by Zhang Zhiming, SDX Joint Publishing Company, 1997.
26. [UK] M.J.C. Vile, *Constitutionalism and the Separation of Powers*, translated by Su Li, SDX Joint Publishing Company, 1997.

Papers

1. Series of papers in *Fangyuan Rule of Law Special Issue on People's Supervisors.*
2. Special papers on the People's Supervisor System on wzjs.jcrb.com.
3. Han Dayuan & Wang Xiaobin, *A Constitutional Perspective on the People's Supervisor System*, Journal of National Prosecutors College, 2005.
4. Mo Jihong, *The Justifiability of People's Superviosr System*, Journal of National Prosecutors College, 2009.
5. Zhou Anping, *Critique of the People's Supervisor System*, Journal of Nanjing Normal University (Social Science Edition), 2007.

6. Xu Xin, *Criticism of the People's Supervisor System*, from a speech delivered at the Seminar on the People's Supervisor System of Southwest University of Political Science and Law, Center for Judicial Studies, Nov. 29, 2005.
7. Zhou Yongnian, *Reflections on Legal Positioning of People's Supervisor System*, Law Science, 2006
8. Chen Zhengyun, *Legal Supervision and the Reform of Procuratorial Functions*, Chinese Journal of Law, 2008.
9. Chen Ruihua, *The Nature of Judicial Power*, Chinese Journal of Law, 2000.
10. Cai Dingjian, *The Transformation of Procuratorial Functions in the Course of Judicial Reform*, Political Science and Law, 1999.
11. Long Zongzhi, *On the Positioning of Public Prosecutors*, People's Procuratorial Semimonthly, 1999.
12. Zuo Weimin & Wu Weijun, *People's Supervisors: Deepening and Developing the Concept and System*, People's Procuratorial Semimonthly, 2005.
13. Wang Jianghua & Li Xin, *Investigation Power of Procuratorial Organs over Duty-Related Crimes and Its Supervisory Constraints*, Journal of Yunnan University (Law Edition), 2006.
14. Zhao Xiumin, *The Relationship Between Power and Rights in the Perspective of Constitutionalism,* Journal of Gansu Political Science and Law Institute, 2004.
15. Yan Hailiang, *An Interpretation of the Democratic Significance of "The State Respects and Protects Human Rights"*, Study & Exploration, 2007.
16. Chen Fukuan, *Application and Rules of the People's Supervisor System*, Law Science, 2008.
17. Ma Changshan, *The Rule of Law Value of People's Supervisor and Its Realization*, Journal of National Prosecutors College, 2006.
18. Gao Yifei, *Exploring the Justification of the People's Supervisor System*, Journal of Guizhou Minzu University (Philosophy and Social Science Edition), 2005.
19. Long Zongzhi, *Discussion of Several Issues Concerning the People's Supervisor System*, People's Procuratorate, 2005.
20. Ji Weidong, *Reflections on the Practice of the People's Supervisor System*, People's Procuratorial Semimonthly, 2005.
21. Xie Hui, *Legal Norms as the Core of the Legal System*, Study & Exploration, 2003.
22. Lin Laifan & Zhai Guoqiang, *Reflections on the Methodology of Social Sciences*, Zhejiang Social Sciences, 2006.
23. Yu Zhong, *The Normative Analysis Method and Its Philosophical Basis in the View of Legal Methodology*, Xinjiang Social Science, 2004.
24. Qin Qianhong, *The Evolution of China's Legislative Model from a Constitutional Perspective: From "Transformative Legislation" to "Autonomous Legislation"*, China Legal Science, 2005.
25. Zhou Wangsheng, *On the Current Legislative System in China*, Journal of Peking University (Philosophy and Social Sciences), 1989.
26. Li Lin, *On the Theory and Practice of Division of Legislative Authorities*, Chinese Journal of Law, 1998.
27. Zhou Wangsheng, *Several Theoretical Issues on Local Legislation,* Administrative Law Review, 1994.
28. Xu Junlun, *Characteristics of Local Legislation*, Science of Law, 1996.
29. Cai Dingjian, *The Development, Achievements and Problems of Local People's Congress Legislation*, National People's Congress of China, 1994.
30. Zhang Zhongqiu & Zhang Mingxin, *Observations and Reflections on the Division of Legislative Authority and the Operation of Legislative Power in China*, Tribune of Political Science and Law, 2000.
31. Ying Songnian, *The Provisions of the Legislation Law on the Principle of Legal Reservation*, Administrative Law Review, 2000.
32. Xue Panlin, *The People's Supervisor System from a Constitutional Perspective,* The Chinese Procurators, 2008.
33. Cheng Weigang et al., *Designs on Improving the Procedures Related to the People's Supervisor System*, Law Science, 2006.

34. Dan Wei, *A Proper Understanding of the People's Supervisor System and the Solid Promotion of Procuratorial Reform*, People's Procuratorial Semimonthly, 2004.
35. Zhou Shimin, *Nature and Function of the People's Supervisor System*, Journal of National Prosecutors College, 2004.
36. Yao Qiang & Mei Yisong, *Discussion on Controversial Issues of the People's Supervisor System*, Law Science, 2005.
37. Tong Jianming, *Legal Basis and Supervisory Nature of People's Supervisor System*, Procuratorate Daily, 2005.
38. Peng Huiling, *Nature and Social Value of the People's Supervisor System*, Journal of Hainan Normal University (Social Sciences), 2004.
39. Han Tie, *The Historical Evolution of Jury Nullification in the United States: The Conflict between Democracy and Modernization*, The Chinese Journal of American Studies, 2008.
40. Song Yinghui, *Analysis on the Latest Reform in Japan's Criminal Procedure System*, Hebei Law Science, 2007.
41. Chen Yuzhong, *On the Principle of Prosecutorial Discretion in Japanese Criminal Procedure*, Japan Research, 1997.
42. Xin Peiyan, *Comparative Analysis and Practical Evaluation of the People's Supervisor System: With Reference to the General Characteristics of Extraterritorial Public Participation in Procuratorial Power*, Justice of China, 2008.
43. Huang He, *Positioning of the People's Supervisor System—From the Perspective of Legal Supervision Classification*, Administration and Law, 2006.
44. Liu Jie, *Constitutional Control of Police Power in China,* Journal of Beijing People's Police College, 2005.
45. Xu Guoping, *Three Improvements to the People's Supervisor System*, Procuratorial Practice, 2004.
46. Jia Zhaoyang, *Studying People's Supervisor System*, Journal of National Prosecutors College, 2005.
47. Bai Gantao, *Rational Reflections on the Implementation of the People's Supervisor System by the Procuratorial Organs*, Journal of Heilongjiang Administrative Cadre College of Political Science and Law, 2005.
48. Liu Tieying, *Thoughts on the Socialization of Law Enforcement by Procuratorial Organs*, Journal of National Prosecutors College, 2005.
49. Song Yuansheng, *On Social Supervision over Investigative Actions: From the Perspective of Specialization*, Journal of Henan Administrative Institute of Politics and Law, 2008.
50. Chen Han, *Legalization, Socialization, and Proceduralization: Prospects for the Development of the People's Supervisor System*, Journal of Guangdong Ocean University, 2007.
51. Xu Weilin, *Rational Reflections on the Legalization of the People's Supervisor System*, Hubei Social Sciences, 2007.
52. Qinggeletu & Wuyunbateer, *Proposal for Connecting the People's Supervisor System with NPC Supervision*, People's Procuratorial Semimonthly, 2005.
53. Niu Baocheng, *The People's Supervisor System Needs to Be Incorporated into Legislative Planning*, People's Procuratorial Semimonthly, 2004.
54. Wang Lei, *On the Legalization of the People's Supervisor System*, People's Procuratorial Semimonthly, 2006.
55. Xu Weilin, *Rational Reflections on the Legalization of the People's Supervisor System*, Hubei Social Sciences, 2009.
56. Chai Chunyuan, *Promoting the Legislation to Highlight the Vitality of the People's Supervisor System*, People's Procuratorial Semimonthly, 2006.
57. Yu Feng & Xie Xiaojian, *Calm Thinking of the People's Supervisor System*, Jiangxi Social Sciences, 2005.
58. Guan Baoying & Zhang Shufang, *Research on the Market Economy and the Transformation of Legislative Models*, Studies in Law and Business, 1997.
59. Luo Changxi & Zhou Jian'gao, *Legislative Thoughts on the People's Supervisor System*, People's Procuratorial Semimonthly, 2005.

60. Ke Hanmin, *The Legislation of the People's Supervisor System Can Proceed in Three Stages*, Procuratorate Daily, November 7, 2005, at 3.
61. Jiang Guohua & Yi Saijian, *On the Legislative Democracy*, Journal of South-Central Minzu University (Humanities and Social Sciences), 2007
62. Zhang Youyu, *Legislative Principles of Socialist Legal System in China*, Dongyue Tribune Dongyue Lucong, 1980.
63. Xiao Jinming & Yin Fengtong, *On Basic Principles of Chinese Legislation*, Literature, History, and Philosophy, 1999.
64. Liu Qingsheng, *Research on the Reform of the System of the Selection, Appointment and Management of the People's Supervisor*, Social Sciences Hunan, 2008.
65. Dai Zhongxiang, *Exploration of the People's Supervisor System*, Exploration and Free Views, 2005.
66. Zhang Lang, *Discussion on Theoretical and Practical Issues of the People's Supervisor System*, Justice of China, 2005.
67. Li Jianming, *A Study on the Effectiveness of People's Supervisors' Opinions*, People's Procuratorial Semimonthly, no. 8 (2005).
68. Li Jianliang, *The Conceptual Evolution and Functional System of Fundamental Rights: Starting from Jellinek's "Status Theory" (II)*, Constitutionalism Era.
69. Xu Hengda, *The Epistemological Formation and Conceptual Archaeology of "Substantive Truth-finding Doctrine": Focusing on the Development of German Criminal Procedure from the Middle Ages to the Early Modern Period*, National Chengchi University Law Review, 2008.

The manufacturer's authorised representative in the EU is Springer Nature Customer Service Centre GmbH, Europaplatz 3, 69115 Heidelberg, Germany. If you have any concerns regarding our products, please contact ProductSafety@springernature.com

Printed and bound by CPI Group (UK) Ltd, Croydon, CR0 4YY
07/10/2026
02229352-0004